Freud

The man, his world, his influence

Freud

The man, his world, his influence

Edited by
Jonathan Miller

WEIDENFELD AND NICOLSON
5 Winsley Street London W1

© George Weidenfeld and Nicolson Ltd, 1972

Designed by John Wallis
for George Weidenfeld and Nicolson Ltd
Printed and bound in Great Britain by
C. Tinling & Co. Ltd., Warrington Road
Prescot, Lancashire

ISBN 0 297 99531 6

Contents

Illustrations

The Young Freud (*between pages 4 and 5*)

The Freud house in Freiberg, Moravia (Courtesy of Mrs E. L. Freud)
Sigmund Freud with his sisters and brother (Courtesy of Mrs E. L. Freud)
Sigmund Freud with his father (Courtesy of Mrs E. L. Freud)
Sigmund Freud with his mother (Courtesy of Mrs E. L. Freud)
View of Vienna (Popperfoto)
Director and staff of Leopoldstätter Communal-Realgymnasium (Austrian National Library)
The Freud family, *c.* 1876 (Courtesy of Mrs E. L. Freud)
The Faculty of Arts and Sciences at the Old University, Vienna (Austrian National Library)
Hall of the Old University (Austrian National Library)
Martha Bernays at 21 (Courtesy of Mrs E. L. Freud)
Freud and Martha Bernays, *c.* 1885 (State Library, Berlin)
Sigmund and Martha Freud in 1886 (Courtesy Mrs E. L. Freud)

A Jew in Vienna (*between pages 20 and 21*)

Vienna : The Jewish quarter (Mary Evans Picture Library)
Page from *Extrablatt*, 29 July 1883 (Austrian National Library)
Karl Lueger (Austrian National Library)
Antisemitic drawing by Hans Schliessmann, 1880 (Austrian National Library)
Antisemitic cartoon from *Krach* (Austrian National Library)
The New University taken over by the Nazis (Austrian National Library)
Antisemitic propaganda (Austrian National Library)
The Burning of the Books, Berlin, 1933 (State Library, Berlin)
Official antisemitic discrimination in Vienna (Austrian National Library)
Jewish resistance plaque (Werner Forman)
The Zentralfriedhof Jewish cemetery (Austrian National Library)
Moses by Michelangelo (H. Roger-Viollet)

Friends, Teachers and Colleagues (*between pages 36 and 37*)

Freud and Wilhelm Fliess (Courtesy Mrs E. L. Freud)
The College of Professors of the School of Medicine, Vienna University (Institute for the History of Medicine, Vienna)

Illustrations

Ernst Wilhelm Ritter von Brücke (State Library, Berlin)
Eduard von Hofmann (Institute for the History of Medicine, Vienna)
Laboratory of the Institute of Physiology (Institute for the History of Medicine, Vienna)
Hermann Nothnagel (Austrian National Library)
Theodor Meynert (Institute for the History of Medicine, Vienna)
The psychiatric ward of the Vienna General Hospital (Austrian National Library)
Nathan Weiss (Institute for the History of Medicine, Vienna)
Josef Pollak (Institute for the History of Medicine, Vienna)
Leopold Königstein (Institute for the History of Medicine, Vienna)
Jean-Martin Charcot (State Library, Berlin)
The Hôpital de la Salpêtrière, Paris (H. Roger-Viollet)
The inmates' cells at the Salpêtrière (H. Roger-Viollet)
Reconstruction of Freud's consulting room in Vienna (Erich Lessing, Magnum)
Jane Avril by H. de Toulouse-Lautrec (Courtauld Institute Galleries, London)
Charcot's electrotherapy cabinet at the Salpêtrière (Ullstein Bilderdienst, Berlin)
Note in Charcot's hand (Editions du Seuil, Paris)
Letter in Freud's hand (Austrian National Library)
Poster of Sarah Bernhardt (John R. Freeman)
The Paris Opera House (Ullstein Bilderdienst)
Painting by André Brouillet of a demonstration by Charcot (Courtesy Mrs E. L. Freud)
Schloss Belle Vue (Austrian National Library)
Ernst von Fleischl-Marxow (Institute for the History of Medicine, Vienna)
Max Kassowitz (Austrian National Library)
Plan of lectures in Freud's hand (General Administrative Archives, Vienna)
Josef Breuer (Austrian National Library)

Freud's Vienna (*between pages* 52 *and* 53)

Portrait of Freud by Ben Shahn (Courtesy of the Lawrence-Myden Foundation; Photo Snark International)
Danaë by Gustav Klimt
Graben Strasse (Popperfoto)
Drawing of Kolomann Moser and Josef Hoffmann by F. König from *Ver Sacrum*
The Washergirls' Ball by Wilhelm Gause (Kunsthistorisches Museum, Vienna)
Viennese skyline (Werner Forman)
Page by Josef Hoffman from *Ver Sacrum*
Furniture design by Hoffmann from *Ver Sacrum*
Judith by Gustav Klimt (Museo d'Arte Moderna, Ca' Pesaro, Venice)
The Secession building, Vienna (Werner Forman)
The Café Griensteidl by R. Völkel (Austrian National Library)

The Middle Years (*between pages* 84 *and* 85)

Theatre poster by Oskar Kokoschka
Sketch of Freud by Hermann Struck (Courtesy Mrs E. L. Freud)
Freud and colleagues at Clark University, 1909 (Courtesy Mrs E. L. Freud)

Illustrations

The International Psychoanalytical Congress at Weimar, 1911 (A. C. Cooper)
Freud and Ernst Freud at Thumsee, 1901 (Courtesy Mrs E. L. Freud)
Freud with Ernst and Martin during the First World War (Courtesy Mrs E. L. Freud)
Freud and Anna Freud in the Dolomites, 1912 (Courtesy Mrs E. L. Freud)
Title page of *The Interpretation of Dreams* (Austrian National Library)
Title page of *Three Essays on the Theory of Sexuality* (Austrian National Library)
Freud at work in his study (Mansell Collection)
Julius Wagner-Jauregg (Institute for the History of Medicine, Vienna)
Stefan Zweig (Popperfoto)
Gustav Mahler
Detail from the triptych of the *Garden of Delights* by H. Bosch (Prado, Madrid)

Freud and Surrealist Painting (*Between pages* 132 *and* 133)

Boy with Playing Cards by Chardin (National Gallery, London)
Card-players by P. Cézanne (Courtauld Institute Galleries, London)
Automatic Drawing by André Masson (Galerie Louise Leiras, Paris)
Decalcomania by Oscar Domínguez (Museum of Modern Art, New York)
Il faisait ce qu'il voulait by Yves Tanguy (Richard S. Zeisler, New York)
Personal Values by René Magritte
Le *dormeur téméraire* by René Magritte (Tate Gallery)
Les amants by René Magritte (Richard S. Zeisler, New York)
From *Une semaine de bonté* by Max Ernst
From *La femme 100 tête* by Max Ernst
Illumined Pleasures by Salvador Dali (Sydney Janis Collection, New York)
Accommodation of Desire by Salvador Dali (Wright Ludington Collection, Santa Barbara, California)

The Later Freud (*between pages* 156 *and* 157)

Portrait sketch of Freud by Ferdinand Schmutzer (Art and History Archives, Berlin)
Anna Freud in 1930 (Ullstein Bilderdienst, Berlin)
Martha and Sophie Freud, *c.* 1912 (Courtesy of Mrs E. L. Freud)
19 Berggasse, Freud's apartment block (Austrian National Library)
Freud and his grandson Stephen Gabriel (Courtesy of Mrs E. L. Freud)
Freud psychoanalyzing Freud. Drawing by Charles B. Slackman (State Library, Berlin)
The 'Seven Rings Committee', Berlin, 1922 (State Library, Berlin)
Freud and two of his chows (Hans Casparius)
Freud in his study in Vienna (A. C. Cooper)
Freud with his daughter Mathilde, Ernest Jones and Lucie Freud (Courtesy Mrs E. L. Freud)
Freud's consulting room at Ellsworthy Road (A. C. Cooper)
Ornaments on Freud's desk (Courtesy of Mrs E. L. Freud)
Sketch of Freud by Salvador Dali (Courtesy Mrs E. L. Freud)
Freud at work on *Moses and Monotheism* (Courtesy Mrs E. L. Freud)

Foreword

Jonathan Miller

THIS essay represents a set of scattered tangents, each one drawn in search of the hypothetical circumference of Freudian influence. I have made no attempt to outline this circumference either directly or completely since the notion of such a figure breaks down under closer scrutiny, suggesting as it does that the influence of a great man's thought comprises a closed, albeit expanding, area of new ideas. However, although the metaphor disintegrates if taken too literally it justifies itself as an editorial device by allowing one to produce lines of argument from topics which are not commonly associated in the same publication. And since it is one of the purposes of this volume to vindicate the disputed judgment of greatness that has been passed on Freud the task is partly accomplished if only by showing the variety of human interest with which his theory has made contact.

Now whether Freud was right or no, and it is still a matter of argument as to what sort of evidence would count for or against him, he has dramatically shifted the perspectives of psychological controversy and created several new ones altogether. In this respect Freud has established what the journalists often like to call 'a world' and what we even more pompously, might term a 'universe of discourse'. That is to say it is now hard to discuss the major themes of human conduct without at least making corrections which allow for the bias of his notions.

Nevertheless many well qualified authorities claim to navigate successfully without introducing any substantial Freudian factors into their calculations. Some clinicians for instance, confronted by the urgent, and in many cases

Foreword

overwhelming, demands of distressing mental illness are likely to dismiss the body of Freudian thought, not only for what they hold to be its practical shortcomings as a source of therapy, but more seriously for its failure to imply, as any physical science should do, the criteria by which its own claims as a theory might be judged. The position is argued energetically by Dr Henry Miller; and whilst I believe that he has interpreted the notion of criteria too narrowly, neglecting for instance the subjective quality of the experience of those who undergo analysis, it would be frivolous to exclude the opinion of someone whose impatience is grounded in the daily practice of hospital medicine.

I have deliberately left out any direct reply to Dr Miller's polemic; partly because the arguments are by now familiar but also because the question of Freud's usefulness is often developed more suggestively outside the strictly clinical sphere. George Lichtheim for instance deals with Freud in the context of Marxist thought, showing among other things how both Freud and Marx arise from the common tradition of nineteenth-century determinism. It is well known of course that Freud did not exactly invent the idea of the unconscious but he broke entirely new ground by describing its activities in more or less mechanical terms, thereby, it might seem, dispossessing the individual of his birthright of spontaneity. Jonathan Glover examines the ethical implications of such a suggestion and discusses how our notions of moral responsibility might change in the knowledge that so many of our actions are pre-determined by influences that lie beyond the subject's conscious control. Anthony Quinton also handles the problem in terms of the philosophy of mind and in doing so touches once again upon the difficulties of entertaining a theory which is not apparently falsifiable.

With regard to this last objection one is left with the uneasy feeling that the insights of Freud have more in common with the intuitions of art than with the disciplines of physical science and that, while Freud himself hoped to see most of his proposals finally incorporated into the growing body of biophysics, it is possible that he may have seriously misidentified the logical status of his own enterprise. It is perhaps significant in this respect that the first friendly review which his 'Study in Hysteria' received came not from a scientist but from a dramaturge in the University of Vienna. It is pleasing therefore to include an essay that maintains this honourable tradition. Professor Heer, who discusses Freud in the light of contemporary European politics, holds the post of Dramaturge to the Burgtheater in Vienna. Martin Esslin's description of Freud's Vienna completes this social

Foreword

background, whilst Professor Rosen elaborates the medical setting of nineteenth-century Austria, providing a full-length portrait of Freud's great teacher Nothnagel.

If Freud's picture of the mind can be faulted as a scientific description there is little doubt that he assumes a significant place in the history of literature and criticism, and Michael Podro consolidates this claim with his investigation of the art historical idioms that are embodied in such works as the *Interpretation of Dreams*. Meanwhile Dawn Ades shows the relationship between Freud's notion of the unconscious and that which was exploited by the Surrealists.

Anthropologists have enjoyed a peculiar, almost flirtatious, relationship with the doctrines of psychoanalysis and a whole volume could be devoted to the way in which this engagement has prospered over the years. I have settled instead for a somewhat idiosyncratic essay by Dr Octave Mannoni, partly because his treatment of the colonialist theme is so unusual, but also out of personal caprice, since I derived enormous inspiration from these ideas when producing a version of Shakespeare's *The Tempest* some years ago at the Mermaid Theatre.

Finally to root the collection in humane common sense I have invited Dr Catherine Storr to discuss the way in which Freudian dogma has helped to change the patterns of European child-rearing, oversensitizing the middle class parent to the developmentalsusceptibilities of their growing infants.

In editing this volume I enjoyed the pure pleasure of issuing invitations with careless flamboyance. The main burden of work fell largely upon Enid Gordon who researched much of the background and maintained the overall design. I would also like to thank Dr Anna Freud and Mrs Lucy Freud for their help and permission to use photographs from their family archives; and Andra Nelki and Ann Mitchell for their ingenuity in finding such an extraordinary range of illustrations.

1

Freud, the Viennese Jew

Friedrich Heer

(*translated by W. A. Littlewood*)

SIGMUND FREUD's work dominated his era and is indeed one of the landmarks of the twentieth century. Its implications have by no means been fully explored and even today there is still much to discover. Some of his more rigidly orthodox disciples have tried to imprison his ideas in a stultifying dogmatism that he himself would never have accepted. In the USA he is often presented as an aloof, conformist figure who observed with complete detachment the great human conflicts and who had experienced no personal revelation of death or tragedy. Freud, like all thinkers of world stature, could be compared both to a quarry and to a volcano: a quarry from which builders fetch stones to construct their own relatively modest homes – i.e. their own psychoanalytical theories and methods; a volcano, in that his ideas and energies erupt unexpectedly like molten lava just when they are thought to be extinct.

There is a good case for re-examining this towering figure of our times, and it is important to remember that the foundations, structure and development of Freud's work, whose influence far exceeds his particular historical and social position, can only properly be understood as the achievement of a Viennese Jew who was constantly fighting a heroic battle for his identity and self-awareness in a hostile milieu, in Vienna – a city he both loved and hated. But it was in this milieu that he found the raw material for his research: from the psychical undergrowth of this Viennese *fin-de-siècle* society, dancing giddily and unknowingly (though some of its shrewder representatives were only too well aware) towards the First World War. They were suicides about to become murderers.

'Personally, I absolutely hate Vienna . . .' wrote Freud on 11 March 1900 to his Berlin-Jewish friend Wilhelm Fliess, for long, lonely years his only intellectual companion. Ernst Lother, the celebrated Austrian poet, novelist and playwright (he followed Max Reinhardt as director of the theatre in the Josefstadt in Vienna) told me that when the Habsburg Empire was breaking up, Freud had said emphatically: 'My whole libido is bound up with Austria-Hungary.'

In 1900, the year that Freud was writing to his friend Fliess about his dislike of Vienna, a booklet was published in St Polten, a town an hour's journey away from Vienna, called *From the year 1920: As dreamed by the Parliamentary Representative, Dr Joseph Scheicher*. Joseph Scheicher, eventually a prelate, was Dr Karl Lueger's closest follower and the strongest supporter of Christian Socialism among the younger clergy; from 1897 to 1909 he was a member of the Lower-Austrian Parliament and was elected three times to the State

Parliament. What did Joseph Scheicher dream in 1900 that was prophetic of 1920 ? He imagined himself in 1920 reminiscing about 'cleansing' Vienna of its Jews. 'Are they hanging many ?' Not now (1920) but before, it was different. . . .

In Vienna we once hanged 300 Jews and 20 Aryans in one day. . . . In the Polish and Ruthenian states we had to hang thousands before the villains realized we were serious. They knew, for example, that beasts of prey have to be destroyed but it was a long time before the unfortunately less educated Jews and natives of those provinces realized that human predators have to be treated in the same way.

We don't know whether Freud – whose *Interpretation of Dreams* had been published the year before – had heard of this book, but the official anti-semitism of Dr Karl Lueger's Christian Social Party, then so strong in Vienna, must have been apparent to him. Ernest Schneider, one of the most active of the young Christian-Socialist campaigners, publicly demanded that Jews be physically rooted out, and suggested 'head money for Jews' for every one shot. Baron von Vogelsang, an important Christian-Socialist theorist, did in fact deplore the anti semitic insignia (a hanged Jew as a watch-chain ornament) worn by Georg von Schönerer's Pan-German Party. The clergyman, Dr Josef Deckert, a widely read folk writer and convinced Christian, Socialist, preached that 'the Jews must be rendered harmless to Christians', and taught that racial anti semitism was in accordance with Catholic doctrine. Lueger himself, in a famous anti semitic speech to the State Parliament, spoke against 'the Jews' unbelievably fanatical hatred, their unquenchable thirst for revenge' and continued : 'What are wolves, lions, panthers, leopards, tigers, men themselves, compared to these predators in human guise ?'

In 1895 Lueger finally gained power as Burgomaster of Vienna (Emperor Franz Joseph had refused four times to confirm the appointment), and instituted a campaign of anti semitic propaganda, thus making himself known to 'his' Jews. Hitler honoured Dr Karl Lueger as a model, the great teacher of his Vienna years – 1909 to 1912 – and acknowledged him as such in *Mein Kampf*. During his rise to power, therefore, quite a few Jews in Vienna (and elsewhere, for example in Berlin and Prague) were to think that Hitler, if he gained office, would behave in the same way as the 'Führer' of Vienna. This was a fateful piece of self-deception on the part of Vienna's Jews and Sigmund Freud's life was a continual struggle against self-deception and the deception of others. It is important to remember that his acceptance of his Jewishness was made in a climate of rabid anti semitism. In *The Interpretation of Dreams*

Freud

Freud recalls an unforgettable episode from his youth. His father told him how, when he was a young man in his native town, a Christian had struck the cap from his head, saying 'Get off the pavement, Jew.' His father, Jakob Freud, had lived in Freiberg in Moravia, where Sigmund was born. In 1859 the family moved across Saxony to Vienna, a Vienna that Joseph Scheicher in his dream hailed as 'a new Samaria, or new Jerusalem'. In 1914 Sigmund Freud's eldest son, Martin, joined the Imperial Army as a volunteer in the second week of the war; the others two sons, Oliver and Ernst, joined up somewhat later, as did one of their cousins, who died in 1917. Freud was deeply troubled by the first heavy defeats of the Imperial Armies.

Nowadays we can laugh at all Franz Joseph's fifty-five subsidiary titles conferring on him imperial, kingly, princely or ducal rights over regions in middle Europe which are now scarcely recognizable under their old names. One title, however, would only raise a bitter laugh: 'Emperor Franz Joseph ... Duke of Auschwitz.' But they were important during a decisive period of Sigmund Freud's life in Vienna, from 1860 to 1918. Eastern European Jews were fleeing from pogroms in lands ruled by the Tsar to find refuge in countries under the protection of the Austrian Emperor, especially in the cities. In 1857, a year after Freud's birth, Vienna had a Jewish population of 6,217 or 1.3 per cent of the total. In 1869 there were 40,227 Jews in Vienna, 6.3 of the total population. In 1890 (the year in which Freud began to practise the cathartic method), the number was 99,444, 12 per cent of the total. By 1910, the year in which the International Psychoanalytical Association was founded and the first issue of its monthly journal *Zentralblatt für Psychoanalyse* was published, there were 118,495 Jews in Vienna and the Vienna area – 8.7 per cent of the population. In 1923 (the year of Freud's first two cancer operations and of the publication of *The Ego and the Id*), there were 201,510 Jews, 10.8 per cent of the population. (Compare these figures with Berlin, which in 1816 had 3,373 Jews, whereas in 1910 the Berlin area held 144,000, 3.6 per cent of the population. Or Prague, with 13,056 Jews in 1869, 8.2 per cent of the population; or Budapest which, in 1869 held 44,890 Jews, 16.6 per cent of the population, and where, in 1910, the number had risen to 203,687, 23.2 per cent of the population. It was from Budapest that Freud's first important colleagues and pioneers of the psychoanalytical movement came, to Vienna, then to Berlin and later to New York.)

There was nothing simple about being a Jew in Vienna during the years between 1860 and 1938; it was a highly complicated business. An exclusive community of upper-middle-class Jews lived there, its ranks closed to the in-

The Young Freud

The house in Freiberg, Moravia, where Sigmund Freud was born, at 6.30 p.m. on 6 May 1856. Drawing by Jungwirth, 1936.

Sigmund Freud (left) with his five sisters and younger brother Alexander. Painting by an unknown artist.

Below Sigmund, aged 8, with his father, Jakob Freud.
Below, right Sigmund at 16, with his mother, Amalie Nathansohn-Freud.

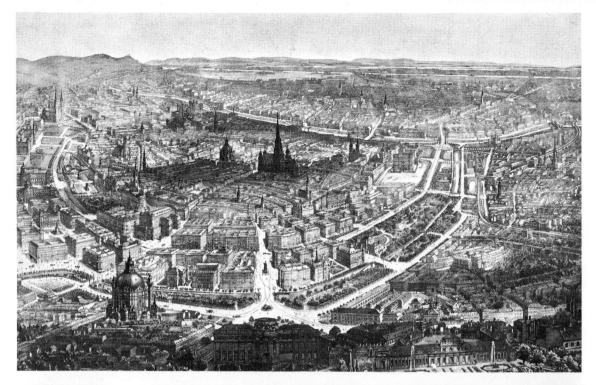

Top In 1860 the Freuds settled in Vienna. Of his early years there Freud said: 'They were hard times and not worth remembering.'
Bottom Dr Alois Pokorny, principal, with the teaching staff of the Leopoldstätter Communal-Realgymnasium, the high school which Freud attended from 1865 to 1873.

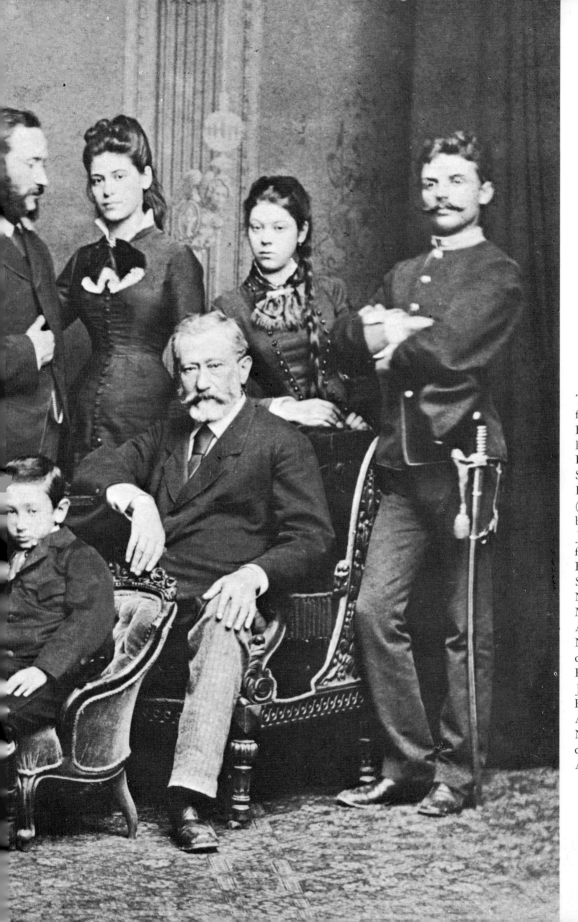

The Freud family, *c.* 1876. Back row, from left to right, Pauline, Anna, Sigmund, Emmanuel (their half-brother from Jakob Freud's first marriage), Rosa, Mitzi, Simon Nathansohn. Middle row, Adolfine, a Nathansohn child, Mrs Freud and Jakob Freud. Front row, Another Nathansohn child and Alexander.

Vienna: the Faculty of
Arts and Sciences at the
Old University where
Sigmund Freud attended
his lectures.

The baroque hall of the
Old University where
Freud's graduation
ceremony took place in
1881.

Left Martha Bernays at the age of 21. Freud wrote to her: 'I know you are not beautiful in a painter's or sculptor's sense. . . .What I meant to convey was how much the magic of your being expresses itself in your countenance and your body, how much there is visible in your appearance that reveals how sweet, generous and reasonable you are.'
Right Sigmund Freud and Martha Bernays during their engagement, *c.* 1885.

flux of Eastern European Jews and to its own lower-middle-class. The leaders of this upper class had been ennobled by the Emperor since the beginning of the nineteenth century and they held important positions in finance and industry. Thus there was an ever-growing Jewish intelligentsia and academic community. Jewish men of letters, writers, novelists began to set the fashion, but alongside all this were the lower middle class and proletariat who had come mainly from the East.

It would be impossible to reduce the spiritual and intellectual life of the Viennese Jewish community to any common denominator. The upper-middle class were staunch supporters of the Emperor and patriotically devoted to the cause of Austrian hegemony until the disintegration of the Empire. Throughout the war for example, strict domestic economy was practised in Baron Edmund de Rothschild's palace (in complete contrast to the behaviour of wealthy 'Aryan' families). One Viennese Jew, Julius Meindl, tried to use his international contacts to negotiate in Switzerland for a separate peace for the monarchy. Joseph Roth, a descendant of an army family of Austrian Galician Jews, gave Austria-Hungary one of its literary monuments in two novels, *Radetzky March* and *Capuchin Crypt*. In March 1938, after the Anschluss, Roth, as an officer of the Imperial Army, challenged Arthur Seyss-Inquart, Austria's first and only Nazi Chancellor, to a duel, charging him with high treason against his country.

Viennese Jewry rejected Zionism; Moritz Benedict (1849–1920), said by A. Fuchs to have been 'for a generation one of the ten or twelve most powerful men in Austria', and from 1881 chief editor of the *Neue Freie Presse*, refused to allow even the word 'Zionism' to be printed. *The Times's* leader of 20 March 1920 described his attitude during the war as 'Jewish Pan-Germanism'. Theodor Herzl (who was to make his mark as a playwright at the Burgtheater) was features editor of the *Neue Freie Presse*. The Jewish Social Democrat leaders had definitely turned their backs on everything Jewish. Under the autocratic rule of Friedrich Austerlitz the *Workers' Newspaper* ridiculed Zionism and later on was to print such comments as 'hooked cross and hooked nose'. Many Viennese Jews were looking for a way of escaping from their race; such notions as 'Jewishness without Judaism' sprang up and a kind of self-hatred expressing itself as Jewish anti semitism, especially around 1918, under Otto Weininger's influence (*Race and Character*), took hold of men like Arthur Trebitsch (whom Hitler, knowing his writings but nothing of his Jewish ancestry, is said to have preferred as late as 1935 instead of Rosenberg as Party Commissioner responsible for the supervision of disseminating party

Sigmund and Martha Freud in 1886

philosophy. [My source for this is a letter written to me by Falk von Gagern on 10 January 1968 referring to his conversation with Hitler at the 'Elephant' in Weimar in March 1935.]) Another important critic and writer who cannot be exonerated of Jewish anti semite feeling was Karl Kraus; he voiced his feeling in his antagonism to the *Neue Freie Presse* and other Jewish-run newspapers. At the general meeting of the Austrian Israelite Union in 1885, the Chairman spoke of the necessity of combating Jewish anti semitism; Jews must learn to stop hating themselves. The forerunner of this campaign for Jewish self-awareness among Vienna's Jewry was Dr Joseph Samuel Bloch (1850–1923). In 1886 he published a booklet entitled *National Enmity and the Jews in Austria*. Jews should not support nationalist parties who were forever quarrelling among themselves. Bloch attacked the 'ridiculous figure' of the Jew adopting German-national or Czech-national postures.

Unless we understand these deep-rooted conflicts in the Viennese Jewish community we cannot appreciate the significance of Freud's work, since it draws its vitality and power from the precarious balance of opposing forces. His work is not linear or one-dimensional: it cannot be understood on one level. All his life Freud's awareness of his own Jewishness was in conflict with his questioning of Jewish existence. This conflict found forceful utterance in his last great work. He began to write *Moses and Monotheism* in the summer of 1934 – a year of civil war in Austria (in July of that year Engelbert Dollfuss, the Federal Chancellor, became the first victim of the Nazi *putsch*). The book was first published in German in August 1938. Freud knew very well how hazardous his 'destruction of the Moses legend' might be, coming at a time when books were not the only things being burned (as his own had been, in the Nazi bonfire in Berlin): as Heinrich Heine had prophesied, preparations to burn human beings were already under way. (Freud cannot have foreseen this, for if he had, he would never have published his *Moses* on the brink of the greatest massacre of the Jews the world has ever known.)

Deep inner conflicts were an integral part of Freud's life and work. In 1878 he had modified his Jewish name, Sigismund (which was Vienna's favourite term of abuse in anti-Jewish jokes) to Sigmund. He certainly did not call himself after the Nibelungen hero, Sigmund, out of admiration for that rabid anti semite Richard Wagner, but probably it was a subconscious withdrawal from his own Jewishness. He had destroyed his manuscripts in August 1885, and his letters in April 1908, as he obviously did not want his own physical development to become common property – his lifelong, love-hate verbal battles with Moses, with the paternalistic God of Jew and Christian, with his loved and hated Vienna, with the Emperor (whose counterpart, his majesty, the ego, waged war against the underground of its own psyche just as war was raging against underground resistance to the Austro-Hungarian Empire).

Everything that is truly dynamic, open and stimulating, the fruitfully problematic and thought-provoking elements in Freud's work, all stem from the unresolved tensions and conflicts of his being, his life and existence as a member of an old Viennese Jewish family. Every attempt to simplify or smooth over his life and his tragic personality inevitably results in an over-simplification of his work, and falsifies it by presenting it as innocuous – something that no school of medicine, dogmatists or disciples would wish to do. In Freud's psyche the soluble and frankly insoluble conflicts of a *fin-de-siècle* society were played out in the metropolis of the declining Austro-Hungarian Empire: a time when many open and secret enemies hoped for its total collapse, while its friends, its sons feared precisely that outcome. Let us look briefly at Freud's life and work in his Vienna, his Austria and with his contemporary society.

As a child Sigmund Freud was powerfully influenced by both Catholic and Judaic tradition. Nanny, his old, ugly nursemaid, terrified him with her descriptions of the torments of hell. When his family moved from Freiberg to Leipzig, then to Vienna, this first train journey seemed to him a journey to hell. At Breslau station his first glimpse of gasflares had conjured up a picture of the damned eternally burning in hell; his consequent phobia against railway journeys was only to be cured by analysis. Human life was to him a journey through hell – and Freud consciously set out to fight it, to challenge Tartarus, and made it his mission to overcome the gates of hell by bringing light to that abyss in the human mind that had been created in his own childish mind by the horrid tales of his deeply religious nurse.

Bible-reading had also made a deep impression on Freud as a boy. His father, whom he both hated and loved, gave him his Hebrew bible on his thirty-fifth birthday, inscribed 'My dear Son, it was in the seventh year of your age that the spirit of God began to move you to learning. . . '. Freud admits openly that his early reading of the Bible had a decisive influence on his intellectual and spiritual development. In the Old Testament (apart from a few very late writings) there is no concept of hell: heaven and hell played no part in the creed of the devout; one's life on earth was the scene of all one's striving and for that one was responsible to God, who is fire, Jahweh, a faceless god, marching in front of his people, the wandering god of a nomad race, a god who represents the future.

In 1865 Freud began his studies at a Humanist *Gymnasium* in Vienna, a type of school that makes a lasting impression on all its pupils. I remember my own school years in the Academic *Gymnasium* in Vienna (1927–34): among my contemporaries were Franz Schubert and Thomas Masaryk and I later had the honour of unveiling a memorial to an earlier generation of pupils, Hugo von Hofmannsthal, Arthur Schnitzler, Richard Beer-Hofmann and Peter Altenberg. In my time, anything from thirty to seventy per cent of the pupils and a slightly lower percentage of the teachers were Jews. In *Psychology of a Gymnasiast* which he wrote for the fiftieth anniversary celebrations of his school, Freud recalls that the way to knowledge was made accessible only by their teachers: 'They encouraged all our deepest inclinations, yet forced us to be completely submissive: we ferreted out their little weaknesses, but were proud of their excellence, their knowledge and their integrity. If they encouraged us at all we were basically very fond of them. . . . From the outset we were as equally inclined towards love as towards hate, towards criticism of them as towards respect. Psychoanalysis describes such an openness towards opposite attitudes as *ambivalence*, and is easily able to trace the feeling to its source.'

Emotional ambivalence: the two extremes of Freud's attitude to his father, towards God the Father, towards the ruler of the Danubian provinces and towards *his Majesty the ego* are expressed here in his recollections of his Viennese teachers: 'Now we can understand our relationship with our schoolteachers. These men, who were not always fathers themselves became father-substitutes for us. . . . We transferred to them the ambivalence that we had developed within our own families and we argued with them because of this disposition within ourselves, just as we were accustomed to argue with our real fathers.'

For eight years Freud was an outstanding pupil and stood at the head of his class. The *Abitur*, the Austrian equivalent of matriculation, was the gateway to all the higher professions and this was also Freud's experience. He began to study at the *Gymnasium* in 1865. The following year, 1886, at the battle of Sadova (Königgratz), the Imperial Armies suffered a crippling defeat by the Prussians, which brought about the disintegration of the old Danubian Empire. The transformation of the unified state into the dualism of Austria-Hungary crippled all prospects for the future, because the Magyar nobility which ruled over all the nations in the Hungarian half of the Empire and the numerically inferior German nationals who were worried about their dominant position in the *cis-Leithan* half of the Empire, refused to accept the dissolution of the monarchy into a federation of states with equal rights. Politics were passionately discussed in Freud's school years, but we do not know whether Freud had, at this early stage, acquired the patriotism towards Vienna and Austria that led him, until 1938, to turn down as a temptation to 'desert the flag' (his own words) any invitation to leave the country.

In 1873 Freud became a student at the University of Vienna, with the intention of becoming a doctor. That year was another fateful one in the history of Vienna and the Danubian provinces. The Viennese World Exhibition had not been the hoped-for starting point for the 'rebirth of the monarchy' but a disaster. The collapse of first the Vienna, then the Berlin stock exchange in 1873 ruined countless lives and unleashed a frenzy of political anti semitism. 'Jewish capitalism', 'Jewish liberalism', 'Jewish love of mammon' were to blame for the catastrophe. Both the conservatives and their opponents were beating the same drum. Freud wrote: 'On starting university in 1873 I was to experience some palpable disappointments. Above all I was wounded by the assumption that, because I was a Jew, I would have a feeling of inferiority and of not belonging.' Stefan Zweig, a friend and patient of Freud, remembers his own university days:

What the S.A. men accomplished for the National Socialists the student corps did for the Pan-Germans. Protected by their academic immunity, they established an unprecedented reign of terror and marched in military formation to every political event. Organized as so-called 'fraternities', brutal, drunken, battle-scarred, they dominated the quads armed with heavy cudgels . . . ; always the aggressors, they turned now on the helpless Slav, now on the Catholic, Italian or Jewish students and drove them out of the university. At each of these 'forays', blood flowed. . . .

Here are some statistics from Vienna University in Freud's day: in 1869 30 per cent of the medical faculty was Jewish (in 1889–90, 48 per cent); 19.8 per cent of the law faculty (in 1889–90, 22 per cent), and 11.7 per cent (in 1889–90, 15 per cent) of the philosophy faculty. An anti semitic pamphlet about the University estimated in 1894 that in the faculty of medicine two full-time, fourteen associate professors and thirty-seven private teachers were of the Hebrew faith. The majority of doctors in Vienna were Jewish and this had both favourable and unfavourable consequences for Freud: favourable, in that he was able to move in a wide circle of Jewish doctors. Almost all his early co-workers,s upporters and opponents were Jewish doctors, either natives of Vienna or people who had emigrated to or from Vienna. However, 'nationalist', German-nationalist and 'Christian' professors waged – virtually up until the present day – a bitter defensive campaign against a 'further Judaicizing' of Vienna University. Freud was never awarded a professorship, and in 1916–7 he abandoned his lectures (in 1885 he had opted for neuropathology). German and Austrian professors continued for more than half a century to 'expose' Freudian psychoanalysis as a 'Jewish swindle'. It is noticeable, however, that none of the insults, disappointments or enmities that Freud encountered all his life from the Viennese university circles was able to annul the ambivalence which he felt even towards them. He preserved a respect for some members of the University; he regarded, for example, his old professor, the physiologist Ernst Brücke, as the greatest authority he had ever met.

It was as a student in his university days that Freud changed his name from Sigismund to Sigmund. He graduated in 1881 and, in 1882, entered the General Hospital of Vienna as a clinical assistant. The conflict between Jewish and German doctors in the hospital was portrayed later by Arthur Schnitzler, himself a doctor, and whom Freud affectionately called his *Doppelgänger*, in his play *Professor Bernhardi*. (Freud wrote to Schnitzler in May 1922 : 'I think I have avoided you from a kind of reluctance to meet my double'.).

We knew nothing of Freud's inner conflicts during these years, but they came to a head dramatically – in a spiritual crisis, the mystery of which has not yet been solved – and the climax was the destruction of his manuscripts in August 1885. In 1887 the Christian Social Society was founded in Vienna, and was the seed from which the Christian Social Party sprang, the first large popular anti semitic party in Austria. The society published the *Illustrierte Wiener Volkszeitung* whose proud sub-title was 'The Organ of Anti semitism'. Lueger's career had begun and Freud came to regard him as a personal and deadly enemy. In 1891 Freud went to live at 19 Berggasse, where he worked until he was forced to leave in 1938. Its political position was not uninteresting : it was in Alsergrund, a district densely inhabited by German-Nationalists (later by National Socialists) but it was near the clinics, the University and the General Hospital. Many 'nationalist' students from German-speaking parts of the Empire had their lodgings here in Währing. Freud achieved his breakthrough to psychoanalysis in the last half of the last decade of the nineteenth century, his own *fin-de-siècle*. Freud's most important works piled up thick and fast between the years 1899 and 1914, while ominous storm clouds brooded over Vienna, and writers, thinkers and politicians were prophesying a world war. On 24 July 1895 Freud analyzed one of his dreams for the first time; in March 1896 he first used the word 'psychoanalysis'; on 4 November 1899 he published *The Interpretation of Dreams*; in 1902 the first meeting of the Psychological Wednesday Society was held; this was to become, in April 1908, the Vienna Psychoanalytical Society. There is no written evidence for my guess that this Wednesday society was an answer, a conscious or unconscious counterblast to the famous Thursday Society which had been founded by Vogelsang and where the inner circle of the Christian Socialists met for debate, training and to expound their ideological campaign against the 'Jewish spirit of the age', the 'Jewish Hydra' which – so they thought – was a shadow double eagle standing for the destruction of the monarchy and its 'Christian basis' and the establishment of 'Jewish Liberal Capitalism' and 'Jewish Socialism'. Freud undertook his investigation of the human Tartarus in a Vienna where high society, petty-bourgeois circles and the proletariat were insurmountably divided. The nobleman's town residence had nothing in common with the hundreds of thousands of hovels where every bed served several occupants (alternating in day and night shifts). The upper and lower circles did however, communicate by means of prostitutes. Lack of a bed and lack of sex were closely connected in Vienna. Stefan Zweig and the young Hitler experienced both: an odd fellowship between the son of a Jewish patrician family and the offspring of the lower-middle class, the humanist and the anti-humanist. Both remembered 'the unhealthy, sticky, sultry over-perfumed air' of unsatisfied lust in which young men were forced to seek out tarts and whores and to suppress their sexuality in the sub-conscious. Zweig wrote: 'How towns love to hide, under clean, busy streets and elegant promenades lined with luxury shops, the subterranean canals in which the filth of the sewers is drained away and where the whole sexual life of the young is supposed to take place invisibly, hidden from the moralistic surface of society.'

This subterranean, sewer-like Vienna, with its slum tenements and low brothels, impressed itself deeply into the consciousness of the adolescent Hitler. The wretchedness of the slums was equated with Babel, a hell caused by the intermingling of nationalities and races, by 'blood defilement'. His sexual problems and his fear of venereal disease became neurotically inseparable from his religio-political fear of the devil – of whom Jews were the incarnation. Jews, prostitution, lasciviousness and debauchery were, for the young Hitler and many Christian Socialists and German Nationalists, all part of the same thing.

Freud

Stefan Zweig described Vienna's prostitution thus:

In a way it was like the dark structure of a cellar that supports the unblemished and brilliant façade of the ceremonial building of middle-class society. . . . As in Japan's Yoshiwara or the fish market at Cairo, row upon row of women sat – perhaps two to five hundred of them, here, in twentieth-century Vienna, crowded together, each at the ground-floor window of her house – cheap goods on display. They work in two shifts, a day and a night shift.

Gustav Kubizek described how his friend Hitler and he would be accosted on their way back from the Burgtheater or the opera by 'loitering streetwalkers'. Because of his lifelong fear of syphilitic infection Hitler wanted to free German women, the German people, to purify mankind of syphilis, of the 'Jewish disease', of the 'Disease of Jewish Marxism'. His sexual neurosis became fully developed in Vienna.

Zweig has also described his own youthful panic:

The fear of infection overshadowed one's whole soul, even one's most intimate relationships . . . and to this fear was added a dread of the rebarbative and humiliating nature of the treatments used in those days. . . . Small wonder, then, that so many young people in whom the infection was diagnosed immediately reached for a revolver. . . . If I really try to remember, there was scarcely one of my youthful friends who didn't turn up at some time with a white face and staring eyes.

Freud was Hitler's great intellectual opponent. *The Psychopathology of Everyday Life* was published in 1904: in 1903 Robert Musil had published *Young Torless* in which his portrayal of the sado-masochistic terrorism of the young with all the horror of a KZ world ('the secret room' is where the boarders torment unpopular 'nonconformists'). The Jewish doctor Edward Bloch who attended Hitler's mother until her death and knew the young Adolf well – Hitler used to send him his drawings of Viennese scenes for which Dr Bloch paid 20 crowns a piece, gratefully received by Hitler – remembered how he had seen Hitler in Linz, just before he moved to Vienna: 'In all my forty years of medical practice I have never seen a young man so completely bowed down by grief and suffering as the young Adolf Hitler was.' In 1933 Alma Mahler Werfel and Franz Werfel saw Hitler in an hotel in Breslau: 'The whole town of Breslau was in an uproar. I waited hours to see that face. . . . A face that had conquered 30 million people must be some face after all! It was some face all right. Hypnotic eyes . . . a young face, full of terror . . . no Duce! but a youth that would never blossom into maturity or find wisdom!'

In the ego, in every person's mind, were the caverns and abysses that were reflected in Vienna's slum dwellings and hellish conflicts, which they had, indeed, helped to produce. Inspired by Freud, Vienna's Jewish doctors, psychologists and writers began to explore the depths of this underworld. They concluded that the sick society (in the ailing city of Vienna) and the sick ego infect and poison each other. The brutality, aggression and rebellion of the young, both Negroes and whites, that was experienced in the nineteen-sixties and seventies in the dehumanized ugliness of America's cities was also a feature of life in Vienna, the melting pot of the twelve nations of the Danube provinces, at the end of the nineteenth and beginning of the twentieth centuries.

Here in Vienna, Freud saw, in a vision of poetic magnitude, that illnesses, the psycho-physical wounds of the ego, indicate wounds experienced in childhood, centuries, millennia ago. In Vienna writers had already anticipated Freud in the interpretation of dreams and of trauma (Freud himself recognized the close connection between his creative fantasy and the 'free play' of poetic imagination): in the *Jewess of Toledo, Libussa* and *Strife in the House of Hapsburg* Grillparzer had explored the wounds in the depths of the souls of the oppressed subject races. Nikolaus Lenau, in his *Albigensians* and *Ziska*, portrays the inner depths, to this day still not healed, of the people in southern France and Bohemia-Moravia, prophetically warning about the coming eruption from the latter volcano. Robert Hamerling (a blood relative of Hitler's) created a sort of precursor of Hitler in the militant regime in Münster described in his *Jan van Leyden, King of Sion*. Franz Theodor Csokor was another writer who, in writing about the Münster anabaptists, was really aiming at Hitler. Freidrich von Reck-Malleczewy was arrested by the KZ, in whose hands he died, for his anabaptist novel of 1933 was also aimed directly at Hitler.

In and around Freud's Vienna proof of the reality of the trauma of the recent, the distant and the far-distant past was given in the novels of Kafka, Brod (Brod says that Kafka was the only person in Prague who still believed in 1918 in the victory of the Balkan powers), Werfel, Kubin, Broch, Musil, Saiko, Doderer and others. Freud was to find this trauma in Vienna, in old Austria, in the immediate present as well as in the furthest past of mankind. He found it in his patients, mostly people in the higher echelons of society who unconsciously were particularly 'good' at the dubious art of concealing their innermost thoughts, silencing their desires and repressing the fires that blazed in their depths. Freud's constant experience in Vienna was that 'all the evil spirits have been loosed upon me' (7 January 1913). In Vienna and in the

13

Freud

Danubian provinces, primeval forces were still atavistically alive in contemporary man. As in the 'dark Middle Ages' a scapegoat was sought and found: the Jews.

On 3 March 1923 Freud wrote from Vienna to Romain Rolland:

... I, of course, belong to a race which in the Middle Ages was held responsible for all the plagues that beset people and which is currently blamed in Austria for the collapse of the empire and in Germany for losing the war. Such experiences are sobering and do not incline one to believe in illusions. A great part of my life's work also (I am ten years older than you) has been devoted to the destruction of my own and mankind's illusions. But if this one is not somehow realized [in an earlier part of the letter he has described this 'illusion' as the 'extension of love to embrace all human beings'], if we don't learn, in the course of our development, to divert our destructive impulses from our own kind, if we continue to hate one another for small differences and to kill one another for small gain, if we always use our progress in mastering natural forces for mutual annihilation, what future will there be for us? It is already difficult enough to ensure the continuance of our race, with the conflict between our natures and the demands of the culture that has been imposed on us.

Faced with the collapse of the old Austria and the middle-European states, with the approaching catastrophe, with man's wretched condition, Freud, the old-Austrian, turned away from the simplest Anglo-American belief in the virtues of progress. He wrote, on 9 December 1928, to Richard Dyer-Bennett who, in his book *Gospel of Living,* had set forth precisely this belief in the golden West and warned him:

To turn human beings into Gods and the earth into heaven would not be an aim of mine. This is too reminiscent of 'vieux jeu' nor is it quite feasible. We human beings are rooted in our animal nature and could never become godlike. The earth is a small planet, not suited to be a 'heaven'. We cannot promise those willing to follow us full compensation for what they have to give up. A painful piece of renunciation is inevitable. ...

Renunciation was the ethos of old Austria's jansenist officials! Renunciation was what Grillparzer and Stifter had taught.

Freud is talking here about a phenomenon first observed by Adolf Loos in 1908 in his essay *Ornament and Crime*: *the uncontemporariness of 'contemporaries'*:

The tempo of cultural development is impeded by the stragglers. I may perhaps live in the year 1908, but my neighbour is living in 1900, and another man in 1880. It is a misfortune for a state when the culture of its inhabitants is spread over such a great timespan. The Kalspeasant is living in the twelfth century, while in the Jubilee

14

Freud, the Viennese Jew

Celebration [1908 in honour of Emperor Franz Joseph] marched people who would have been thought backward during the time of the great dispersal of populations.

Freud warned Dyer-Bennett: 'What also seems over-optimistic to me is your judgement that humanity has progressed far enough to react to an appeal such as yours. A very thin top stratum may come up to your expectations, but otherwise all the old levels of culture – that of the Middle Ages, of animistic earlier times, of the Stone Age itself – are still active in the great mass of the people.' Watching Bosnians, Montenegrians, Tyrolers daily in the Vienna streets, Freud saw the centuries passing by in the Prater, in the many snackbars and suburban restaurants. 'Then what can one do to make life better? In my opinion, be patient and accept that there is still a long way to go.'

One must be patient, and dare to take the 'long way' through a distant country (the title of one of Schnitzler's plays) equipped with the Jewish experience of suffering, the experience of Vienna, that highly complex, many-layered entity where 'on the ground and first floors' upstairs and downstairs, masters and servants, the open and hidden layers of the consciousness, and the twelve nationalities at once so near and so widely separated, co-exist.

Freud saw all this, from a detached standpoint as a Jew. He was aware of the connection between his unconscious and his Jewishness, and in 1926 admitted to Enrico Morselli: 'I don't know whether you're right in thinking that Psychoanalysis is a direct product of the Jewish spirit, but if it were I wouldn't feel ashamed.' Freud's unconscious is as much a direct product of the Jewish spirit as it is of Vienna, of the old Austria.

In 1910 Karl Kraus published an essay entitled 'The Chinese Wall'. This was a Viennese catchphrase at that time (also used in the following context: 'the Austrians are the Chinese of Europe'). Count Heinrich von Lützow, a diplomat in the imperial service as ambassador to Rome in the difficult years between 1904 and 1910 when Austria was trying to reach an agreement with Italy, often refers to this 'Chinese Wall' in his memoirs, *In the Diplomatic Service of the Imperial Monarchy*, published in Vienna in 1971. The Great Wall was, in 1911–4, as Lützow emphasizes, what divided the 'society', that is those nobles eligible to be received at court (you had to be able to trace your family back through eleven ancestors on both your father's and on your mother's side of the family), from all the rest of the population, and particularly from the middle-class intelligentsia.

Freud

For Karl Kraus the 'Wall of China' in Vienna – and the legal aspect was not the least – was the

. . . pathological result of allowing morality to cripple sexual feelings. . . . Perversion is rampant in the world. . . . For us things have become problematic that for thousands of years were perfectly natural. We have built our dwellings on what we thought was an extinct volcano. . . . Eros, starving, was supposed to sublimate his tastes; he has become not more selective, but fiercer, and chooses what has been denied him. . . . He pretends to feel brotherly love and feasts on wounded warriors. . . . We have sat down to warm our toes at the sacred flame that used to inflame men to great deeds, and it has set fire to our homes. The social structure designed for its own and our protection has become highly inflammable. We built an oven to contain a flame, and now the oven itself is burning.

Kraus goes on to say that the so-called Christian, bourgeois, European, Caucasian morality had 'built iron-clad ships but was performing a ritual dance round the fetish of the hymen', that the Chinese in Europe

. . . would find a race whose people overwhelmed one another with wars and with 'brotherly love' and who combined only to despise all those of a different colour or different habits. East and West saw each other as devils and held their noses. . . . *The Great Wall of Western morality* protected sex from those who wanted to force an entry and at the same time protected people from sex, thereby creating a traffic between innocence and greed and the more doors were slammed on pleasure, the more eagerly people awaited experience. People beat at the great gates and the tumult caused the wall to shake. Chaos was welcomed because order had failed.

That was the situation in Europe before 1914 in terms of personal life; the oppressed but lively sexual urges exploded. Men and boys hastened to the battlefields in order to be 'free' and courted death as the experience of orgasm. They thought of being 'reborn' through war, becoming 'manly', of being able to prove their virility in an experience akin to sexual ecstasy. Thus they rushed to war, in the Kaiser's Germany, in France (the military academy of Saint-Cyr was nicknamed 'La Jésuitière', the jesuitry, where chauvinism and a narrow Jansenist code were preached) and in the German-speaking provinces of Austria-Hungary, urged on by their women-folk who longed to experience openly *their* orgasm in submission to the 'heroic' ideal.

Leon Trotsky (who had been living in Vienna since 1907) was walking with Victor Adler, a Jewish doctor and the grand old man of Austrian Social democracy (Freud was to live at Adler's old address, 19 Berggasse), through the streets of Vienna after the outbreak of war. Trotsky was astonished by the air of horrible excitement among the crowd, composed of all the nationalities of the empire. He thought that they were aware of an increased intensity, of imminent change, and that great hopes had begun to stir in them. Victor Adler remarked upon the 'festive atmosphere': 'They are all rejoicing because they don't have to go to war. And also all the extremists, all the crazy people are out on the streets. This is their day. Jaurès's murder is just the beginning; war unchains instincts, all forms of madness.'

Trotsky wrote in his autobiography: 'A psychiatrist by profession, Adler approached political events, especially Austrian politics – as he often ironically remarked – from a psycho-pathological viewpoint.'

In 1898 Freud and Dr Karl Lueger, 'the Master of Vienna' (as Freud called him), happened to visit the St Caugian caves on the same day. The caves contained subterranean stalagmites and stalactites of demoniacal aspect: Lueger, the man whom the Nazis later described as 'the first Führer' who knew so well how to manipulate for political ends the hidden unconscious of the 'little man' and how to direct his love and hatred in his own service; and Freud, who wanted to help people to live in harmony with their own subconscious natures. When, in 1898, Tsar Nicholas through his foreign minister, Muraview, invoked the powers to a peace conference, Freud wrote in a letter from Ausee: 'The news of the day, this manifesto from the Tsar, also concerns me personally. . . . If I could meet him, two people might perhaps be helped. I could go to Russia for a year and remove just enough, so that he wouldn't suffer, and leave enough to prevent him starting a war. Subsequently we would hold three conferences a year, exclusively in Italy and I would give my services free.'

When Freud was made a professor by Emperor Franz Joseph in 1902 (he received the title but was never given a chair), he wrote: 'There is such a shower of congratulations and floral tributes that it's as if his majesty had officially recognized the role of sexuality, and the Cabinet ratified the interpretation of dreams, or the necessity of psychoanalytical therapy in the treatment of hysteria had been passed by Parliament with a two-thirds majority.'

Outside the Vienna Parliament, on the Ring stood statues of charioteers. They were supposed to represent man's ability to control his urges. (According to the Platonic parable, the soul is a chariot from which the mind must direct the horses or passions.) But inside Parliament – as both the young Hitler and the already 'elderly' Freud (he felt himself to be old in 1913: 'Yes, I really am already 44 years old, an elderly, somewhat shabby Israelite') along with millions of other observers had noticed – endless ugly scenes were being enacted; 'German nationalists and Czech delegates hurled themselves on one another, fought and roared like wild animals.'

How was one to tame this fearful man-animal that was in the process of tearing itself to pieces? Freud saw the individual as a state and in many respects his view of it was an old Austrian one.

Even Freud, a linguistic scholar of the first order, did not realize how closely his concept of a hierarchy within the personality was modelled on the complicated orders within the Hapsburg monarchy. Thus the 'id' forms the lowest level of the state within each person, the spiritual underworld; in the often unruly id are found Eros and the death-wish (the urge of the peoples of the Danubian provinces to embrace death in war, civil war and rebellion). The sub-strata of the Habsburg Empire, the volcanic depths, correspond to the id; it expresses the Christians', and indeed the Jews' permanent revolt against the 'loved', but secretly hated, God the Father, the all-powerful Jehovah – a subconscious hatred whose outward manifestation was especial zeal in the performance of secular and religious duties.

Life, the personality, had to carry the troublesome burden of the id. As the personification of unbridled pleasure (Freud was a puritan) it needed the stabilizing power of a realistic principle to keep it in check: the ego. The ego bore a heavy responsibility, like all politicians in the non-Hungarian half of the Empire. The ego had to be the buffer between the blind urges of the populace, of the id and the wearisome external realities of life in those days, from 1866 to 1914! The ego had to mediate between the ever-rebellious lower regions, the id, and the above-stairs or super-ego. In these upper regions, the super-ego, are situated laws, precepts, order, religion and the arts; all the higher cultural achievements of mankind. Characteristically Freud considered these 'higher cultural achievements' to be the repressive achievements, just as under the imperial government the ministry for culture and education had ruled, from above, repressively.

The super-ego is like Emperor Franz Joseph, but even surpasses and transcends him. It is also impossible in our day and age to imagine what the position of the Emperor was during the Empire, or how it was that turbulent German Nationalist students could have turned into true-blue civil servants and officers. There was a very deep-rooted belief in the Emperor which united Czech, Polish, Croatian and German 'empire loyalists'.

The internal disintegration of this belief in the Emperor between 1880 and 1914 provides the background to the birth of psychoanalysis for Freud, who called upon the super-ego to be an artificial omnipotent father in the place of the rapidly weakening Emperor Franz Joseph. The super-ego had a truly imperial function, fulfilled in the same way as the paternalistic, apostolic sovereign, Emperor Franz Joseph, fulfilled his function or as God the Father acted as protection for the Son of Man.

And what means did the super-ego have to keep its pre-eminence in the Person-State ? First and foremost, censorship. In Metternich's regime censorship reached a high enough level in the press, theatre and literature. As world war became imminent censorship was increased until during the war years it reached unbelievable proportions. During the nineteenth century censorship was particularly sensitive to any insult to the almighty imperial dynasty which, according to the imperial family, could be damaged not only by attack, conspiracy, outbursts of hatred, but also by love, by faithful service. Grillparzer's play *A true Servant of his Master* seemed to the Emperor Franz to be an attack. The servant was not supposed to approach too near to His Majesty, not even in an excessive display of love.

Freud knew Viennese censorship in old Austria in all its many colours : its direct form, as the voluntary censorship exercised by journalists and writers who already eliminated or suppressed anything in their thinking that might give offence to the high-ups if they were written down. Freud knew the neo-puritan self-censorship of a middle-class 'good society' which, beginning with the 'unmentionable', underclothes, censored, repressed and suppressed everything to do with sex. 442,092/920/FRE

Freud's 'censorship of dreams' is an imitation and offshoot of the many direct and indirect forms of censorship in Austria that formed a permanent 'Brothers' Quarrel' (*Bruderzwist im Hause Hapsburg* is the title of another play by Grillparzer). There was a civil war in the individual heart, in the Austrian state, in the Habsburg family. The super-ego. Emperor Franz Joseph, knew that his wife, the Empress Elizabeth, hated him, as did his son, Crown Prince Rudolf, who committed suicide three months before Hitler was born. He knew that his heir, Archduke Franz Ferdinand, hated him and made him sign a formal declaration in council on 28 June 1900 in the presence of all the notables of the empire renouncing all rights of succession on behalf of his children. Fourteen years later to the day, on 28 June 1914, Franz Ferdinand was assassinated at Sarajevo. The fall of the House of Habsburg had the dimensions of a classical tragedy. Freud, living eye to eye with the Greek tragic writers, had no doubts on the subject. The drama in the human heart is really tragic and ends only too often with the total disintegration of the personality. *Finis Austriae, finis hominis*. Austria's end is man's end : the 'final

solution' of the Jewish question, the final solution of the human question.

Faced with an extraordinary human situation in that Viennese world Sigmund Freud became a saver of souls. He opposed the dangerous political soul-savers, charismatic leaders like Karl Lueger, against church or religio-political leaders like Pastor Wilhelm Schmidt, the eminence and rise of the First Republic which was dominated by Christian Socialist regimes. Freud declared himself openly to his friend Oskar Pfister who was a doctor, an evangelical theologian, cleric and psychologist, as the founder of a new order of new soul-savers: 'I do not know whether you have come across the hidden link between "lay-analysis" and "illusion". In the former I want to protect analysis from doctors, and in the latter from priests. I want to put it in a position that doesn't yet exist, in the care of temporal soul savers who don't have to be doctors and who are not allowed to be priests.' (25 November 1928.)

Sigmund Freud reflected in his personal life and work the collapse of internal and external hierarchy of the Habsburg Empire. He saw how old-established authority as represented by religion had failed, how they could no longer control the upheavals from beneath. Heinrich Heine had foreseen the chaos. The Church, all churches, were losing their power over men's minds. The Jewish religion watched helplessly as more and more Jews were lost to it, drawing away from their faith, being baptized and emancipating themselves.

Who was to take on these 'lost souls'? They were burning in hell at the mercy of uncontrollable urges, like the poor souls in hell whom Freud as a child had seen by gaslight on Breslau station. Who was to be the new pastor? Freud was convinced that this was *his* task. Therefore he campaigned for fellow-workers, apostles of his 'great good news'; and was appalled to discover that some of the faithful had betrayed his work, and become Judases who perverted his teaching. In 1902 came the final break with Fliess, in 1911 Adler abandoned him, Stekel in 1912. C. G. Jung severed contact with him in October 1913, in 1924 Rank, then a few years later Ferenczi, dissociated themselves from him.

One must, nowadays, consider Freud's international pre-eminence in the light of his string of betrayals on the personal level. Freud could have adopted Emperor Joseph's much-used phrase that he repeated almost mechanically every time he was told of a fresh disaster in his family, or his Empire or among his subjects: 'I am spared nothing.' The Emperor was resigned, but not Freud: 'the sovereign ego' could not afford to give up the struggle: the cause of mankind is not yet lost.

A Jew in Vienna

Vienna: The Jewish quarter.

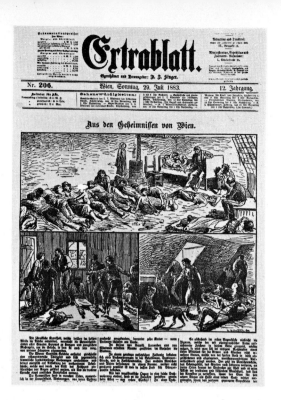

Antisemitic drawing by Hans Schliessmann, 1880.

Above, left Front page of *Extrablatt*, 29 July 1883, with drawings of slums. The conditions in Jewish slums were to make a deep impression on Stefan Zweig and the young Adolf Hitler alike.
Above Karl Lueger, who was appointed Burgomaster of Vienna in 1895, had long been an antisemite and when he came into office he instituted widespread propaganda. Freud came to regard him as a personal and deadly enemy and Hitler as a prophetic master.

Opposite Antisemitic cartoon published in *Krach*.

Overleaf The New University taken over by the Nazis in 1938. The banners proclaim 'Ein Volk, ein Reich, ein Führer'.

Top, left Viennese antisemitic propaganda in 1932.
Top, right Among the books burnt in Berlin in 1933 were Freud's works. Freud's comment was 'What progress we are making. In the Middle Ages they would have burnt me, nowadays they are content with burning my books.'
Bottom Official discrimination against a Jewish shop-owner in Vienna.

Plaque on a house in the Jewish district, commemorating the resistance of Viennese Jews during the Nazi occupation. It reads: 'Before 1942 Place of Refuge; on 28 May 1942 Place of Deliverance; until 1945 Place of Defiance in the service of the Resistance for Austria.'

The Jewish cemetery in Vienna. Freud's feelings for Vienna and his Jewishness alike were often ambivalent. Of the cemetery he wrote: 'A grave in the Zentralfriedhof is the most distressing idea I can imagine.'

2

Freud and Medicine
in Vienna

George Rosen

The figure of Moses obsessed Freud for many years. In 1914 he published anonymously an essay on Michelangelo's statue, but the symbolic figure of the prophet continued to engross him, particularly towards the end of his life.

WILFRED TROTTER, surgeon and pioneer social psychologist, observed in 1915 that 'however much one may be impressed by the greatness of the edifice which Freud has built up and by the soundness of his architecture, one can scarcely fail, on coming into it from the bracing atmosphere of the biological sciences, to be oppressed by the odour of humanity with which it is pervaded. One finds everywhere a tendency to the acceptance of human standards and even sometimes of human pretensions which cannot fail to produce a certain uneasiness as to the validity, if not of his doctrines, at any rate of the forms in which they are expounded.'[1] The sense of unease noted by Trotter, the psychological tension experienced by a physician oriented to pathology in biological terms, is of more than casual interest for it echoes Freud's own experience twenty years earlier when he began to treat hysteria.

'I was not always a psychotherapist,' Freud wrote in 1895, 'having been trained in localized diagnosis and electroprognosis like other neuropathologists ; and it still seems strange to me that the case-histories which I write read like short stories, and lack, so to say, a serious scientific character. My consolation must therefore be that this situation is apparently due more to the nature of the subject than to any predilection on my part. Localized diagnosis and electrical reactions simply have no significant place in the study of hysteria.'[2]

With these words Freud placed himself in a specific social and intellectual milieu, in the medical world of Vienna during the last decades of the nineteenth century. At the time he made these comments Freud was forty-one and had been active for some twenty years as a laboratory investigator and medical practitioner. His initial aim when he enrolled as a medical student at the University of Vienna in 1873 was apparently to become a research biologist. Nor did he abandon this goal even when he realized during his first years at the university that 'the peculiarities and limitation of my talents denied me any success in the several scientific disciplines into which I had plunged with youthful eagerness'.[3]

In 1876, after having completed his studies in comparative anatomy with the zoologist Carl Claus, Freud entered the Physiological Institute directed by Ernst Brücke, one of the leading physiologists of the nineteenth century. Here, except for a few brief interruptions, he remained until 1882, occupied with the microscopic anatomy of the nervous system. Also indicative of Freud's inclination to medical research is the circumstance that in 1878 he spent a semester and part of his summer vacation working in the laboratory of Salomon Stricker, professor of experimental pathology. During this period, on 6 August 1878, he wrote to his friend Wilhelm Knoepfmacher, 'I have entered another laboratory during the vacation and am preparing myself for my real occupation. To flay animals or to torture people, and I incline more and more to the former alternative.'[4]

Even after turning to clinical practice, Freud maintained his original role as a medical scientist. Indeed, in 1882, when he applied to Hermann Nothnagel[5] for a position in internal medicine at the Allgemeine Krankenhaus, Freud supported his request by stressing his experience as a researcher in zoology, physiology and histology, a qualification consistent with Nothnagel's emphasis on scientific investigation in clinical medicine.[6] This view of the physician as a man of science, and the ideology which provided its rationale, were reinforced by Freud's professional environment. As a medical man and a very hard-working one, the kind of life he led kept him out of the mainstream of avant-garde culture. Freud's Vienna was only tangentially the city of Hermann Bahr, Hugo von Hofmannsthal, Richard Schaukal, or Arthur Schnitzler.[7] His personal associations were almost entirely with physicians like himself, almost all Jewish.[8] Of these, Oscar Rie (1863–1931) and Leopold Königstein (1850–1924) are perhaps best known. Freud wrote his clinical studies on hemiplegia in children with cerebral palsy together with Rie, a pediatrician, who was his colleague at the Kassowitz Institute, and who also attended the Freud children. Königstein, an ophthalmologist, was another close friend, who confirmed Carl Koller's announcement of the use of cocaine as an anesthetic in eye surgery. Even better known and of whom less need be said is Josef Breuer, a talented experimental physiologist and successful practitioner (1841–1925) with whom Freud became acquainted in Brücke's laboratory and with whom he later collaborated in the *Studien über Hysterie*.

Clearly, during the two decades preceding the appearance of psychoanalysis, Freud had been deeply and actively involved in the medical world about him as scientist and practitioner. Knowledge of the concepts, the values, the attitudes which characterized this milieu, and the ways in which they were applied, is necessary to understand the intellectual and cultural influences which Freud absorbed and which he utilized in various ways in his evolution toward psychoanalysis.

When Egon Friedell quipped, 'Is Freud, then, a metaphysician? Yes, but he doesn't know it,' he struck closer to the mark than he himself may have realized.[9] For Freud did have a metaphysic which is only partially stated or is implicit throughout the body of his writings, and which became more prominent only toward the end of his life when he loosened the reins on his imagination. Fritz Wittels suggested that Freud's bent toward abstract speculative thought was so overpowering that his fear of being dominated by it led him to curb it by dealing with scientific problems involving concrete data.[10] This view is supported by Freud's comment to Ernest Jones that as a young man he 'felt a strong attraction towards speculation and ruthlessly checked it'.[11]

But what led Freud to restrain his speculative tendencies, to discipline his imagination, and to aim at becoming an exact scientist? The major influence in this respect was his teacher Ernst Brücke. On various occasions Freud himself attested to the importance of this man, referring to him as the teacher whom he honoured above all others, and as 'the greatest authority who affected me more than any other in my whole life'.[12] What kind of man was Brücke to make such a profound impression on the young Freud, and what was the nature of his influence? A lead to an answer is provided by Freud's statement in 1925 that 'in Ernst Brücke's physiology laboratory I found . . . men whom I could respect and take as models.'[13] The men were Brücke himself, and his assistants Ernst von Fleischl-Marxow and Sigmund Exner.[14]

When Biff in Arthur Miller's *Death of a Salesman* says, 'I just can't take hold, Mom, I can't take hold of some kind of life', he expresses the problem with which Freud dealt by adopting Brücke and his associates as models. Freud was casting about for some way of taking hold of his life and developing a professional identity, and the physiologists provided him with a social role, with a pattern of behaviour and set of values which he could accept and use to satisfy his own needs. The model which Freud saw in Brücke and his associates was not peculiar to them, though Brücke was one of its most prominent exemplars. It was the social aspect of a scientific movement which dominated medicine in the later nineteenth century and was a major influence in the formation of contemporary medicine. Although not limited to the German-language area of Europe, this movement was most vigorously developed there, chiefly by students of the German physiologist Johannes Müller.[15]

For this movement the goal of medical science was to achieve an understanding of pathological processes for clinical application. The French experimental physiologist François Magendie had emphasized in 1836 that pathological phenomena were a consequence of altered physiological processes. In principle there was no essential difference between physiology and pathology;

both had to be studied by the same scientific methods. Similar views on the need to develop normal and pathological physiology as a basis for clinical medicine were also advanced by Johannes Müller, and enthusiastically accepted as a programme for action by his students, who were to influence not just German medicine, but more broadly medicine in Europe and America during the later nineteenth century.

Representative are the remarks of Rudolf Virchow (1821–1902). In 1845, he defined life as 'the expression of a sum of phenomena each of which follows ordinary physical and chemical laws'.[16] Four years later he noted that 'disease is nothing more than life under altered conditions'.[17] Virchow and the many contemporaries with whom he shared these views were an avant garde of medical science whose aim, as he phrased it, was a 'mechanical analysis of nature'.[18]

Enthusiastic crusaders for this cause were four young physicians who in the early 1840s undertook to propagate their scientific faith and to demonstrate its truth by research. Emil du Bois-Reymond and Ernst Brücke, both in their early twenties, met in Müller's laboratory while still students and became the nucleus of the group. About this time, in 1841, Brücke made the acquaintance of Hermann Helmholtz, an extraordinarily gifted medical student, who had also been influenced by Müller. Recognizing that they were kindred spirits, both in terms of common interests and as personalities, the three young men soon became fast friends. In 1847, in the course of a visit to Berlin, Carl Ludwig, the fourth member of the group, met Brücke, du Bois-Reymond and Helmholtz, the men who were to be his life-long friends and companions in the creation of modern physiology.[19]

This was the year in which Helmholtz, then twenty-six, presented his classical paper on the conservation of energy, '*Über die Erhaltung der Kraft*', to the Berlin Physical Society, an event which illuminates the aims of their research as well as the atmosphere in which it took place. Opposed to the idea of a specific vital force in living organisms, which had dominated German biology and medicine during the earlier decades of the century, they resolved to demonstrate that vital processes could be investigated and explained in physio-chemical terms. In a letter of 1842 to a friend, du Bois-Reymond formulated their programme. 'Brücke and I solemnly pledged,' he wrote, 'to assert the truth that no forces other than the common physio-chemical ones are active within the organism. Where these forces do not yet suffice for an explanation, one must seek for their specific nature or mode of action in concrete cases by means of the physico-mathematical method, or assume new forces equal in significance to the physico-chemical forces inherent in matter which are always reducible to components that attract and repel each other'.[20] In applying it, physiological problems were to be elucidated by combining the study of the anatomy of an organ with a knowledge of the physico-chemical changes taking place during its function. Conversant with anatomy, Brücke and his friends were also students of physics and chemistry, aware of the newest developments and methods in these sciences.

What this approach meant in practice is evident from the dissertation offered by Carl Ludwig in 1842 for appointment to the medical faculty of Marburg. In this work, published in 1843 as *Beiträge zur Lehre vom Mechanismus der Harnsekretion*,[21] he developed a physical theory of renal secretion. The structure of the kidney glomeruli suggested that the first stage in renal excretion would be a diffusion of liquid through a membrane due to a difference in pressure between the two sides. Ludwig supported this work by further experiments published in 1849 and 1856. Through these investigations he created the foundation of our knowledge of diffusion through membranes.

By one of those historical coincidences that seem to lend credence to the idea of a *Zeitgeist*, 1842 was also the year when Brücke received the degree of doctor of medicine with a dissertation on the diffusion of fluids through inanimate and live membranes, *De diffusione humorum per septa mortua et viva*.[22] In this study he endeavoured to prove that the phenomena of resorption and secretion were not due to some vague vital force, but to physical and chemical forces that could be determined and measured experimentally. Imbued with this ideology, Brücke pursued a wide range of investigations as Professor of Physiology and Pathology in Königsberg (1847–9), and after 1849 as professor of physiology for forty years in Vienna. Among these were the physiology of vision, where Brücke identified the function of the ciliary muscle in accommodation, and made the first studies that led to the discovery of the ophthalmoscope by his friend Helmholtz. He also studied how the vocal cords, the tongue, lips and other structures produce vocal sounds in different languages. As a result Brücke was able to make a practical artificial voice box for the first patient whose larynx had been successfully removed by Theodor Billroth in 1873. Other areas investigated were digestion, where Brücke was a major pioneer of enzyme research, and the physiological and anatomical aspects of aesthetics.

In a similar spirit, Helmholtz who in 1849 succeeded Brücke in Königsberg, and then became Professor of Physiology in Bonn (1856) and Heidelberg (1859), and Professor of Physics in Berlin (1871), applied physical concepts and methods in physiological research, devoting his attention chiefly to the physiology of perception. In 1850 he measured the velocity of the nerve impulse, and in succeeding years he introduced the ophthalmoscope (1851) for examination of the retina, and the phakascope (1852) an instrument to study changes in the lens during accommodation. With these instruments and the ophthalmometer, an instrument for measuring the refractive power of the eye, he investigated the mechanism of accommodation and more broadly physiological optics. The results of this research were embodied in his classic *Handbuch der physiologischen Optik* (1856–66). During this period Helmholtz had also been investigating the physiology of hearing, an activity which in 1863 produced *Die Lehre von den Tonempfindungen*,[23] a fundamental work on the physics and physiology of sound perception.

The fourth member of the quadrumvirate, du Bois-Reymond, devoted his research to the electrical phenomena of animal tissues. Recognizing that the electrical activity of the nervous system could be used to study its function, he employed this type of experimentation to develop the discipline of electrophysiology. Du Bois-Reymond interpreted the electrical activity of tissues in terms of a theory of electric molecules, possessing negative and positive facets, which produced a current when stimulated.

Within a period of some twenty-five years these four men had in large measure achieved what as students they had resolved to do. They had become the leaders of scientific physiology in the German-language area, and their students and writings exerted a major influence on medical science from Russia to the United States. Advances in medicine were not absent in the clinical area, but during the latter half of the nineteenth century they were most evident in the basic branches of medicine, physiology and pathology. This was due almost entirely to the circumstance that these areas of knowledge had largely freed themselves from clinical medicine so that it was possible to apply to them the precise methods of the natural sciences and to turn them into independent disciplines.

Brücke and his friends were in the forefront of a generational movement. They were members of a generation of young physicians who insisted that medical problems receive scientific treatment based more on laboratory experimentation and less on clinical observation. In 1846, for example, Ludwig Traube[24] prefaced his *Beiträge zur experimentellen Pathologie und Physiologie* with a programmatic statement insisting on the need for scientific method in medical research, and asserting that pathology could become an exact science only by combining vigorous experimentation with precise observation.[25] Achievement of these aims required an intimate connection between experimental studies and clinical work, as well as facilities for their purpose. In consequence, medical scientists, pressing forward, sought to obtain the necessary buildings and equipment, and some even made the creation of such facilities a condition for accepting a position. Virchow, for example, came to Berlin in 1856 on condition that the Prussian government would build a pathological institute for him.

As a result of these developments, experimental physiology and pathology received a powerful impulse. Throughout Germany and the German-language area, universities created numerous laboratories or institutes associated with their medical faculties for the study of these and related disciplines. Most of these laboratories were not established until after 1860. Particularly noteworthy were those of Ferdinand Cohn for botany (Breslau, 1866), where Robert Koch first demonstrated the anthrax bacillus in 1876; of Carl Ludwig for physiology (Leipzig, 1869); E. F. Hoppe-Seyler for physiological chemistry (Strasburg, 1872); and Max von Pettenkofer for hygiene (Munich, 1879).

As late as 1865, however, Brücke's Institute, located on the second floor of an old rifle factory (*Gewehrfabrik*), was still quite primitive. It comprised a large lecture room, also used for microscopy, on either side of which were several smaller rooms, one serving as Brücke's office and work space. The Institute was not supplied with gas for illumination, and when anything had to be heated it was done on an alcohol burner. Nor was there any piped water; every morning the single *Diener* had to fill a tub with water in the yard and carry it upstairs for the use of those working there. In 1871, the Institute was enlarged by three additional rooms on the ground floor, of which one served as a dark room for optical experiments, and another was set up as an electrophysiological laboratory. This was the Institute in which Freud worked until 1882.[26]

Brücke never obtained the new Physiology Institute that he wanted. When he retired in 1890 he had worked for forty years under conditions which from our viewpoint appear wretchedly inadequate. Yet the number and quality of those who did scientific work under Brücke offer a very sharp contrast to the limitations and inadequacy of the physical facilities. Usually organized around some outstanding teacher and investigator, such as Brücke or Virchow, the institutes and laboratories were used to develop new knowledge and to instruct students attracted to the men who guided them. Students investigated subjects proposed by the professor, subjects often related to his own research, and thus learned to become independent investigators. Brücke visited the workplaces of the students at least once every day, listened to reports of work in progress, discussed problems that may have arisen, and offered suggestions on how to deal with them. The student was taught how to carry out research with attention to precise detail, to check his findings critically, and to formulate them clearly, reporting the truth as he saw it, in short, to fulfil to the best of his ability the ideal of scientific integrity. As E. Lesky, the historian of the Vienna medical school, has put it, 'In Brücke's laboratory they learned not just physiology, but rather a new form of medical thinking.'[27]

Underpinning this mode of thought was a philosophical position which has already been mentioned. The investigation of normal and pathological phenomena in living organisms required the rejection of any *a priori* metaphysical system. Description of such phenomena was only the beginning. Life was equated with matter and energy, so that their genesis and development had to be studied and explained in material terms, that is, in terms of the chemical and physical forces that determine these processes, and thus ultimately on the basis of the impersonal, objective laws of nature. Intention and purpose had no place in such an approach to biological phenomena. This doctrine, combining positivism, mechanism and materialism, was the philosophy to which Freud was exposed during his formative years as a medical student and young physician. Transmitted to him by those with whom he had chosen to identify, it was a major factor in the formation of his mode of thought and of his self-image as a medical scientist.

Freud received his medical degree in 1881, and the following year left Brücke's laboratory, because he recognized that to be able to marry Martha Bernays, to whom he became engaged in June 1882, he would have to earn a living by private practice.[28] For this purpose he entered the Allgemeine Krankenhaus, the great teaching hospital of Vienna, to gain clinical experience. But when Freud turned his attention to clinical medicine, he did not completely give up the goal of a scientific career. As he wrote to his fiancée in 1882, the separation from science was painful, but perhaps not final.[29]

Freud entered the hospital in July 1882 as an *Aspirant*, a position roughly the equivalent of an intern, which would enable him to become a candidate for the post of *Assistant* or *Sekundararzt,* that is, an assistant physician or resident.[30] He chose to begin in surgery, but after two months applied to Hermann Nothnagel, who had just become Professor of Internal Medicine, for a position on his service, and on 12 October 1882 began as an *Aspirant* in medicine. Freud worked in Nothnagel's clinic for six and a half months until

April 1883. Then on 1 May he was appointed *Sekundararzt* in the Department of Psychiatry headed by Theodor Meynert, a position he held for five months until September 1883. While still a student, Freud had been attracted by Meynert's personality and work. In the autumn of 1882, at the same time as he began to work under Nothnagel, Freud entered Meynert's laboratory to do research on cerebral anatomy, an activity which he continued until he left for Paris in 1885.

Meynert's significance for Freud's development is clearly reflected in his reference to 'the great Meynert, in whose footsteps I followed with veneration', and has been fully documented.[31] Noteworthy, however, is the relative lack of attention given to Freud's relations with Nothnagel and the influence the latter seems to have exerted on him. Freud referred to him in 1885 as 'the man who was so often decisive for me',[32] an accurate summation of one aspect of their relationship. There is no question that Nothnagel helped to further Freud's career with counsel and active intervention on a number of occasions. In May 1884 he discussed with Freud the economic realities associated with his desire to pursue an academic career in neurology, advised him how to prepare to apply for appointment as *Privat-Dozent*, urging him to publish clinical papers, and counselled him to acquire skill in electrotherapy. Implicit in the discussion, as Freud recognized, was an assurance that Nothnagel would sponsor him and refer patients to him. Then, in January 1885, upon Freud's inquiry, Nothnagel urged him to apply for the position of *Privat-Dozent*, and was a member of the committee that recommended the appointment. He also sponsored Freud for promotion in 1897, and again in 1902. Moreover, when Freud began his practice in 1886, Nothnagel referred patients to him.[33]

Yet Freud's attitude to Nothnagel was ambivalent. At the first meeting with him in 1882, Freud recognized his honesty and forthrightness, and there can be no doubt that in general he respected him as a man and a medical scientist.[34] Nonetheless, in a letter of 29 January 1884 to his fiancée, Freud refers to a medical meeting where he sat behind Theodor Billroth, the surgeon, and Nothnagel, and 'with outrageous impudence thought to myself: Just wait, the time will come when you will greet me as you now greet the others'.[35] A year later he noted in another letter: 'Nothnagel attended the session today, but was very impatient to get home. Either one of his children was sick or ten patients at ten gulden each were waiting for him.'[36] Again, on 2 February 1886 in a letter from Paris discussing his own character and abilities, Freud asserted that 'under favourable conditions I can achieve more than Nothnagel, to whom I consider myself far superior'.[37]

Nothnagel was the very model of a successful academic clinician, a man who had achieved the pinnacle of his career. In the eyes of the fifteen-year younger Freud, he was obviously a person worthy of emulation, against whom he could measure himself in terms of scientific and professional achievement, and perhaps for that very reason a focus of envy and resentment. Ernest Jones disposes rather casually of Freud's relationship with Nothnagel, alleging that his inability to emulate the professor's enthusiasm for medicine led him to leave the clinic after six and a half months. This may be true, but it is certainly not the whole story, for Freud clearly regarded his relationship with Nothnagel more seriously. Freud's attitude toward Nothnagel becomes more comprehensible if one remembers that he persistently pursued the goal of a career in academic medicine. At the point where the aim of becoming a laboratory scientist, as exemplified by Brücke, became impossible of attainment, Nothnagel presented Freud with a way of successfully combining medical science with practice in an academic setting. Moreover, Nothnagel's philosophy of clinical research was entirely compatible with the ideology Freud had learned in the physiology laboratory. At their very first meeting Nothnagel urged Freud to continue working in a scientific spirit, emphasizing that 'medicine can indeed be scientifically investigated.' To which Freud replied: 'I know that, it is not very different from the way the physiologists work.' 'It is the same', Nothnagel interjected.[38]

The point of view expressed by Nothnagel represented a trend of which he was a major exponent. After 1870, the idea developed among German-speaking clinicians that a thoroughly equipped laboratory for the scientific investigation of clinical problems should be an integral part of a teaching hospital. When Bernhard Naunyn was called to Königsberg in 1872, he insisted on the immediate establishment of a suitable laboratory for experimental studies as well as adequate budgetary appropriations for the pathological research to be carried on there.[39] Other clinicians also established laboratories and from these facilities, associated with medical faculties and teaching hospitals, issued valuable investigations which contributed in considerable measure to the flowering of scientific medicine in this century.[40]

The clinical laboratory is the product of trends in nineteenth-century medicine that developed in several countries but most importantly in Germany. One was the creation of the research laboratory for studies in chemistry, physiology and pathological anatomy. A second was the development and application of the concept of experimental pathology. Related to these developments was the movement designated as 'physiological medicine' with its emphasis on the examination and quantification of physiological processes in health and disease, as exemplified by thermometry, determination of blood-pressure variations, and methods for counting blood cells. Finally, there was the development of 'functional diagnosis', so called by Ottomar Rosenbach (1861–1907), assistant of Nothnagel at Jena. In this approach clinicians endeavoured to obtain information about the early stages of disease not by ascertaining anatomical changes, but rather by testing the functions of an organ physiologically. Methods of functional diagnosis were derived from experimental physiology, or new ones were devised and employed in clinical investigation, but all involved the laboratory.[41]

Nothnagel was in the forefront of this movement, having been associated at Freiburg with Adolf Kussmaul, the German clinician, whose use of the stomach pump in cases of gastric dilatation led to its employment for the study of gastric disease, thus inaugurating functional diagnosis.[42] His inaugural lecture at Vienna in 1882 contains a clear formulation of his position. For the clinician, Nothnagel said, 'the symptomatic picture is incomplete, the anatomical diagnosis is insufficient, only when we are able to derive the functional disturbance from the corresponding changes in the organ and to explain them physiologically, only then is the diagnosis a scientific one'.[43] Firmly convinced of the need for the closest possible connection between clinical observation and laboratory experimentation, Nothnagel remained primarily a clinical scientist who insisted that exact investigation in the laboratory must go hand in hand with the precise collection of information at the bedside by every available scientific means. Furthermore, he asserted, the physician deals with sick people, not diseases, so that the symptoms, signs and laboratory data must be seen in relation to the whole person.[44] These principles permeated his clinical teaching. When a patient was presented in the lecture hall, the intern to whom the case had been assigned for a work-up was required to read the case-history which had to be not only medically but also stylistically perfect. (It would certainly be of interest to know how many and what kinds of cases Freud worked up, but so far no one seems to have looked at the patient records in internal medicine for this period – if they still exist.) Using the information provided by the intern and the findings elicited by examination of the patient, Nothnagel developed the diagnosis on the basis of the anatomical and physiological relationships, and discussed the prognosis and therapy.

Nothnagel's clinic provided sufficient opportunity to study diseases of the nervous system, conditions involving the brain, the spinal cord or the peripheral nerves, according to the principles described above. Neurology was an area of major interest for Nothnagel, to be studied, as he told Freud, in terms of anatomy, physiology and pathology.[45] This was in line with his own experience and his development as a clinician. A younger member of the Berlin medical avant-garde, Nothnagel first studied pathological anatomy with Virchow, then in Königsberg turned to neurology under the influence of the clinician Ernst Leyden (1832–1910). Using animal experiments and clinical material, he became a neurophysiologist and neuropathologist. Among Nothnagel's numerous studies are investigations of epilepsy, a description of acroparesthesia and experimental demonstration of the primary role of vascular changes in vasomotor neuroses. His research was not limited to factual description, but endeavoured wherever possible to elucidate functional relationships. This approach assumed even greater significance with the demonstration by Gustav Fritsch and Eduard Hitzig in 1870 that stimulation of definite areas of the cerebral cortex activated localized muscle groups, and that removal of these areas led to paralysis or loss of function of the corresponding parts of the body. Here was a new mode of research and Nothnagel applied it energetically. However, in his enthusiasm for experimental neurophysiology, he did not forget the clinical aspects. As a result of his neuropathological investigations, he was recognized as a leading authority in this field and the publication in 1879 of his *Topische Diagnostik der Gehirnkrankheiten*, in which he summed up his experience of the clinical pathology of cerebral disorders and their localization, led to Nothnagel's appointment to the chair of internal medicine in Vienna.[46]

Freud was acquainted with this book, as indicated by a reference to it in his monograph on aphasia,[47] and undoubtedly read the numerous papers on neurological subjects which Nothnagel published in the 1880s and 1890s.[48] Moreover, as an intern in his clinic, Freud had undoubtedly been present at discussions of the numerous neuropathological cases demonstrated in the lecture-room and on ward rounds. Nothnagel also had a comprehensive command not only of the research techniques available at the time, but also of the current diagnostic and therapeutic methods and instruments. In addition to percussion and auscultation, his auditors were urged to learn the use of the laryngoscope, the ophthalmoscope and the microscope, how to perform the most important qualitative and quantitative chemical tests, and to acquire competence in electrodiagnosis and therapy. Alongside the limited pharmaceutical armamentarium of his day, Nothnagel stressed physical therapy, employing not only electrotherapy but also hydrotherapy and spa cures.[49]

Freud

Sometime in 1883, Freud decided to specialize in neurology and in December 1883 (or perhaps January 1884) received a position as resident (*Sekundararzt*) in the neurological division of the Medical Department, where he spent fifteen months acquiring a knowledge of clinical neurology.[50] Freud's version of this stage in his career, as recounted in 1924 when he was sixty-eight, cannot be accepted as it stands:

At that time this speciality [i.e. neurology] was hardly cultivated in Vienna. The clinical material for its study was scattered over various sections of internal medicine, and there was no adequate opportunity to acquire training in it, so that one was compelled to teach oneself. Even Nothnagel, who had been appointed shortly before on the basis of his book on cerebral localization, did not single out neuropathology among other separate areas of internal medicine.[51]

That neurology was not yet a fully accepted speciality in 1884 is true, but that this branch of medicine was neglected is not in accord with the picture of clinical and laboratory activity described by E. Lesky, the historian of Viennese medicine.[52] Nor does Freud do justice to Nothnagel's contribution to neurology. One cannot avoid the feeling that even two decades after the death of his former teacher and patron, Freud still felt the need, consciously or unconsciously, to diminish the significance of a man whom he had in some degree taken as a model and whom he also consequently saw as a competitor. Indeed, his remark in a letter of 29 August 1888 to Wilhelm Fliess seems in part to echo Nothnagel, perhaps with an overtone of sarcasm. 'To be a physician instead of a specialist, to use all means of examination and to take possession of the whole patient, that is certainly the only method which promises personal satisfaction and financial success.' But he continued, 'I did not learn enough to become a physician. . . . I was able to learn just enough so that I became a neuropathologist.'[53]

But what Freud learned in terms of diagnostic methodology and therapeutics was essentially what Nothnagel taught. In the latter's view, no physician can

. . . be a good diagnostician and clinician, though he may be the most outstanding experimenter, microscopist, bacteriologist or chemist, if he is not a good pathological anatomist. . . . But the anatomical diagnosis alone remains incomplete and insufficient, if it is not supplemented and expanded by the physiological comprehension and penetration of the [morbid] processes, if it is not developed into a functional diagnosis. . . . Yet we should never forget that in the specific case we must be clear about the anatomical situation.[54]

In short, pathological structure and function must be considered together and the diagnosis must be made in terms of their reciprocal relationship.

As evidenced by three papers published in 1884–6, and by his studies of children with cerebral palsy, this is the way Freud worked as a resident and later as chief of neurology in the Kassowitz Pediatric Institute. Freud's awareness of this viewpoint and methodology is clearly shown in the preface to his translation of Charcot's *Policlinical Lectures*, where he discusses the differences between German and French neurology. Toward the end of the nineteenth century French and German clinicians reasserted the scientific autonomy of clinical medicine. The French, continuing a tradition established by Paris clinicians, emphasized the methodological primacy of observing patients and of demonstrating post mortem the lesions underlying the disorders, *la méthode nosologique,* as Charcot called it. As part of this approach, French clinicians tended to emphasize the establishment of disease types on the basis of such data, as well as the concept of *formes frustes,* less typical examples encountered in clinical practice which could be grouped around the most characteristic forms. This approach was particularly well adapted to the development of neurology (or neuropathology as it was then called), and made possible important advances in this branch of medicine. Charcot's work in establishing such clinical entities as amyotrophic lateral sclerosis and disseminated sclerosis exemplifies its successful application. Freud noted that this characteristic of French clinical medicine was foreign to German practice where the concept of the typical case, the morbid entity, had no major role. On the other hand, a salient characteristic of the German clinicians was the tendency, understandable in the light of their history, to interpret physiologically the morbid condition and the interrelations of the symptoms.[55]

Despite some inclination to the French position, Freud remained within the conceptual and practical framework of German clinical neurology as developed and exemplified by Nothnagel, Meynert, Obersteiner and others.[56] His efforts to correlate psychological phenomena with physiological function and anatomical structure, best known at present through the 'Entwurf einer Psychologie' of 1895, are in line with certain aspects of scientific neurology at the end of the nineteenth century. However, Freud's interest in this problem was present much earlier, and is already evident in his study of aphasia (1891) where he discussed the form of psychophysical parallelism to which he adhered and which he derived from Hughlings Jackson.[57] According to Freud, 'The chain of physiological processes in the nervous system is probably not causally related to psychological processes. The physiological processes do not cease as soon as the psychological ones have begun. Rather the physiological chain continues, except that from a certain moment on every link of that chain (or some of them) corresponds to a psychological phenomenon. Consequently the psychological process parallels the physiological one (a dependent concomitant).'[58] Adherence to this position was compatible, however, with the thesis that mind could not exist apart from a brain. For Freud there was no evidence that mental processes occurred apart from physiological ones; they must therefore somehow be linked.[59] The nature of this linkage remained to be determined, but it seemed obvious that in some way it occurred in and through the structures of the brain, however they functioned. In a general sense, this position was commonly held in the medical circles in which Freud moved, and was put in very specific terms by Theodor Meynert, the psychiatrist and brain anatomist, with whom he worked for a number of years. Meynert had a continuing interest in linking mental phenomena to the anatomy and physiology of the brain. Assuming a single type of excitation in the nervous system, he expressed its operation in terms of quantitative variation related to as yet unknown chemical changes. For Meynert all nervous activity was based on innate reflexes mediated subcortically, or acquired responses determined by experience which followed cortical pathways, leading to normal and abnormal behaviour.[60] This basic neural pattern was intimately interwoven with an associationist psychology derived from Herbart and the British sensualist-empirical philosophers. Early responses to pleasure or pain led to the formation of a primary ego. 'Goal ideas' implanted in the ego then enabled it to gain control of cortical processes and develop organized logical thought. Meynert applied this theoretical analysis to psychopathological problems, for example, in the mental condition which he called *amentia,* a condition in which patients exhibited delusions and incoherent hallucinations, seemingly unrelated to their history or current circumstances, and in general a state of confusion (*Verwirrtheit*).[61]

The degree to which Freud absorbed the teachings of Meynert may be illustrated by a passage from *Jenseits des Lustprinzips* published thirty years later. Freud wrote: 'In psychoanalytic theory we assume unhesitatingly that the course of psychological process is automatically regulated by the pleasure principle. That is to say, we believe that a given process is always stimulated by an unpleasant state of tension, and then takes a path so that the final result coincides with a relaxation of this tension, that is, with an avoidance of the unpleasant or a production of pleasure.'[62]

Friends, Teachers and Colleagues

Freud and Wilhelm Fliess. They were very close friends from 1895 to 1902. Freud's
intense correspondence with Fliess did much to encourage his self-analysis.

Top The College of Professors of the School of Medicine, University of Vienna, 1881.
Bottom, left Ernst Wilhelm Ritter von Brücke (1819–92), director of the Institute of
Physiology at the University of Vienna, 1819–60, was one of Freud's favourite teachers, later
his supervisor and friend.
Bottom, right Eduard von Hofmann (1837–97), Professor of Forensic Medicine, 1875–89,
was Freud's examiner in the final examinations for his medical degree.

Top The laboratory of the Institute of Physiology where Freud worked as a research scholar from 1876 to 1882. The laboratory had no water supply, no gas and no electricity but it was the pride of the medical school on account of the distinction of its students.

Bottom, left Hermann Nothnagel (1841–1905) was Professor of Internal Medicine, 1882–1905. Freud served an apprenticeship in his department at the General Hospital in 1882–3.

Bottom, right Theodor Meynert (1833–92). Another favourite teacher of Freud's at the University and head of the Psychiatric Clinic where Freud worked in 1883. Freud described him as 'a more stimulating person than a host of friends'.

The psychiatric ward of the Allgemeine Krankenhaus, the Vienna General Hospital which Freud entered in 1882 after leaving Brücke's laboratory.

Top, left Nathan Weiss (1851–83), a hospital colleague whom Freud liked; he hanged himself in a public bath ten days after returning from his honeymoon.

Top, right Josef Pollak (1850–1916), another colleague of Freud's at the General Hospital.

Bottom, left Leopold Königstein (1850–1924), an opthalmologist, was one of the three men (the others being Freud and Koller) involved in the discovery of cocaine as an anaesthetic of great importance in eye medicine.

Bottom, right Carl Koller (1867–1944), took the lion's share of the glory in the discovery of the clinical uses of cocaine although Freud had been the first to point the way.

Paris 1885–6

Jean-Martin Charcot (1825–93). 'He engrosses me,' Freud wrote during his visit to Paris in 1885–6; 'when I go away from him I have no more wish to work at my own simple things. My brain is sated as after an evening at the theatre.'

Top The Hôpital de la Salpêtrière in Paris, where Charcot worked.
Bottom The inmates' cells at the Salpêtrière.
Overleaf, left Reconstruction of Freud's consulting room in Vienna.
Right Jane Avril, by Toulouse-Lautrec. Jane Avril, a dancer at the Moulin-Rouge, was a hysteric and a patient of Charcot's at the Salpêtrière.

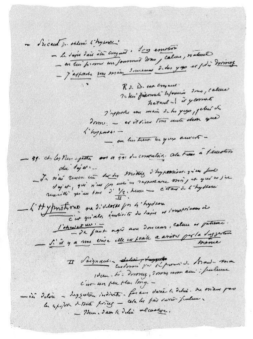

Top Engraving of Charcot's electrotherapy cabinet in the Salpêtrière.
Bottom, left Notes in Charcot's hand on the use of hypnosis.
Bottom, centre and right Letter in Freud's hand applying to the Faculty of Medicine board for a travelling grant to see Charcot in Paris.

During his stay in Paris, Freud went to watch Sarah Bernhardt and was enthralled. 'How that Sarah plays! After the first words of her vibrant, lovely voice I felt I had known her for years.'

Overleaf A demonstration of Charcot's use of hypnosis on hysterical patients. Freud attended Charcot's demonstrations for four months. Painting by André Brouillet.

Below 'Paris had been for many years the goal of my longings,' wrote Freud, 'and the bliss with which I set foot on its pavements I took as a guarantee that I should attain the fulfilment of other wishes also.'

Schloss Belle Vue, the restaurant in which, on 24 July 1895, Freud first glimpsed, through the analysis of one of his own dreams, his future theory that the essence of a dream is the fulfilment of a hidden wish.

Above, left Ernst von Fleischl-Marxow (1846–91), was one of Freud's closest friends. Freud's researches into cocaine had been prompted in part by his desire to help Fleischl who had been living in pain for years. Freud wrote to Martha about Fleischl, 'I admire him and love him with an intellectual passion, if you will allow such a phrase. His destruction will move me as the destruction of a sacred and famous temple would have affected an ancient Greek.'

Above Max Kassowitz (1842–1913), was the head of the first public Pediatric Institute where Freud worked for several years as director of the Neurology Department.

Left Plan of lectures in Freud's hand, enclosed in an application for habilitation, 1885.

Another worker who endeavoured to link nervous function and mental phenomena was Sigmund Exner (1846–1926), student of Brücke and Helmholtz, assistant to the former and eventually his successor, and one of the men whom Freud took as a model when he joined the Physiological Institute. Exner worked on optical physiology, particularly on the retina; on the physiology of voice and speech, as a result of which he investigated the tonal qualities of various languages and dialects, acquiring a large collection of phonograph records of dialects; and on cerebral physiology, where he helped to establish that localization in the brain was not sharply defined and that cortical areas tended to overlap. In 1894 Exner published an *Entwurf zu einer physiologischen Erklärung der psychischen Erscheinungen*, a work which Freud certainly knew.[63] Using the neurone theory, as well as ideas of Brücke and Meynert, Exner also developed a hypothetical neuro-logic psychology by means of which he endeavoured to explain a variety of mental processes, among them perception, memory and thinking. Underlying this theoretical structure were the concept of nerve excitation with quantitative variation, postulated emotion centres, and a mechanism for the association of ideas.

These efforts to ground mental phenomena on cerebral anatomy and physiology belong to the genre which Ellenberger has appropriately labelled 'brain mythology'.[64] Freud's *Entwurf* of 1895 belongs within this context, but with a difference. During his four months with Charcot in 1885–6 Freud was impressed with the French neurologist's views on hysteria, traumatic neuroses and hypnosis, and there is no doubt that this 'existential encounter', as Ellenberger terms it, opened up a new world of ideas to him. Freud later abandoned Charcot's views, as he did those of Breuer; in the 1890s he had already begun to occupy himself with the neuroses and was making psychological discoveries which to him were of the greatest moment. As he wrote to Wilhelm Fliess on 21 May 1894, 'I am pretty much alone here in elucidating the neuroses. They consider me almost a monomaniac, but I have the definite impression of having come upon one of the greatest mysteries of nature.' Part of the problem was how to explain the mystery, but as he noted in the same letter: 'There are still a hundred larger and smaller gaps in the neurosis story, but I am closer to an overall picture and general viewpoints.'[65] An obvious approach was to provide a physiological underpinning for the new discoveries, in the style of Meynert, Exner and others, and so the *Entwurf* was created. But to Freud's disappointment it was of no use in furthering his investigations and was abandoned. An echo of this situation may be found in a statement made in 1915. 'It is an unshakeable result of research,' he wrote,

Joseph Breuer (1842-1925), another close friend of Freud's and one of his greatest sources of inspiration. It was the discussions Freud had with Breuer which started him towards psychoanalysis 'that psychological activity is linked with the functioning of the brain as with no other organ. The discovery of the differentiation of the parts of the brain, and their special relationship to specific body parts and mental activities leads a bit farther – but how far is not known. For all efforts to uncover a localization of psychological processes, that is, efforts to think of ideas as stored in cells and to allow stimuli to wander along nerve fibres, have failed completely.'[66]

Freud's decision to abandon such efforts and to deal with psychological processes in the language of psychology, as Breuer proposed in 1895, did not mean that he dealt with his psychological discoveries totally *de novo*.[67] As he proceeded to separate the psychological from physiological considerations, much that was new still bore tell-tale characteristics of its ancestry. Freud's thought was formed in the context of nineteenth-century mechanistic physiology and medicine, and throughout his life he employed mechanistic terms and concepts. To be sure these were metaphors, but they were drawn largely from electrophysiology and physics, particularly hydraulics. Even after sloughing off the mentality of the nineteenth-century medical scientist, the vocabulary still remained. Certainly this was a factor underlying the sense of unease expressed by Wilfred Trotter in 1915. Yet Freud had to deal with a problem not unknown to other creative scientists: to develop a terminology and a conceptual structure appropriate for the description and explanation of categories of phenomena. To create a satisfactory terminology for his purpose, Freud made use of the materials available to him in nineteenth-century medical science. This was also true of his therapeutic methods. At first he seems to have relied on current methods of treatment: electrotherapy, baths, massage, spa cures, and the rest cure of Weir Mitchell. Indeed, Freud was still using them in the 1890s.[68] Nor was hypnosis new. Freud turned to it only in 1887, but he knew of it earlier since he had seen it in Paris, and it was a subject of considerable interest in medical and lay circles in the later nineteenth century.[69] Not until these had been tried and found wanting did Freud abandon them and turn to free association.

There were other influences upon Freud on his way to psychoanalysis. His indebtedness to Hughlings Jackson has been mentioned, but one cannot omit his use of Jackson's doctrine of the evolution and dissolution of function to develop the principle of regression which is basic to the genetic propositions of psychoanalysis.[70] The influence of Romantic science on Freud has also been explored and seems to have stemmed chiefly from Gustav Fechner,[71] a number of whose ideas were used in his metapsychology (topographical concept of mind, concept of mental energy).[72] A claim has also been made for an influence on Freud from German Romantic medicine, chiefly through Fliess, but this was not a major scientific source of Freud's thought.[73] Fliess was more a foil than a contributor.

Just as Marx was allegedly not a marxist, so Freud was not a freudian. He began his career by accepting the role of the man of science as defined by the scientific and medical milieu which he entered when he became a medical student and he behaved accordingly. As part of this role he internalized a philosophy of positivism and mechanism, and a methodology of clinical research, to which he remained in some degree formally faithful practically to the end of his life, even though he abandoned the substance. Into this form he fitted the new theory of the neuroses which he developed from 1886 to 1896, and later the depth psychology which he developed thereafter. For this reason the basic scientific sources of Freud's thought are to be seen in the physiology, pathology and medicine of the later nineteenth century as they developed in the German-language area of Europe, and specifically in Vienna. Without Freud there would probably not be psychoanalysis as we know it, but without the medical Vienna of Brücke, Nothnagel, Meynert, Exner and Breuer, Freud would not have developed as he did.

3

Freud's Vienna

Martin Esslin

THE thought of Vienna oppresses me', Freud wrote to his fiancée on 10 March 1886 from Berlin. Again and again, during his long engagement to Martha Bernays, when renewed difficulties in creating a sound financial basis for their marriage had further delayed their chance of setting up house together, Freud toyed with the idea of emigrating – to England, North or South America, or Germany – or moving to some small town in Austria and becoming a country doctor. Yet, although in his letters he spoke of 'the abominable steeple of St Stephen's cathedral' and declared that 'a grave in the Zentralfriedhof is the most distressing idea I can imagine', he never actually put his plan of leaving the city into practice. 'I feel full of fight and am not thinking of giving up my future in Vienna', he wrote to his fiancée shortly after he had once again raised one of those plans to leave. And even after Hitler had occupied Austria, he assured Ernest Jones who was urging him to get out: 'This is my post and I can never leave it.' And he only left when the situation for him had become plainly untenable.

Freud's ambivalent attitude to the city where he spent most of his life is highly characteristic of most Viennese intellectuals. They know far too well that the image of Vienna in the minds of those who only know it through operettas, Hollywood films and romantic novels, or even the image which remains in the mind of tourists who briefly pass through, is utterly false. The veneer of politeness, gaiety and good living certainly is there. But the politeness frequently turns out to be no more than a hard-headed desire to give good service in a city dependent on tourist traffic. Behind the façade of good living there was, certainly in Freud's times, if less so today, a great deal of the bitterest poverty. And underneath the gaiety there always boiled fierce political and personal hatreds and rivalries, much brutality and aggression. The very ease of life in Vienna appeared to some of its best creative brains as a threat to their ability to work. As Franz Grillparzer, one of Vienna's greatest poets, put it as early as 1843 :

> Schön bist du, doch gefährlich auch
> Dem Schüler wie dem Meister
> Entnervend weht dein Sommerhauch,
> Du Kapua der Geister.

> (You're beautiful but dangerous
> To Pupil and to Master,
> Your summer winds, they sap our strength,
> You Capua of the spirit.)

Freud's Vienna

(It was in Capua that ease of living had demoralized Hannibal's army before the assault on Rome.)

And yet, however restless and discontented the intellectuals of Vienna felt in their city, however much they might have complained that the complacency of its citizens, their mindless concern with good food and good wine, their unreliability, their concern for empty titles and their servility towards those who bore them, made the place a stagnant backwater where serious creative thought was quite impossible ('I have lived here for fifty years and have never come across a new idea here', Freud barked at Ernest Jones when he praised the creative atmosphere of Vienna), the fact remains that in the period around 1900 Vienna was in fact the crucible of many of the most important ideas which have most deeply shaped our century, for good or for ill: it was in Vienna – and in the Austrian cultural sphere of which it was the centre but which comprised the German-speaking populations of Prague, Budapest and Trieste – that Mach, Schlick, Carnap and Wittgenstein laid the foundations of logical positivism and linguistic philosophy; that Schönberg developed twelve-tone music; that Adolf Loos pioneered modern architecture: that Kafka revolutionized modern literature, together with writers like Musil, Broch, or Svevo (a very Austrian Triestine, although he wrote in Italian); and that Freud created psychoanalysis. And on the debit side: the greatest destructive force of the twentieth century also came out of Vienna: antisemitism, the ideology of politicians like Georg von Schönerer and Karl Lueger – who was Burgomaster of Vienna in Freud's time – and of Adolf Hitler.

Why should this city, the centre of an anachronistic supranational Empire in the process of dissolution, have been the cradle of so many world-shattering developments? What gave it the distinctive intellectual flavour from which they sprang?

Undoubtedly one of the elements that shaped Vienna's intellectual atmosphere was the heterogeneous nature of its population which had expanded so rapidly in the second half of the nineteenth century that it made the city into a veritable melting pot: from 1840 to 1910 the population of Vienna quintupled from 440,000 to more than two million – most of them drawn from the outlying and relatively underdeveloped parts of the Habsburg monarchy into what was one of its few areas of rapid industrial expansion: from Hungary, Poland, Galicia (the area of the densest Jewish population in Eastern Europe), Croatia and above all from the Czech- and German-speaking peoples of Bohemia and Moravia, where the home of Freud's family was. So numerous was the influx into Vienna of immigrants from Moravia and the Austrian part

43

of Silesia that in my own family (which partly came from there) this area was referred to as 'the cradle of humanity', because 'everybody one knows comes from that part of the world'. It was the development of the railways which speeded the rapid influx of these new populations. The terminal of the line from the area in question, the Northern Railway, was situated in the second *Bezirk* (*arondissement*) of Vienna, the Leopoldstadt; the new immigrants tended to settle near there; the district which had been the ghetto in the Middle Ages again became the centre of the Jewish population. It was here that Freud's family also lived after they had moved to Vienna from Freiberg in Moravia in 1860. And it was here that Freud frequented the local *Gymnasium* (grammar school) in the Sperlgasse.

A fair proportion of the new population *were* Jews. Moreover, while the large bulk of the immigrants from rural areas and peasant stock turned into industrial proletarians, the Jews tended to start as merchants or entrepreneurs and thus formed a much higher proportion of the lower middle class. Being resourceful and enterprising, they tended to thrive. It was one of the clichés of Viennese folklore that the first-generation Jewish immigrant to Vienna would have been an itinerant merchant, peddling his pots and pans, buttons, or samples of cloth from house to house. His sons would become wealthy industrialists or bankers, while the third generation would be made up of intellectuals: lawyers, doctors, writers, journalists. And there was a grain of truth in this pattern: the Jews of Hungarian, Bohemian, Moravian or Galician origin had a long tradition of abstract reasoning in the Talmud schools behind them: once they had secured the economic base of their family they wanted to better themselves in their sons and sent them to university, even if that meant considerable sacrifices for them. In 1890 one third of all students at the University of Vienna were Jewish. Here lay the roots of the antisemitism of Schönerer and Hitler. The rapid rise of the Jews to intellectual influence was also helped by the fact that, in contrast to the gentile Czechs, Croats, Hungarians and Rumanians who streamed into Vienna, they were largely German-speaking (or at least spoke Yiddish, a German dialect) and were thus free from one of the main handicaps under which members of the other nationalities suffered. Once they had emancipated themselves from the more rigid orthodoxies of Judaism, they became fervent admirers and upholders of German culture. Freud is quoted as saying: 'My language is German. My culture, my attainments are German. I considered myself a German intellectual until I noticed the growth of antisemitic prejudice in German Austria. . . .'

Freud's Vienna

Until the latent, or largely verbal, antisemitism of the nineties finally erupted into genocide under Hitler, the Jews of Vienna did not suffer too overtly under it. Burgomaster Lueger, who by violent antisemitic outbursts, gained electoral support among the lower middle classes, jealous of the rapid rise to wealth and professional status of their Jewish neighbours, in fact had Jewish friends and collaborators. When tackled about this, he is said to have replied: '*I decide who is a Jew and who isn't!*' And while it was difficult for Jews to reach the highest rungs of office, exceptions were always made in a society where personal influence (*Protektion* is the Austrian term for it, a clear remnant of a feudal way of thinking) could achieve a good deal and was eagerly solicited by the ambitious.

Indeed, the tensions and the competitiveness, which this relatively mild antisemitism gave rise to, might have had a stimulating effect on the intellectual life of the city. That so many of the major figures of Austrian intellectual life of the period were, in fact, Jews may have something to do with this need to prove themselves better than they were made out to be by the racial fanatics who argued that an inferior tribe like the Jews was incapable of any truly creative effort.

Various other factors account for the liveliness of Vienna's intellectual life in Freud's time. One of these may well have been the size and structure of the city itself: Vienna had grown in the course of centuries around a very compact central area, the inner city, in the exact middle of which stands St Stephen's Cathedral with the steeple which has become the emblem and symbol of Vienna. There are two concentric circles of outer suburbs around this centre – the first, where the old city walls used to stand, marked by a wide road called the Ringstrasse, the second, outer, circle by a second ring-road, the Gürtel. This concentric structure makes access to the centre relatively short from the inner ring of suburbs, so that anyone living in these can walk there quite comfortably. Combined with the fact that the centre contained many of the peculiarly Viennese coffee-houses this made for an ease of intellectual interchange and cross-fertilization which was quite unique.

The Viennese coffee-house (reputedly the fruit of the abortive siege of Vienna by the Turks in 1683, when, after the withdrawal of the besiegers vast stores of coffee were found in their abandoned camp) combined the features of a London club (and the London clubs, after all, spring from coffee-houses that opened when the Viennese fashion caught on in England) with an unparalleled ease of access. The typical Viennese coffee-house at the turn of the century was large, well-furnished and so spacious that there was no need to turn away customers : as a result it was an unwritten law that the purchase of a single small cup of coffee entitled the guest to remain in the coffee-house for the rest of the day. To show him that he was welcome the waiter would place a fresh glass of cold water on a silver tray before him at half-hourly intervals. Newspapers and periodicals in a multitude of languages were supplied free ; billiard tables, chess sets and playing cards were at the disposal of the guests ; on demand pen, ink and writing paper would be produced ; most better coffee-houses had a set of one of the large encyclopaedias and other reference books for the use of their customers ; messages could be left with the waiters who would conscientiously pass them on ; letters could be addressed to regular guests at their coffee house. As a result many writers and students spent their working day in the pleasant and comfortable surroundings of these hospitable establishments rather than in cramped furnished rooms or small flats filled with crying children. A large part of the city's intellectual life thus took place in the coffee-houses : the main personalities in literature, the law, music, the theatre, medicine or science constantly met each other and engaged in heated debate. New ideas would instantly be tested by discussion and, even more important, personal contact between members of the different branches of the intellectual life produced a healthy cross-fertilization between them. Psychoanalysis might be regarded as the fruit of just such cross-fertilization between medicine, psychology, philosophy, anthropology, and the study of literature, especially classical tragedy and myth. Freud was very typical of the Viennese medical man who, throughout his life, remained interested in the theatre, art, archaeology and literature. Only a medical man with a deep classical culture could have produced the synthesis of science and symbolical thought which is psychoanalysis.

Another source of this cross-fertilization, undoubtedly, was the ideal of a universally educated man which inspired the curriculum of the Austrian educational system, particularly in the 'middle school' (between the elementary and university levels), the *Gymnasium* or grammar school. The emphasis here was heavily on the classical languages, Greek and Latin, but natural sciences and mathematics were also taught very thoroughly, and – in marked contrast to the English-speaking countries – there was practically no specialization at this middle level : the examination which gave access to the University, the *Matura* (maturity examination) had to be taken in humanist *and* science subjects. Moreover, so powerful was the ideal of universal culture (*Allgemeinbildung*) that even those who, on entering university, specialized on subjects like law or medicine, continued to regard it as incumbent upon them to show their appreciation of the humanities by an interest in music, painting and literature. Anyone who had access to the University and thus belonged to the privileged class of the *Akademiker* (a position which also resulted in the immense practical advantage of having only one year of compulsory military service instead of three) felt he had to show his status by being able to talk about the arts, to quote from the classics, to go to the opera, the theatre, picture galleries and concerts. The book-case with the uniformly bound standard sets of the German classics was an indispensable status symbol even in the homes of dentists or agronomists or graduates of the technical universities who sported the academic title *Herr Ingenieur*.

Vienna was a very large city, one of the biggest in Europe; yet, at the same time, it was compact enough to enable the intellectual community to be in close physical and personal contact, with members of each branch of the intellectual life interested in what was happening in the others. Medical students and doctors would be hotly engaged in the veritable battles which raged about the music of Wagner between the conservatives and the innovators, while classical scholars, having had to pass their *Matura* in higher mathematics and physics as well, were still able to get excited about the theories of Einstein or Max Planck.

This compact and highly personalized intellectual life, moreover, rested on a broad base of popular respect and interest. While there were considerable class distinctions as far as income, occupation and living standards were concerned, culturally Vienna was an almost classless society; the reason for this probably lay in the late development of industry in the Habsburg Empire: well into the middle of the nineteenth century Vienna was essentially a city of artisans and small merchants. The popular comedies of that classic of the Viennese folk theatre, Johann Nestroy (1801–1862) portray a society of wealthy cabinet-makers and drapers ambitious to win the hand of some young baroness whose impoverished papa needs funds to keep up his country estate; the professional classes, doctors, lawyers and civil servants in these plays are seen also as artisans, craftsmen of a different sort; and the aristocracy, the vast majority of which belonged to the lower orders of nobility, was far from rich and by no means much more refined. (The exceptions, of course, were the grandee families who owned vast estates in Hungary and Bohemia, the Eszterhazys, Kinskys, Lobkowitzes and their kind whose vast baroque palaces are the chief adornment of cities like Vienna and Prague: they, and the court of the Habsburgs, were so elevated and remote that they played little part in the life of the city). One can glimpse this state of affairs in

Hofmannsthal's *Rosenkavalier,* where, after all, a member of one of the noblest houses marries into a merchant's family and the lower order of the aristocracy, represented by Baron Ochs, is shown as coarse and certainly on no higher level of refinement than the well-to-do tradesman.

The result of this state of affairs in Freud's time was a truly remarkable cultural homegeneity: the broad masses of the people, for example, were – and still are – as fond of the opera as the intellectual elite. A change in the artistic direction of the Vienna State Opera still makes headline news in the papers and is given precedence over international affairs of far greater import, while, on the other hand, the intellectuals are as passionately interested in soccer and the other popular sports as the lowest orders of the populace. The gap between popular music and more serious fare is, or at least was in Freud's time, not as wide as elsewhere : and musical controversies also become topics of very general interest.

The advantages of such a state of affairs are evident : not only does personal contact and proximity stimulate intellectual debate, but the fact that even the broad masses hold intellectual debate in respect and take an interest in it, enhances the intellectuals' status and gives them a feeling that their efforts are of importance.

On the other hand the close physical proximity of the debaters and the public's tendency to regard such debates as popular entertainment creates a fertile ground for acrimonious controversy in which personal malice and pride play an unduly prominent part. A good many of the early quarrels among psychoanalysts, and the atmosphere of personal acrimony with which they were pursued, were in fact simply typically Viennese intellectual rows. Another very characteristic example of the same phenomenon is the case of the philosopher Otto Weininger (1880–1903) which involved Freud in a war of pamphlets and letters to newspapers. Weininger, who had committed suicide at the age of twenty-three, was the author of the savagely misogynist book *Geschlecht und Character* (Sex and Character) in which he made use of the idea of bisexuality which Freud's Berlin friend and correspondent Fliess claimed was *his* discovery. Fliess accused Freud of having communicated the idea to Weininger. To defend himself Freud wrote a letter to the periodical *Die Fackel,* published by one of the central figures of Viennese intellectual controversy, the great satirist and polemicist Karl Kraus (1874–1936). Freud was an assiduous reader of Kraus's publication, which appeared at irregular intervals and was written entirely by Kraus himself. Kraus always conducted a whole gamut of intellectual polemics at the same time : he castigated the illiterate style in which the newspapers were written, attacked narrow nationalism and militarism, took sides for and against leading contemporary writers, propagated the rediscovery of neglected classics – and also conducted a relentless battle against hypocrisy in matters of sex. It is characteristic of the Viennese cultural climate that this highly intellectual – though brilliantly witty and amusing – writer should have become one of the city's best-known personalities, whose antics, affairs and adventures were followed by the entire population. Young people instantly judged each other as being either pro-Kraus (*Krausianer,* i.e. Krausians) or against him. Although a fervent advocate of a more humane treatment of prostitutes and sexual perverts, Kraus was essentially a puritanical moralist and rejected psychoanalysis – probably on account of the hysterical controversies amongst its adherents – as 'the disease of which it purports to be the cure'.

Kraus, with his savage indignation against impurity of all kinds, whether of language or moral intention, a hunch-backed Central European reincarnation of Dean Swift (if such a thing can be imagined), was far from representative of the general temper of Vienna: the homogeneity of Viennese culture manifested itself not only in the close personal contact of intellectuals and the absence of an unbridgeable gulf between the intellectual élite and the masses, it went even further: in Viennese eyes there was no gulf set even between the material and the spiritual sphere; it may be mere superficiality, but it might also be regarded as some sort of profound wisdom, that good food, drink, entertaining sports and pastimes, walks in the mountains or in a beautiful countryside were not regarded as different in kind from the more refined pleasures of the intellect: people who appreciated a Beethoven symphony as essentially a good tune could also derive pleasure from a popular song, as performed in a music hall or one of the open-air wine-drinking places; and if they exclaimed, on tasting a particularly delicious cream-cake: '*Ein Gedicht*!' (A poem!) they really did mean that for them the aesthetic pleasures of great literature were essentially on a par with the delights of good cooking. And if they followed Kraus's violently intellectual polemics, they did so only because they thought them entertaining, 'good fun'.

Essentially, then, Vienna was a place in which the whole of life tended to be seen and judged from a hedonistic point of view ('the pleasure principle', to use Freud's formulation); even its cultural and intellectual heights were seen in terms of sensual pleasure.

No wonder then that this city, at the turn of the century, appears in its literature as veritably obsessed with sex and sexual pleasure.

Freud

Basically there may have been little difference in this respect between Vienna and its eternal ideal and model, Paris, as it appears in the operettas of Offenbach and the farces of Feydeau. Here as there, beneath a thin veneer of surface respectability, the actual, as against the ostensible, code of morals, demanded from the men the maximum number of conquests, from married women the acquisition of discreet and faithful lovers. But there were significant differences too between the two cities: if Paris was grander, more vicious, if it had more style, Vienna seemed homelier, cosier, more good-natured. Arthur Schnitzler (1862–1931), like Freud a medical man, and much admired by Freud for his subtle insights into the hidden motivations of human behaviour, has left us in his plays, novels and stories as well as in his auto-biographical fragment, a vivid picture of this aspect of Viennese society. His series of one-act plays, *Anatol* (1893), shows us the typical upper-class sensualist, who oscillates between affairs with working-class *grisettes*, ballet-dancers and prostitutes and romantic passions for respectable ladies, married and unmarried. The same picture appears, in harsher colours, in Schnitzler's famous series of dialogues, *Reigen* (Round-dance, 1900), in which at the centre of each conversation there appears a row of dots, indicating the moment when the sex act takes place, between the prostitute and the soldier; the soldier and the servant girl; the servant girl and the young gentleman; the young gentleman and the married lady; the married lady and her husband; the husband and 'the sweet girl' (i.e. a working-class girl of easy virtue); the 'sweet girl' and the poet; the poet and the actress; the actress and the count; and, finally, the count and the prostitute. These dialogues not only play upon the ironic contrast of feelings before and after the sex act, and the part played by overtones of social class, dominance and inferiority in such sexual encounters; they also underline the ease with which, in this astonishingly homogeneous society, class barriers were overcome, and demonstrate yet again the essential unity of manners and morals among the differing social strata of Vienna. It is no coincidence that a central position in the chain is occupied by '*das süsse Mädel*' (the sweet girl), Vienna's most original contribution to the typology of sex: the working-class girl who so respects and admires the young men of the class above her, i.e. young doctors and law students, junior officers and poets, that she is only too eager to be picked up by them, lavishes real affection on her lovers, perhaps in the hope that they will eventually marry her, and is then abandoned in favour of some respectable virgin whose family can give her a good dowry. In Schnitzler's most famous play, *Liebelei* (Playing with Love, 1896), the sweet girl must actually stand by while her beloved, a young man from a good family, has himself shot in a duel about a married woman for whom, because she was of a socially superior class, he is presumed to have felt 'real', romantic love as distinct from the sensuous pleasure he derived from his working-class mistress. What strikes one in this play, however, is precisely the closeness – in social terms – between the supposedly superior and inferior classes. The barrier between them is purely notional : there *are* differences in wealth and rank, but no cultural barrier, no difficulty in communication.

On the occasion of Schnitzler's sixtieth birthday, in May 1922, Freud wrote to him and confessed that he had always been strangely shy of closer personal contact : 'I think, I avoided you, because of a kind of "*Doppelgängerscheu*" [fear of one's own double] . . . again and again, in immersing myself in your creations I have had the impression of finding, behind the poetic fiction, the same presuppositions, interests and results, which I already knew as my own. Your determinism as well as your scepticism – what people call pessimism – your awareness of the truths of the subconscious, of the instinctual nature of man, your destruction of the conventional cultural certainties, the preoccupation of your thought with the polarity of love and death, all this appeared to me uncannily familiar.'

The sensuality of Vienna at the turn of the century was characterized by an openness, a lack of guilt feelings which radically distinguish it from the sex obsessions and repressions of, say, late Victorian England or America. It is as though Vienna had escaped the wave of pietistic puritanism which swept the Protestant countries after 1850; as though the spirit of London in Restoration and Regency times had simply maintained itself undisturbed for another century. This may have been one of the fruits of the counter-reformation which ruthlessly suppressed all manifestations of protestant feeling in the Habsburg lands. Even in rural areas, where the Church held absolute sway over the peasants, illegitimacy rates were astronomical and it was no secret that in many cases the nephews and nieces which peopled the parsonage were in fact the offspring of the Roman Catholic parish priest and his 'house-keeper'. Guilt feelings could readily be dissolved by confession and absolution at regular intervals. It is this atmosphere which made it possible for Vienna to produce one of the few really hilarious pornographic novels of world literature, *Josefine Mutzenbacher* (1906), the life story of a whore told by herself, which is generally held to be the work of Felix Salten (1869–1947) a well-known critic, novelist and writer of children's books, the most famous of which achieved world renown as the Walt Disney film *Bambi*. Only a total absence of sexual guilt feelings in the local cultural climate could explain the gaiety with which episodes like the seduction of the schoolgirl by the parish priest during confession are here described, quite apart from incest between father and daughter and a whole host of other outrageous, but always wildly funny episodes. What makes this book a valuable source of insight into the Viennese brand of sensuality is the obvious authenticity of the descriptions it contains : to anyone familiar with life in Vienna the basic correctness of its, admittedly, heightened and exaggerated picture is only too evident. If confirmation were needed one need only refer to so obviously authentic a document as the *Tagebuch eines halbwüchsigen Mädchens* (The Diary of an Adolescent Girl) which appeared in 1919 with a commendatory letter by Freud. Here nothing outrageous happens, but the basic attitude, if one allows for the social difference, the all-pervading preoccupation with sex is very much part of the same pattern.

The development of psychoanalysis must be seen against this background : there can have been few urban societies in history in which the facts of sexuality were more avidly discussed and pondered (*vide* Schnitzler and a host of other writers) than Vienna around 1900, few societies where the lower classes (*vide Josefine Mutzenbacher*) were more openly devoted to sexual activity in all its forms and equipped with a vocabulary of fantastically graphic coarse language to describe it. If the bourgeosie was more refined in its speech, in its habits of life it was even more deeply obsessed by sexual matters.

Amid all this sensuality – whether it preoccupied itself with food, drink, music, literature, the pleasures of intellectual discussion, or sex – this society so deeply devoted to pleasure was in fact dancing on a very thin crust over a volcano about to erupt. That the Austro-Hungarian Empire was heading for a profound crisis was obvious to all open-eyed contemporary observers. Various solutions to the nationality problem were discussed, everybody agreed that a solution must be found, but none of the numerous vested interests was prepared to yield an inch, and the country gradually slithered into the war which was bound to spell its dissolution and end.

It is this juxtaposition of an intellectual elite, universally educated, closely knit, with all the stimulus to lively debate on the one hand, and the feeling of impending doom on the other, which seems to me to provide the explanation why so much of the seminal thought of our century originated in Vienna. As Dr Johnson so rightly observed, 'when a man knows he is to be hanged in a fortnight, it concentrates his mind wonderfully'. Here a whole intellectual

Portrait of Freud by Ben Shahn.

Freud's Vienna

Left Viennese *fin-de-siècle* society was café society *par excellence*. Here, in Graben Strasse, the café stood in the middle of the street.

Right Drawing by F. König of Kolomann Moser and Josef Hoffman, two of the major Secessionist artists, responsible for the face-lift of much of Vienna at the turn of the century.
Below The famous Washergirls' Ball, at the height of the carnival season, was much patronized by the pleasure-loving Viennese aristocracy. Painting by Wilhelm Gause.

The Viennese
skyline. Not
for Freud the
lyrical
descriptions of
St Stephen's
cathedral. To
him it was
merely 'that
abominable
steeple'.

The Vienna Secession

Below The genius of the movement lay above all in the graphic arts. Kolomann Moser, Klimt, Adolf Böhm, Joseph Hoffman, J. M. Olbrich, all contributed to *Ver Sacrum*, the movement's journal. A page of *Ver Sacrum*, by Hoffmann.

Far right The Secession building was designed by Josef Olbrich and built in 1897–8. The metal doors were designed by Klimt and the decoration around them by Kolomann Moser.

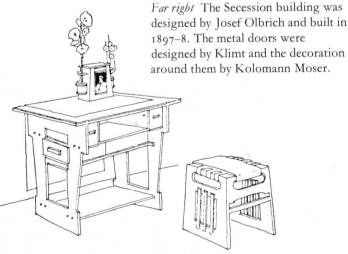

Above Furniture design by Hoffmann.
Right Gustav Klimt, *Judith*.

Freud's Vienna

elite of brilliant intelligence had its mind stimulated to concentration by the certain knowledge that the end was near.

And if the city's sensuality provided Freud with a backdrop to his thought about the roots of the sexual impulse, the tensions inherent in a political system about to break up also pointed to the wellsprings of aggression. It can be argued that the terrifying forces of destruction which swept through Europe in the mass murders of the concentration camps and the mass destruction of populations in Russia during the Second World War are the direct fruits of the tensions and frustrations which built up in the poorer quarters of Vienna in the first decade of this century.

For the reverse side of the coin which on its obverse shows the brilliant intellectual elite of the Vienna coffee-houses is the sullen hatred, the frustration of the semi-educated and not too bright pseudo-intellectuals who, precisely because intellectual achievement carried such high status value in their society, burned with envy at being denied recognition. The theories of Schönerer, Hitler and all the other antisemitic 'thinkers' of the period can be seen as imitations of the sweeping and daring thought systems produced by the genuine intellectuals of the time, attempts to emulate and surpass their sweep, their insight and their search for a practicable way out of the deadlock. If the coffee-houses in the city's centre were swarming with philosophers and poets, political theorists and socialist visionaries, the innumerable beer-halls and wine-taverns of the outer suburbs were filled with half-educated imitations of these brilliant figures, who brooded over their beer, producing the wildest pseudo-philosophies. In my childhood in the Vienna of the nineteen-twenties I met dozens of these : they were so eager to find a listener for their fantasies that they were content even with a child. Hitler to me was merely one, very typical specimen of this breed, who, by a combination of manic drive and energy with exceptional luck actually got into a position to put these fanatical fantasies into practice. *Mein Kampf* is merely one long monologue of a typical Vienna beer-hall pseudo-philosopher.

After the collapse of the Habsburg Empire in 1918, Vienna outwardly remained essentially the same as the imperial city. It was merely more poverty-stricken, more sordid, its intellectual controversies more bitter and intense. The influx of people from Eastern and South-Eastern Europe continued, even at an increased rate : the number of Jews reached its highest point in 1923, largely because of a wave of refugees from Rumania and Poland. This gave renewed impetus to antisemitic propaganda. What had been a society on the brink of disaster now became one in open dissolution. The deep pessimism of

Top The Cafe Griensteidl, one of the meeting places of literary and artistic Vienna. On the left are Arthur Schnitzler and Hermann Bahr. Watercolour by R. Volkel.
Bottom Gustav Klimt, *Danaë*.

the later Freud about the discontents of civilization should be seen against the background of this profound malaise. Galloping inflation had wiped out all private fortunes at one stroke, the very fabric of society had crashed and released swarms of unpleasant profiteers, political opportunists, gangsters and gunmen. The city still had two million inhabitants – a third of the total population of the small remnant of the Empire which still called itself Austria. What made matters worse was the fact that this industrial capital had a socialist administration while the rural areas of the mountains and backwoods remained deeply Catholic and anti-socialist.

By about 1930 an uneasy balance was at last reached. But after Hitler's rise to power in Germany in 1933 everyone knew that Austria was doomed. The country's efforts to assert its independence lacked conviction. At best they amounted to attempts to gain a little more time. A new wave of refugees arrived: German Jews and anti-Nazis fleeing from Hitler. For a while this produced another era of intense intellectual and artistic activity. The conversation in the coffee-houses between 1933 and 1938 was as hectic and as brilliant as it had ever been.

But then, on 13 March 1939, Hitler entered Vienna as its conqueror. The beer-hall fanatics had won and were ready to drive the thinkers into exile or death. Sigmund Freud was among those who succeeded in getting away. In a letter, dated 6 June 1938, from 39, Elsworthy Road, London N.W.3, he wrote to one of his friends: 'The feeling of triumph at being free is strongly mixed with sadness, for we loved the prison from which we have been released. . . .'

With the entry of German troops Vienna ceased to be a capital and became a provincial city on the fringe of Hitler's empire. After the war it became a capital once more, of a prosperous, thriving, politically far more stable country, in many ways a far happier town than that in which Freud had lived from 1860 to 1938. But a city with a new, a different personality, totally unlike that of its former imperial self.

4

Freud and Marx

George Lichtheim

OUR theme is the relation of Marx's thinking about society to Freud's analysis of the individual. The validity of Marxian sociology and Freudian psychology will be taken for granted. The question is to what extent they overlap.

Any serious consideration of this topic must from the outset exclude the politically motivated polemics which have grown up around it, in consequence of the mutual animosity displayed by Freudian and Pavlovian psychiatrists ever since the Soviet regime in the 1930s placed a ban upon Freud. We are not concerned with Soviet Marxism and its East European derivatives.

To start with, it is important to recognize that Marx's materialism, unlike that of Lenin and the Soviet Marxists, did not centre upon metaphysical notions concerning matter as the ultimate constituent of the universe. The materialism of the French Enlightenment could not account for the human mind and its achievements.[1] In consequence Marx operates with a concept of nature which is more comprehensive than that of matter.[2] Man is a natural entity, and from this it follows that his mind is a part of nature, to be investigated by the same methods as those employed in the natural sciences generally. So far there is nothing to which Freud might not have subscribed, although in point of fact he was not influenced by Marx. Both men took for granted the naturalist outlook common to European thinkers who had emancipated themselves from theology and idealist metaphysics. Both held that religion is an illusion. Neither believed in an immortal soul enclosed in a carnal tomb from which it will arise after death. Marx (1818–83) and Freud (1856–1939) stand at different points in the evolution of European society, inasmuch as Marx was a Victorian, whereas Freud lived to witness the disintegration and collapse of bourgeois civilization in Central Europe. Nonetheless they shared certain general assumptions about man and the world, ultimately rooted in the philosophy of the Enlightenment since its beginning in Bacon, Descartes, Hobbes and Spinoza.

Where Marx diverges from these thinkers is in holding that man was from the start a social being. There never was a state of nature from which civilization emerged as the result of a social contract. The social whole is prior to the individual, for man becomes self-conscious only by interacting with his fellow-men. Society is not an aggregate of individuals, but the product of men's reciprocal action.[3] This line of thought goes back to Aristotle, while among the moderns it is associated with Montesquieu and the Scottish philosophers of the eighteenth century, notably Adam Ferguson and John Millar. In contrast, Freud stands closer to the tradition of Hobbes, Locke and

Rousseau, for whom society is an artificial construct established by men for the protection of their interests. The social philosophy of Freud is that of John Stuart Mill, for whom the study of man was ultimately reducible to psychology, society being an aggregate of independent individuals who have come together for their mutual benefit. This psychological individualism ties up with liberalism, whereas Marx's conception of man leads to socialism, for the simple reason that it envisages the human collective as a totality within which men interact by exchanging their products. They do so even in bourgeois society, whose philosophy – liberalism – operates with a set of concepts derived from a naive individualism, and for this reason Marx assigns these concepts to the realm of what he terms 'ideology' (false consciousness). Modern sociology is to a large extent the offspring of Marxism, while psychology is the legitimate child of Mill's concern with the isolated individual. To the extent that liberalism and socialism operate with incompatible notions as to the nature of society, Marx and Freud stand at opposite poles. Nonetheless they hold in common the rationalism of the Enlightenment and its belief in progress : there is such a thing as social evolution, and in the final analysis it rests upon men's ability to bring nature (including human nature) under conscious control.

Evolutionary theories about human history, for which Darwin provided the scientific basis with his *Origin of Species* (1859), had to some extent been anticipated by Auguste Comte in his *Cours de philosophie positive* (1830–42). Marx, who read Comte for the first time in 1866, promptly conceived a violent aversion for him, whereas he thought highly of Darwin, notwithstanding the latter's Malthusianism.[4] The year 1859 was likewise the date of publication of Marx's *Zur Kritik der Politischen Oekonomie*, in the Preface to which he gave a brief summary of what in later years came to be known as historical materialism. It is here that there occurs the celebrated passage which runs :

> In the social production of their life, men enter into definite relations that are indispensable and independent of their will, relations of production which correspond to a definite stage of development of their material productive forces. . . . The mode of production of material life conditions the social, political and intellectual life process in general. It is not the consciousness of men that determines their being, but on the contrary their social being that determines their consciousness.

How then are revolutions possible ?

At a certain stage of their development, the material productive forces of society come in conflict with the existing relations of production, or – what is but a legal expression for the same thing – with the property relations within which they have been at work hitherto. From forms of development of the productive forces these relations turn into their fetters. Then begins an epoch of social revolution. . . . No social order ever perishes before all the productive forces for which there is room in it have developed; and new, higher relations of production never appear before the material conditions of their existence have matured in the womb of the old society itself. Therefore mankind always sets itself only such tasks as it can solve; since, looking at the matter more closely, it will always be found that the task itself arises only when the material conditions for its solution already exist or are at least in the process of formation.[5]

The conviction that mankind 'always sets itself only such tasks as it can solve' was central to Marx's mature theorizing. Freedom consists in mastering social necessity. In the course of history, men have hitherto permitted themselves to be ruled by the product of their own alienated social forces. Once they learn to understand the historical mechanism, they will be able to transcend it. Marx's materialism is meant to result in its own supersession.[6] Similarly, Freud conceives the task of psychoanalysis as a liberating one: the therapeutic method is grounded in the conviction that when once the conscious part of the mind learns to understand the significance of the repressed instinctual drives, and by this means brings to the light of day what had been thrust out of sight, the ego will be able to confront the id in all its literalness and thus be relieved of the pain that its symbolic expression had caused. But Freud did not hold that mankind sets itself only such tasks as it can solve. *Civilization and its Discontents* (1930) develops the thesis that civilized existence is only possible at the price of very heavy inroads upon human felicity. Social life is both cause and consequence of frustrations which may become intolerable and for which psychology has no remedy to offer. This gloomy strain in his cast of mind is elaborated in the correspondence between Freud and Einstein published under the auspices of the League of Nations in 1933. In regard to human evolution, Freud appears to think that intra-specific conflict is natural to man and animals, biologically healthy and practically unavoidable. Moreover, a 'death instinct' operates in every organism, causing it to revert to inert matter. In the process of civilization innate aggression may assume the guise of wars which are repudiated by pacifist individuals. But this does not as yet occur with the masses who refuse to subordinate their instinctual pleasures to the dictates of reason.[7]

It is thus legitimate to say that Freud was a pessimist so far as human society is concerned. Unlike his contemporary Alfred Adler (1870–1937), who held socialist views and correspondingly attached more importance to the cultural conditioning of the ego than to repressed instinctual drives, he did not believe that neuroses were the product of a particular civilization: the bourgeois one. Moreover, Adler rejected the concept of the Oedipus complex, which was central to Freud.[8] He also maintained that there was some circularity to Freud's view that civilization is based on the repression of the instincts, while repression for its part is an aspect of civilization. The break between Freud and Adler in 1911 was never healed, and the Adlerian school came to represent a 'revisionist' departure from Freudian orthodoxy. In due course, Adler was succeeded by Wilhelm Reich, whose *Einbruch der Sexualmoral* (1931) allotted pre-eminence to the factors of social domination and repression. Meanwhile on what might be termed the 'right wing' of the psychoanalytic movement, C. G. Jung became the head of a rival school which located the origin of neuroses and psychoses in archetypes whose seat is the collective unconscious. 'The myths of creation, the virgin birth, the forms of the snake, the Great Mother, the eternal feminine, Paradise, fourfoldness, the number three, all these are archetypical figures and formations of the Collective Unconscious.'[9] In holding to a central position, midway between the ego psychology of Adler and the obscurantist mythology of Jung, Freud remained faithful to his liberal-individualist philosophy, itself a heritage of the Darwinian age.

In the later development of the psychoanalytic movement, a cleavage developed between Erich Fromm, who tried to revise Freud's view of man in the light of Marx's early writings, and Herbert Marcuse, who attempted to combine Marxian materialism with Freudian metaphysics.[10] The prime difficulty with this particular dispute is due to the fact that Marcuse appeared simultaneously in the role of an orthodox Freudian and a revolutionary Marxist. Freud, according to him,

... had recognized the work of repression in the highest values of Western civilization – they presuppose and perpetuate unfreedom and suffering; the Neo-Freudian schools propagate the very same values as cure against unfreedom and suffering – as the triumph over repression. This intellectual feat is accomplished by expurgating the instinctual dynamic and reducing its part in the mental life. Thus purified, the psyche can again be redeemed by idealist ethics and religion; and the psychoanalytic theory of the mental apparatus can be rewritten as a philosophy of the soul.[11]

In his reply Fromm emphasized that while Freud was indeed a critic of society, 'his criticism was not that of contemporary capitalistic society, but of civilization as such'.

✕On the basis of his concept of man, that of his inherent wish for unlimited sexual satisfaction, and of his destructiveness, Freud must arrive at a picture of the necessary conflict between all civilization and mental health and happiness. Primitive man is healthy and happy because he is not frustrated in his basic instincts, but he lacks the blessings of culture. Civilized man is more secure, enjoys art and science, but he is bound to be neurotic because of the continued frustration of his instincts, enforced by civilization.[12]
✕

As Fromm saw it, Freud had adopted a Hobbesian view of man because, like most nineteenth-century thinkers, he envisaged nature in terms derived from bourgeois society, much as Darwin had insisted upon the survival of the fittest : a Malthusian notion which guided him in his study of animal life.

If professed Marxists like Marcuse and Fromm are unable to agree on the compatibility of Marxian and Freudian notions, it seems perilous to venture onto this particular piece of ground. Fortunately we are not obliged to take sides. There was something artificial about a controversy in which (to cite an anonymous critic) 'whereas Fromm has claimed for a long time that Freud has erred and then proceeds to practise psychoanalysis under the pretext of having reformed it, Marcuse now charges Fromm with revisionism, insists that Freud has been right all along and then proceeds to revise psychoanalysis under the pretext of defending its orthodoxy.'[13] Before we engage this topic once more, let us retrace our steps and try to locate the naturalistic view of man which Marx and Freud held in common.

In Hegel's philosophy, God comes to himself in the history of salvation. In Marx's theory, man comes to himself in mundane history. Progress is real, its principal achievement being the liberation of man from the curse of labour. As a natural being, man is alienated and under the domination of his own products. Marx deals with labour in its modern form : labour producing a commodity for another person, i.e., labour formally paid but actually exploited ; formally free, actually enslaved ; formally the independent labour of an individual worker, actually collective labour performed by wage-slaves. The value relations appearing in the exchange of products of labour as 'commodities' are not relations between things, but an expression of the underlying social relation between the human beings who cooperate in their production. This process comes to its climax in bourgeois society, which is just that particular kind of society in which the most basic relations established between human beings in the social production of their lives take on the phantasmagoric appearance of commodities bought and sold behind the backs of the actual producers. What Marx in *Capital* describes as 'the fetishism' of commodities is only another aspect of what in the Paris Manuscripts of 1844 he had termed 'human self-alienation'.[14] Alienation is a calamity which befalls Hegel's 'Idea' at a certain stage of its speculative development. Feuerbach's transformation of philosophy into anthropology had done away with this particular mystification. German idealism stood for the primacy of spirit over matter. Feuerbach inverted this relationship without, however, treating 'matter' as an absolute substance involved in the constitution of the universe. In particular, he defined the religious phenomenon as the projection and hypostasis of an element of human experience into an object of worship.[15] In *Capital* Marx took up this theme as an illustration of what he termed 'fetishism':

> The religious world is but the reflex of the real world. And for a society based upon the production of commodities, in which the producers in general enter into social relations with one another by treating their products as commodities and values, whereby they reduce their individual private labour to the standard of homogeneous human labour – for such a society, Christianity with its *cultus* of abstract man, more especially in its bourgeois developments, Protestantism, Deism, etc., is the most fitting form of religion.[16]

It may be useful to compare this passage with Freud's treatment of religion as an illusion.[17] The common ancestor of both Marx and Freud in this respect is Democritus, with his conviction that belief in the gods stems from fear; or if one prefers it Epicurus and the transmission of his message by Lucretius. From there the line runs by way of Hobbes, Spinoza, Hume, Holbach and Feuerbach to Marx and Engels.[18] Freud is in the same tradition, with the difference that his treatment of religion in *Totem and Taboo* and *The Future of an Illusion* is not explicitly related to any particular school of philosophy. Religion, the reader is told in *The Future of an Illusion*, has come into being, like all the other acquisitions of culture, from the need to guard oneself against the overwhelming pressure of human destiny. Men personify the powers of nature in the same way that the infant deals with his environment. Religion is essentially anthropomorphic. Its genesis is understandable in terms of the human need for an explanation of the universe and the powers encountered within it. There is no particular problem to be solved in accounting for the rise of religion: Freud is in the tradition of the eighteenth-century Enlightenment, for which fear and ignorance are adequate explanations of the phenomenon known as religious faith. For the rest, his standpoint has something in common with that of Comte, for whom the 'positive' age had succeeded the reign of theology and spiritualist metaphysics.

It is arguable that the Marx of *Capital* (1867) had arrived at similar conclusions. His starting point, however, was different. The emancipation from theology, which by the time of Freud had become an accepted fact for the majority of scientists, was the central issue within the Hegelian school in the 1840s when Marx's orientation took shape. Freud's disillusioned view of mankind derived from Schopenhauer, a pessimistic thinker who began to make an impact in the 1850s and 1860s, by which time the spell of Hegel had been broken. For the Young Hegelians, who had come under the influence of Feuerbach in the stormy 1840s, the critique of religion was an aspect of the political struggle against State and Church. The *mésalliance* between philosophy and theology,[19] which was central to German idealism, had to be dissolved in the interest of making philosophy 'practical' and this-worldly. In consequence Marx's atheism acquired a revolutionary character foreign to the mind of Freud. The *locus classicus* is Marx's 'Contribution to the Critique of Hegel's Philosophy of Right' (1844)[20] which starts off by announcing: 'For Germany, the criticism of religion has been largely completed, and the criticism of religion is the premise of all criticism.' Marx goes on to develop the Feuerbachian analysis of religion, and then gives a political edge to it which had been lacking in Feuerbach:

The *profane* existence of error is compromised once its *celestial oratio pro aris* and *focis* has been refuted. Man, who has found in the fantastic reality of heaven, where he sought a supernatural being, only his own reflection, will no longer be tempted to find only the *semblance* of himself – a non-human being – where he seeks and must seek his true reality.

The basis of irreligious criticism is this: *man makes religion*; religion does not make man. Religion is indeed man's self-consciousness and self-awareness so long as he has not found himself, or has lost himself again. But *man* is not an abstract being, squatting outside the world. Man is the *human world*, the state, society. This state, this society produce religion which is an *inverted world consciousness*, because they are an *inverted world*. . . . The struggle against religion is therefore indirectly a struggle against *that world* whose spiritual *aroma* is religion.

Religious suffering is at the same time an *expression* of real suffering and a *protest* against real suffering. Religion is the sigh of the oppressed creature, the sentiment of a heartless world, and the soul of soulless conditions. It is the *opium* of the people.

Freud and Marx

The abolition of religion as the *illusory* happiness of men is a demand for their *real* happiness. The call to abandon their illusions about their condition is a *call to abandon a condition which requires illusions*. The criticism of religion is therefore *the embryonic criticism of this vale of tears* of which religion is the *halo*. . . . Religion is only the illusory sun about which man revolves so long as he does not revolve about himself. . . . Thus the criticism of heaven is transformed into the criticism of earth, the criticism of religion into the criticism of law, and the criticism of theology into the criticism of politics.

Marx in the 1840s, then, had adopted Feuerbach's Promethean ethic which sees man as the ultimate subject of philosophy.[21] Man is a species-being who shapes himself and understands himself in relation to other men. For Marx as for Feuerbach there is such a thing as a 'real man', one who realizes all the possibilities that are specifically human. The contribution Marx brought to this theme was the recognition that the alienation of man from his own nature was not simply due to error, but had its roots in the condition of human society: an 'inverted world' which necessarily produces an 'inverted world consciousness'. From this it followed that the world must be 'stood on its feet', a task Marx allotted to the revolutionary class *par excellence*, the proletariat: a class which has nothing to lose but its chains. Needless to say, there is no trace of this world-revolutionary optimism in Freud. Had he come across Feuerbach's critique of religion (there is no evidence that he did), he would presumably have accepted its central thesis, namely that all religious concepts can be explained in terms of human experience. For Freud as for Feuerbach, religion must be treated on the analogy of dreams, fantasies or works of art. Religious concepts do not portray a supranatural world – they merely rearrange materials drawn from this world.[22] But Feuerbach's rather simplistic ethic, with its stress on love as 'the substantial bond, the principle of reconciliation between the perfect and imperfect', would not have appealed to him. One cannot imagine Freud subscribing to the statement 'Love is God himself and apart from it there is no God.'[23] For that matter, Marx and Engels had no use for the religion of love, just as they steered away from that aspect of 'materialism' which in 1850 induced Feuerbach to pen the notorious phrase 'man is what he eats' (*der Mensch ist was er isst*).[24]

This may be the place to utter a warning against the habit of treating Marx and Engels as the twin originators of a world-view subsequently known as 'dialectical materialism'. There is no disputing the fact that Engels was a materialist in the philosophical sense of the term; that is to say, he held that matter is the ultimate constituent of the universe. The case of Marx is much more complicated. The *Theses on Feuerbach* (1845) start off with a frank recognition that 'all hitherto existing materialism', that of Feuerbach included, has shown itself inadequate, whence it happened 'that the *active* side ... was developed by idealism...'. Materialism cannot account for what is specifically human, a theme developed in the *Holy Family* (1845) notwithstanding the generous recognition given in that work to the Anglo-French materialist tradition in general. Marx's treatment of the subject is not altogether consistent. Cartesian metaphysics is said to have had materialism as its antagonist from the very start,[25] while a few pages later one may read: 'As Cartesian materialism merges into natural science proper, the other branch of French materialism leads direct to socialism and communism.'[26] This conclusion follows because 'if man is shaped by his surroundings, his surroundings must be made human'. Perhaps it is safest to classify Marx as a thinker for whom materialism, naturalism and humanism all have the same goal. Certainly the anthropological naturalism of Feuerbach had nothing to do with the mechanical movements of the atom, but with man as a sensuous and active being.[27]

How far does philosophical materialism enter into a theory according to which the production and reproduction of man's material existence determines the historical movement of society? In the *Holy Family* materialism is described as 'the teaching of real humanism and the logical basis of communism'.[28] But the 'materialists' cited in this connection include Locke and his French followers, Helvétius and Condillac, who cannot be claimed for 'historical materialism' as defined by Marx in his 1859 preface to the *Critique of Political Economy*. The distinction between 'economic base' and 'political superstructure' owed something to Feuerbach's inversion of Hegel's philosophy, but the connection is tenuous. In order to arrive at his mature standpoint Marx had to assimilate the teaching of the classical economists and the Scottish philosophers. The theory of social class, which explains the *modus operandi* of social change, had been anticipated by Ferguson, who in 1767 noted that 'by unequal shares in the distribution of property the ground of a permanent and palpable subordination is laid'.[29] In bringing these and other notions up to date and fusing them into a theory of society, Marx was undoubtedly helped by his antecedent commitment to philosophical materialism, but this materialism was not the ontological doctrine it later became for Engels and his pupils. Marx was not a materialist in the metaphysical sense of the term and his theory of society cannot be deduced from general principles applicable to nature and history alike. In particular, the distinction between state and society, which had been worked out by the British and French writers of the eighteenth century, owed nothing to metaphysical materialism properly so described. It proceeded from the discovery that social development occurs in accordance with objective laws which can be analyzed. It then appears that individual actions enter into a process whose logic becomes clear after the event. 'As one cannot judge an individual by what he thinks of himself, just as little can one judge such a revolutionary epoch by its own consciousness.' This statement in the 1859 *Preface* may be said to represent a link between Marx's manner of thinking and that of Freud. What both have in common is the conviction that surface phenomena are to be understood in terms of objective laws of development.

Given the intellectual climate of Central Europe in the 1920s and 1930s it was inevitable that an attempt should be made to bring about a fusion of Marxism and psychoanalysis. No time need be wasted on the eccentric Wilhelm Reich who in 1933-4 suffered the misfortune of being expelled from the Communist International and the International Psychoanalytical Association alike. But Herbert Marcuse cannot be ignored. Something has already been said about his controversy with Erich Fromm in the 1950s. The question now before us is to what extent his writings promoted that fusion of Marx and Freud which Soviet Marxism systematically opposed, and which had come to nothing in the Vienna of pre-Hitler days.

Marcuse adhered to the Frankfurt school of neo-Marxism founded by Max Horkheimer and Theodor Adorno around 1930, a school whose special mark was the synthesis of Hegelian and Marxian thinking. His first major publication dealt with Hegel's philosophy,[30] as did the massive work through which he became known to the English-speaking world.[31] First published in England in 1941 and later reprinted with a supplementary chapter in 1955, this study of Hegel was solidly anchored within the tradition of German philosophy. It displayed no interest in psychology, whereas from 1955 (the date of publication of *Eros and Civilization*) onwards its author became known as the protagonist of a synthesis of Marxian and Freudian concepts. The fusion was carried further in *One-Dimensional Man* (1964) and in the lecture series published under the title *Psychoanalyse und Politik* in 1968.

The key to Marcuse's later standpoint is furnished by the concept of repression which in his writings is invoked to characterize the institutions of contemporary society and the existence of modern man alike.[32] In the postscript to the second edition of *Reason and Revolution* (1955) this theme is given a philosophical interpretation:

Freud

From the beginning, the idea and the reality of Reason in the modern period contained the elements which endangered its promise of a free and fulfilled existence: the enslavement of man by his own productivity; the glorification of delayed satisfaction; the repressive mastery of nature in man and outside; the development of human potentialities within the framework of domination. In Hegel's philosophy, the triumph of the Spirit leaves the State behind in the reality – unconquered by the Spirit and oppressive in spite of its commitment to Right and Freedom.

This criticism of Hegel stems from the tradition of thought associated with Feuerbach and Marx, but Marcuse had by 1955 come to believe that the social revolution had been defeated:

Reason is in its very essence contra-diction, opposition, negation as long as freedom is not yet real. If the contradictory, oppositional, negative power of Reason is broken, reality moves under its own positive law and, unhampered by the Spirit, unfolds its repressive force. Such decline in the power of Negativity has indeed accompanied the progress of late industrial civilization. With the increasing concentration and effectiveness of economic, political and cultural controls, the opposition in all these fields has been pacified, co-ordinated, or liquidated. . . .

The decisive importance of the relation between the pre-revolutionary and post-revolutionary proletariat has been demonstrated only after the death of Marx, in the transformation of free into organized capitalism. It was this development which transformed Marxism into Leninism and determined the fate of Soviet Society – its progress under a new system of repressive productivity.

In *One-Dimensional Man* this theme is developed further. The 'power of the negative' has vanished, not only because the working class has been integrated into the system, but because the psychic mechanisms which had previously stored up popular dissatisfaction have been remoulded. 'Today's novel feature is the flattening out of the antagonism between culture and social reality through the obliteration of the oppositional, alien, and transcendent elements in the higher culture by virtue of which it constituted *another dimension* of reality.'[33] Ironically, this assessment of the contemporary situation was put forward in 1964 by a philosopher domiciled in the United States on the eve of the greatest crisis American civilization has yet undergone.

Marcuse's lack of success as a social prognosticator need not, however, invalidate his fusion of Marxian and Freudian concepts. The question which has to be asked is to what extent it is possible to operate simultaneously with the Marxian model of social development and the neo-Freudian concepts which Marcuse shares with other members of the Frankfurt school. The interpenetration of Marxian and Freudian notions in the work of Jürgen

Freud and Marx

Habermas and Alexander Mitscherlich suggests that the pioneering labours of Horkheimer, Adorno and Marcuse have not been in vain.[34] Nonetheless there remains the problem of overcoming the deep gulf dividing the two great thinkers who have placed their stamp upon the consciousness of the modern age.

The principal difficulty clearly has to do with Freud's ingrained pessimism concerning man's search for happiness in a civilization built upon the denial of sensual gratification. By contrast, there is a utopian streak in Marx – not only in the young Marx of the 1844 Paris Manuscripts, but also in the author of the *Grundrisse* (1857–8) and of *Capital* (1867). In the concluding third volume of *Capital* there occurs at the very close a passage in which Marx sets out his considered view concerning the existence of man under socialism. The passage is of importance precisely because its author had by then emancipated himself from the romantic Feuerbachian attitude of the 1844 Manuscripts :

... the realm of freedom actually begins only where labour which is determined by necessity and mundane considerations ceases ; thus in the very nature of things it lies beyond the sphere of actual material production. Just as the savage must wrestle with nature to satisfy his wants, to maintain and reproduce life, so must civilized man, and he must do so in all social formations and under all possible modes of production. With his development this realm of physical necessity expands as a result of his wants ; but at the same time the forces of production which satisfy these wants also increase. Freedom in this field can only consist in socialized man, the associated producers, rationally regulating their interchange with nature, bringing it under their common control, instead of being ruled by it as by the blind forces of nature ; and achieving this with the least expenditure of energy and under conditions most favourable to, and worthy of, their human nature. But it nonetheless still remains a realm of necessity. Beyond it begins that development of human energy which is an end in itself, the true realm of freedom, which, however, can blossom forth only with this realm of necessity as its basis. The shortening of the working day is its basic prerequisite.[35]

Marcuse is of course familiar with this passage. Remarkably, he has argued that Marx, so far from being too optimistic about the transition from capitalism to socialism, was not radical and utopian enough.[36]

He underrated the level which the productivity of labour under the capitalist system itself could attain and the possibilities suggested by the attainment of this level. The technical achievements of capitalism would make possible a socialist development which would surpass the Marxian distinction between socially necessary labour and creative work, between alienated labour and non-alienated work, between the realm of necessity and the realm of freedom. In Marx's time, this vision was indeed premature and unrealistic, and therefore his basic concept for the transition to socialism remained that of the development and rationalization of productive forces; their liberation from repressive and destructive controls was to be the first task of socialism. But in spite of all qualitative differences this concept of a 'development of the productive forces' establishes a technological continuity between capitalism and socialism. . . . It seems to me that this conception corresponds to a stage in the development of the productive forces that is already being surpassed by the advanced industrial societies. [37]

The argument ties in with the central theme of *One-Dimensional Man*, namely that industrial society has evolved means of domesticating the class struggle. 'The new technological work-world thus enforces a weakening of the negative position of the working class: the latter no longer appears to be the living contradiction to the established society.'[38] 'Domination is transfigured into administration.'[39] By 1967 Marcuse had caught up with the crisis of American society:

Within the system of repressive affluence, a conspicuous radicalization of the youth and of the intelligentsia takes place. This is far more than a mere ideological development; it is a movement which, in spite of all its limitations, tends toward a fundamental transvaluation of values. It is part of the human or social forces which, on a global scale, resist the oppressive power of the affluent society.[40]

The revolt of the students is an aspect of a global confrontation which opposes the backward countries to their imperialist exploiters. 'What happens in Asia or Africa is not external to the system, but has become an integral part of the system itself.'[41] National liberation movements in the backward sections of the globe have become a factor in spreading discontent among the intelligentsia of the affluent society.

The link between this prophecy of doom and the theory of human motivation remains obscure.[42] Marcuse appears to hold that there exists a boiling-point beyond which oppression automatically transforms itself into rebellion. There is a flow of primeval energy within the human organism, Freud's *libido* which corresponds to Spinoza's *conatus*.[43] This natural drive for self-preservation and the extension of personal power and energy may be blocked or dammed by social institutions, in which case it is liable to assume an oppositional or even revolutionary form, where it is not sublimated into 'higher' activities. In general Marcuse operates with the Freudian concept of repression, according to which the achievements of civilization have been attained at the expense of sexual gratification. At the same time he looks forward to a possible social order so constituted that human relationships will no longer be distorted by the renunciation of sexual happiness. This future state of affairs is described as 'socialism', at which point Marcuse finds himself in the company of Charles Fourier, the principal figure of pre-Marxian 'utopian socialism'. In *One-Dimensional Man* Fourier is approvingly cited as a critic of bourgeois society, whereas his contemporary Saint-Simon is described as a precursor of positivism.

The universe of discourse and behaviour which begins to speak in Saint-Simon's positivism is that of technological reality. In it, the object-world is being transformed into an instrumentality. Much of that which is still outside the instrumental world – unconquered, blind nature – now appears within the reaches of scientific and technical progress. The metaphysical dimension, formerly a genuine field of rational thought, becomes irrational and unscientific. On the ground of its own realizations, Reason repels transcendence.[44]

The concluding sentence may stand as a reminder that Marcuse had begun his philosophical career in 1932 under the intellectual patronage of Heidegger.[45]

What then is the relationship of Freud to Marx? If Marcuse is to be taken as the principal theorist of a Marxism brought up to date with the aid of Freudian concepts, the link appears to lie in a critique of civilization which differentiates between the inevitable degree of repression common to all forms of culture, and the surplus repression peculiar to bourgeois society. History has brought us to the threshold of the promised land, inasmuch as it has now for the first time become possible to do away with a particular kind of sexual repression necessitated by a particular form of social organization: that of late-capitalist industrial society. If one accepts this thesis, one may wonder why socialism has hitherto failed to create a conflict-free society. The explanation plainly has to do with the fact that the Western labour movement has inherited the technological rationality of positivism, while Communism has hitherto gained power only in backward societies in urgent need of modernization and the degree of surplus repression that inevitably goes with it. Human liberation requires that sexual libido should burst the bonds set by economic scarcity and the resultant political pressures. In the sense allotted to this theme in the philosophy of Herbert Marcuse, the preconditions of liberation are currently lacking in East and West alike.

5

Freud and Philosophy
Anthony Quinton

FREUD was not a philosopher and certainly did not think of himself as one. In his own eyes he was a scientist. He committed himself, at an early stage of his career, to the ascetic ideal of true scientific inquiry that Helmholtz had established for the scientific, and in particular medical, profession of the German-speaking world. Helmholtz, who was something of a universal genius, with interests covering the whole field of natural science from mathematics to the physiology of sensation, was a most resolute mechanist. He was hostile to metaphysical speculation in general and, more specifically, to vitalism, the idea that some principle beyond the reach of physics and chemistry must be called upon to explain the nature of living organisms. But he was not averse to *scientific* theorization. He did not agree with Mach that the concepts of unobservable entities that occur in scientific theories are simply linguistic devices for the representation of regularities in the sensations that we immediately perceive. Helmholtz took them to be genuinely descriptive of the real nature of things hidden from our direct perception. The theoretical part of physical science, he said, 'endeavours to ascertain the unknown causes of processes from their physical effects; it seeks to comprehend them according to the law of causality'. Freud's doctrine of the unconscious conforms with this realistic conception of the nature of unobservable theoretical entities. The influence of Helmholtz's ideas can also be seen in Freud's persistent hope that an independent physiological confirmation would in the end be forthcoming for his theories about the real nature of the human mind.

Freud's commitment to this austerely mechanistic ideal is shown in the rigidly objective style and the emphatically scientistic vocabulary of his writings. At the outset this was, perhaps, a self-imposed discipline, which Freud embarked on to control a leaning towards speculative extravagance that he discerned in himself. It was a disposition that eventually broke out in his late, more adventurous writings on primitive society, war, religion and civilization. In the period of his major innovations in psychology, when he was tracing a host of things – neurotic symptoms, dreams, everyday errors and slips of the tongue, even works of art – to hidden causes in the domain of infantile sexuality, this uncompromisingly scientific stance had two noteworthy effects. On the one hand it provoked opposition by the ambitiousness of its claims; on the other, it somewhat mitigated the scandalous character of the detailed content of his views by the impersonal seriousness with which they were put forward. By choosing to present his revolutionary innovations as standard pieces of scientific theory, on a par with the molecular theory of gases or the germ theory of disease, he made the largest possible claim for their objective truth. Although this aspect of his doctrines excited less opposition to start with than their seemingly outrageous content, it has been that which has been most exposed to the criticism of philosophers, especially in the last few decades.

According to Ernest Jones, Freud attended the philosophical seminars of Franz Brentano during his period of medical study in Vienna in the late 1870s. At the time Freud joined the course it had been for two years no longer compulsory for medical students. This fact suggests that he had a distinct interest in philosophy. But there are no appreciable signs in his work of the influence either of Brentano himself or, for that matter, of Aristotle, with whom in these seminars Brentano was mainly concerned. In 1879, during his military service, Freud tried to earn a little money by translating some of John Stuart Mill's essays into German. Jones suggests that it was from one of these essays that Freud obtained his knowledge of Plato's doctrine of reminiscence. All that seems to have caught Freud's explicit attention in Mill himself is the variability of his prose style.

As has often been noticed, there are many correspondences between Freud's doctrines and the philosophy of Schopenhauer. Freud's conception of the unconscious as a reservoir of primitive and irrational energies parallels Schopenhauer's theory that the true self is unconscious will. For both of them, consciousness is no more than a device which the unconscious will makes use of to secure the preservation of the individual and the species. Schopenhauer's ideas were certainly available to Freud. When he was thirteen, in 1969, a popularized version of them was published : von Hartmann's *Philosophy of the Unconscious*. Von Hartmann laid a special, *fin-de-siècle* emphasis on the pessimistic side of Schopenhauer. The idea that death is the only solution to the problem of human existence has an echo in Freud's notion of the death-wish.

But, for all his formal detachment from philosophy, Freud produced ideas whose generality made them of irresistible philosophical interest. In the broader, and more speculative, extensions of his strictly psychological findings, furthermore, he advanced opinions that are indubitably philosophical in a reasonably inclusive sense of the word.

In the psychological theories prompted by his clinical work Freud began by offering explanations only of neurotic symptoms. But the style of explanation contained in these theories was soon seen by him to be applicable to a wide range of other mental phenomena. Dreams, errors and verbal slips appear at first glance to be pointless and irrational waste-products of ordinary, rational, purposive mental activity, as much as neurotic symptoms do. Freud's recognition of unconscious purposiveness in the latter prepared the way for a similar interpretation of the former. The result was a complete inversion of older ideas about the relative importance of rational and non-rational elements in mental life.

The prevailing secular view about the nature of the mind was the variety of psychological determinism derived from Hobbes by the thinkers of the Enlightenment, the Utilitarians and the classical economists. In this view man comes into the world with an initial apparatus of instinctive desires and elemental likes and dislikes. Under the influence of the environment and of ever-increasing knowledge of the causes of pleasure and pain this primordial repertoire gets transformed into a complicated system of preferences and aversions. It is not doubted that man always has a clear idea of what he wants and of what motivates him to act as he does. To the extent that his actions are irrational it is because his beliefs about what will give him pleasure or pain are ill-founded. The apparently purposeless or counter-productive thoughts and actions which were the essential evidence on which Freud based his account of the nature of the mind are brushed aside as of only marginal interest. Either they are purely random phenomena that could be attributed to some merely mechanical feature of the human organism, as dreams might be seen as the idling of the cerebral engine between bouts of genuinely engaged activity, or they are the result of some breakdown within it.

Freud turned this picture of the mind and of the voluntary behaviour which manifests it upside down. What had formerly been seen as an unimportant miscellany of disconnected exceptions to the generally conscious purposiveness of mental life became, in Freud's hands, the point of entry into a massive domain of unconscious mentality. Its hidden, primordial energies were soon taken to account, not merely for the apparently irrational odds and ends which first revealed their existence, but also for all or most of conscious mental life as well. This amounted to a new form of epiphenomenalism: the idea that consciousness is a by-product of other aspects of the total person, influenced by, but exerting no influence upon, those other aspects: in T. H. Huxley's phrase, 'the smoke above the factory'. In earlier versions this theory had taken consciousness to be an epiphenomenon of the body, in particular of the brain and nervous system. Freud made it primarily dependent on the unconscious and its elemental drives. But he connected this, in a speculative way, to the body by expressing the hope, which was mentioned earlier, that a

physiological interpretation could be found for the ingredients of the unconscious.

Philosophy has always shown a proprietary interest in the study of the
human mind. This attitude is embalmed in the old-fashioned designations of
university philosophy departments, current until quite recent times, as departments of mental or moral, as contrasted with natural, science. It is not
surprising that idealists should define philosophy as mind's knowledge of
itself, since they believe that, in the end, everything real is mental. But a concern with the nature of mind has not been peculiar to idealists. The solid
triumphs of the sciences of nature have long secured their emancipation from
philosophy. Since the eighteenth century, at any rate, philosophers have for
the most part followed Locke and Kant, two thinkers particularly enthralled
by the magnitude of Newton's achievement, in conceiving the relation of
philosophy to knowledge of the natural world in comparatively humble
terms, as a matter of systematizing and critically assessing its principles and
not as providing the truest kind of natural knowledge. Full-blooded philoso-
phies of nature, claiming to deduce its character from metaphysical axioms,
have been a minority, in more or less defiant retreat.

The absence from philosophy of a similar modesty about the study of mind
can be reasonably attributed to the later and much less complete emergence
of a science of psychology, with a body of precise and generally agreed-upon
findings to its credit and a generally accepted method of investigation to make
possible the decisive resolution of disputed issues. It was not until the late
nineteenth century that psychological inquiry became recognizably scientific
in its methods. The securest achievements of scientific psychology began with
the adoption of the principle that its proper subject-matter is inter-subjectively
observable behaviour. Its chief successes have been in the field of those rather
elemental aspects of mentality that men share with animals: perception and
learning from experience, for example.

There are still many philosophers who would deny the pretensions of
psychology, even in its more academic form as the experimental study of behaviour, to be a science at all. Support for this denial is provided by the thin-
ness of its agreed findings, at least as compared with those of physics and
chemistry, and by their confinement to the least characteristically human, and
thus least humanly interesting, aspects of the mind. In the writings of Collingwood, for example, psychology is allowed to be the science of feeling but is
stigmatized as a pseudo-science when it claims to understand the nature of

thought. Between body and mind, Collingwood maintains, there is what he calls the *psyche*, to whose contents the distinction of truth and falsehood does not apply. The sub-rational events and processes that it contains are a proper field for the exercise of the experimental methods of natural science. But mind as reason, mind engaged in thinking, truly or falsely, is not a topic for empirical science at all. It can be understood only by the traditional, 'criteriological', sciences of logic and ethics. (See his *Essay on Metaphysics*, chapters ix-xii.) I think that Collingwood is making an important point here, although in a confused and confusing way. This is that knowledge of the causes of our beliefs does not, in itself, entail anything whatever about their validity. But it does not follow from the fact that inquiry into the causes of belief is logically independent of inquiry into their truth or justification that inquiry into their causes is improper or impossible. What is relevant at this point, however, is the confusion: the denial to psychology of a crucial range of mental subject-matter.

At least Collingwood allows *a* field to psychology, conceived as a science emancipated from philosophy, that of the 'psyche' with its sub-rational feelings. Wittgenstein seems to go further. There is to be found in his later writings the outline sketch of a theory of human action which has been extremely influential. Its main theme is that actions are not mere natural happenings for which causal explanations can be sought. An action, such as raising one's arm, will typically involve or contain a bodily movement, such as one's arm going up, which is a causally explainable natural event. But thought about action proper moves on a completely different level. To conceive something as an action is to conceive it as realizing an intention, as something that is intelligible only in the light of the agent's reasons for performing it, which are of quite a different nature from the causes of the bodily movement involved in it.

It is significant that Wittgenstein disparagingly rejects the common idea expressed earlier according to which the limited emancipation of psychology from philosophy is the result of its undeveloped state as compared with the physical sciences. 'The confusion and barrenness of psychology', he wrote, 'is [sic] not to be explained by calling it a "young science". . . . In psychology there are experimental methods and *conceptual confusion*. . . . The existence of experimental methods makes us think that we have the means of solving the problems which trouble us; though problem and methods pass one another by.' This quotation is, indeed, consistent with the idea that once the conceptual confusion has been cleared up the experimental methods can, so to speak, be given their head. But he really means more than that. Once the conceptual confusion which is involved in taking behaviour to be, not actions from reasons, but natural events with causes is cleared up the greater part of what psychologists have taken it to be their business to investigate will be revealed as altogether beyond the competence of the essentially causal methods of inquiry they use.

In a more or less Freudian spirit it might seem inviting to explain this refusal by philosophers to relinquish the study of the mind to psychologists as the expression of a retentive hostility excited by the threat of superannuation. But it is just the relevance of this kind of explanation of beliefs to their validity which is the most substantial part of the point at issue. Whatever the emotional origin of the convictions of anti-psychological philosophers that their methods are more calculated to produce an understanding of the mind than those of the psychologists they criticize, it may still be the case that their conviction is well-founded. To take an extreme case: even if the ultimate source of the determination with which a physicist seeks to discover the fine structure of matter is his frustrated infantile curiosity about the sexual activities of his parents, it does not follow that his physical findings will be illusory. The unusual and even laughable character of the fuel has nothing to do with the capacity of the vehicle to reach its destination.

The type of objection I have been considering applies to any form of psychological inquiry that is or claims to be scientific, in that it attempts to discover the *causes* of mental phenomena and of the actions that manifest or express them. A cause-seeking psychology does not have to assume that strict, absolute determinism is true: to try to explain something is not to be convinced that you can explain everything. But it must assume that some mental phenomena and actions have causes if it is to be embarked upon sensibly at all. This assumption touches a sensitive area and comes into collision with two sorts of resistance which are widespread not only among philosophers but among reflective people generally. The first is the common conviction, already discussed, that if our beliefs are causally determined they are invalid. If this were true there would, in a way, be nothing to fear from scientific psychology. For in any comprehensive form such a psychology would include itself in the scope of its theories about the causation of beliefs. The beliefs of psychologists, even their professional ones, must have causes as much as any others and so suffer with them the common fate of invalidation. A consistent causal psychologist, then, cannot assert that the causal determination of beliefs entails their invalidity. The second sensitive point is the equally widespread conviction that if actions are causally determined their agents cannot be held morally responsible for them. This is the topic of another essay in this book so I shall not pursue it here.

The philosophical criticisms of psychology that arise from hostility to determinism are directed against psychology in general and not at Freud and psychoanalysis specifically. If he is often mentioned by the proposers of criticisms of this kind it is simply because of his eminence or notoriety as a cause-seeking psychologist. The main burden of recent philosophical criticism of Freud, however, is directed specifically at him and psychoanalysis as contrasted with academic, predominantly behavioural, psychology. It maintains that, while behavioural psychology is a genuine science, the doctrines of Freud and his followers, although emphatically claimed to be scientific, are in fact nothing of the sort. In its standard version it simply condemns Freud's theories as a kind of arbitrary metaphysical speculation, masquerading as science.

What Freud's ideas have fallen foul of is the latest developments in the working-out of a leading theme of philosophy of science for more than a century. This is the attempt to supply an account of the logical relations between theory and experience without which, all parties agree, no theory can claim to be scientific. One doctrine in this field, that of instrumentalism, holds that if theoretical concepts of unobservable entities cannot be empirically defined the theories in which they figure cannot be taken as descriptions of reality but are no more than calculating devices, rules of inference with whose aid one observable state of affairs can be predicted from another. On this view Freudian theory is a pragmatically convenient myth which connects getting neurotics to talk about infantile sexual experiences with making them better. This would certainly be entirely unacceptable to Freud who was uncompromisingly realistic about his theoretical constructions.

Another doctrine is inductivism which requires theories, if they are to count as scientific, to be capable of being confirmed by observable states of affairs. An inverted form of this requirement, proposed by Popper, has come to be widely accepted as a criterion for the scientific status of a theory. This is that for a theory to be scientific it must be empirically *falsifiable*; there must be some possible and empirically observable state of affairs which, if it occurred, would refute the theory in question. Since theories are unrestrictedly general they can never be conclusively established by particular observations, however numerous. But they can be overthrown by a single contrary instance. Popper argues persuasively that the more a theory rules out, the more possible falsifiers it has, the greater is its empirical content, the more, in other words, it actually says. Conformably with this, if a theory is unfalsifiable, it is simply vacuous and devoid of empirical content and certainly is no part of science. The manoeuvres which Freud makes to meet this demand make it clear that it is one that he himself implicitly accepts.

In what respects are Freud's theories held to fail by this standard and thus to forfeit their scientific status ? Popper himself illustrates his criterion of falsifiability by applying it first to such acknowledged pseudo-sciences as astrology and alchemy. He then goes on, more audaciously, to apply it, with condemnatory results, to the doctrines of Marx and Freud. In Freud's case he does not go into much detail. His argument turns principally on the familiar Freudian tactic of disparaging hostile criticism of psychoanalysis as being nothing more than the expression of emotional resistance to it. There is, indeed, a certain intellectual vulgarity about this type of polemical stratagem which is more at home in domestic quarrels and knockabout debates on social occasions than in controversy about serious and carefully formulated opinions. It is also an invalid argument, for reasons that have already been touched on. The emotional hostility of a critic is no guarantee of the invalidity of his criticism. It is not much of a ground for even suspecting it. If passionate involvement may blind the critic to the good arguments in support of the view he opposes, it may also inspire him to seek out good arguments against it. To admit this is perfectly compatible with recognizing that a calm desire to discover the truth is more likely than partisan passion to lead to valid reasoning.

The real point here is that the doctrine of resistance is not a central and crucial part of psychoanalytic theory. If it were, Popper would be wholly justified in dismissing psychoanalysis as what he calls a 'reinforced dogmatism', a body of theory which insulates itself against any possibility of refutation by including within itself a thesis about the necessary misguidedness of its critics. That Freud should so often have chosen to resort to this rather low-grade intellectual trick is unfortunate. But his offence is to some extent mitigated by the level of intense critical hostility to which his theories were subjected when they were first expounded and before they became, first, a fashion, and then a more or less habitual persuasion of everyone with more than the humblest educational attainments.

In fact Freud did modify his theories as he went along and, if he did excommunicate a good many of his followers when they dared to dissent from him, some of the modifications he made were at the prompting of critics of his theories other than himself. Perhaps the most important revision of basic doctrine, rather than addition to it, that Freud made was the abandonment of his original view that the traumatic events in infancy that gave rise to his patients' neuroses were actual seductions. Here, it seems, his own common sense was enough to convince him that the statistical mass of parental misbehaviour the theory would imply cannot have actually taken place.

What is interesting about this example is that in replacing actual seduction by sexual fantasy with a parent as object as the infantile causal factor lying behind adult neurosis, Freud replaced a conjecture that was hard to falsify with one that is practically unfalsifiable. If the hypothesis is that an adult's neurosis is the result of parental seduction in infancy there are two good reasons for thinking it will be very hard to refute. The alleged event is remote in time from the neurotic condition it is invoked to explain and its private and shameful nature makes it difficult to verify that it actually occurred. But a seduction is at least a fairly definite historical occurrence, in principle accessible to observation. If, in its place, an infantile *state of mind* is held responsible for the neurosis it becomes practically impossible for there to be any independent check on its having happened. If, as is further suggested, the traumatic desire in the infant is unconscious from the outset, is prevented by repression from ever breaking through into consciousness and is not simply repressed into the unconscious at an early stage, a truly independent check is rendered impossible.

Freud has two answers to this line of criticism, neither of which is, on inspection, very convincing. The first is that the neurotic patient can be got to 'recall' the long-repressed desire in question. But, in the first place, there are good reasons for distrusting memory-claims that reach back to such a very early stage of life. Furthermore the supposed recollection is always prompted by the analyst, trying out his interpretation on the patient's symptoms. The second is that the Freudian hypothesis about the character of the feelings young children have about their parents can be established by the direct observation of children's behaviour. To the extent that this observation reveals such desires, as it is held to, in nearly all children, the unfortunate consequence ensues that either the desires are not necessary conditions of neurosis in adult life or that most adults are neurotic, a proposition that has the near self-contradictory character of the thesis that nearly everyone is much taller than the average. Freud sidesteps this difficulty by invoking further untestable factors: the quantitative strength of the desires involved, for which no technique of measurement is suggested, and the inherited constitution of the patient, which is simply a promissory note that no steps are taken to honour and has the effect of turning the originally challenging theory into the vacuity that certain repressed desires cause neurosis in those of the majority of human beings who have such desires who happen to be constitutionally disposed to become neurotic. Here again the contentious issue of interpretation emerges. Freud admits that the desires mentioned by his theory are not to be discovered by straightforward observation of children's behaviour. They are revealed only to the true believers who know how to interpret the seemingly innocuous conduct of the very young.

So even if Popper rests too much weight on the pseudo-scientific character of the doctrine of resistance the point he is making remains untouched. The item on which he fastens is representative of a vast array of refutation-avoiding devices which permeate Freud's writings. Besides the examples I have given there should be mentioned the extension of terms, conspicuously 'sexuality', well beyond the limits of their conventional application, a linguistic reform misrepresented as a discovery. Then there is the practice of taking the contrary of what the theory predicts as being as much a confirmation of the theory as its originally predicted opposite. A man's strict upbringing should have made him aggressive towards his father. If he turns out to be notably polite to him that is just as good for Freud: politeness is simply the brilliant disguise the unconscious puts on to conceal its actual aggressiveness. There is no room here to follow the tactics Freud uses to preserve his theories from any possibility of empirical falsification in any greater detail. There is an admirable account of them in Cioffi's essay 'Freud and the Idea of a Pseudo-Science' in *Explanation in the Behavioural Sciences*.

Before leaving the subject of the unfalsifiable and thus pseudo-scientific nature of psychoanalytic theory a word should be said about a practical test of its efficacy, if not of its descriptive truth, on which its exponents rely, that of therapeutic success. Because of the difficulty of defining the notions of neurosis and of cure with sufficient precision for definite statistics to be assembled this is an issue that is hard to resolve decisively. But it does appear that the condition of neurotic patients is not changed for the better in a significantly higher proportion of cases when the patient has been psychoanalyzed than when he has been treated by an ordinary medical practitioner or even than when he has been left to cope with his problem on his own. But even if psychoanalytically treated patients did get better significantly more often than others it is as likely that the mere fact that someone took a protracted and sympathetic interest in their condition is responsible for the improvement as that the psychoanalytic beliefs of the therapist had anything to do with it.

Finally I want to comment briefly on two points at which the philosophy of Wittgenstein comes into direct contact with the doctrines of Freud. He shared the view that psychoanalytic theory is not a science, though more because of his view that human thought and action cannot be causally explained than because of its unfalsifiability. But he was not content to leave the matter negatively there and to remit psychoanalysis, by implication, to the same intellectual Alsatia as homeopathic medicine, numerology and measurements of the Great Pyramid. He freely acknowledged what he called its 'charm' and thought that it could be explained why generally sophisticated and unsuperstitious people should endorse it. He makes two suggestive points in this connection. The first is that, far from outraging and shocking people, the emphasis of Freudian theory on the ultimately sexual source of mental energies and the actions in which they are expressed is for many agreeable and exciting. (Freud himself was prepared to admit this at times.) Secondly, the idea of the unconscious going with one everywhere, with all its hidden power and wisdom, was a comforting thought in a generally hostile and obdurate world, paralleling the common childhood fantasy of an invisible companion or guardian angel.

He went on to say that Freud was not a scientist but something quite different, the proposer of a 'new notation', a new and poetically exciting way of describing familiar things. This does seem applicable to the Freudian technique of extending the range of application of terms like sexuality. There is, after all, a certain analogy between a child's affection for his mother and the literally sexual devotions of adult life. But this account of the 'real nature' of Freud's work is remote from any intention it would be reasonable to ascribe to Freud. At best it is an explanation of the charm that Wittgenstein finds in his ideas. In either case it is somewhat faint praise and was surely meant as such.

That suggests that the enthusiastic development of a more or less parenthetical comparison Wittgenstein made of his method in philosophy with psychoanalytic therapy, a development found in its most opulent form in the work of Lazerowitz, is something that he would not have endorsed. The basis of the comparison is that Wittgenstein does not take traditional philosophical problems at their face value, any more than Freud took neurotic symptoms. Rightly interpreted the ancient problems of philosophy are simply puzzles, states of conceptual bewilderment brought about by unconsciously perceived, but nevertheless mistaken, linguistic analogies. The relief of these puzzled states has something in common with Freudian therapy. It consists in lengthily talking out the problem until the patient recognizes the hidden spurious analogy that misled him. Lazerowitz takes this modest, and perhaps even playful, comparison and blows it up into a fully-fledged theory about the nature of philosophy. The theory is that traditional philosophical doctrines are really disguised linguistic proposals and not the assertions about the nature of the world that they outwardly seem, and are taken by their exponents, to be. He then goes on to maintain, not that the proper way of handling such expressions of conceptual puzzlement is *like* psychoanalytic therapy, but that these doctrines or unconscious proposals are literal neurotic symptoms in Freud's sense and should be treated accordingly.

This position has a noticeable power to infuriate philosophers. Those who keep their heads soon perceive that few arguments have ever more compellingly invited a *tu quoque* retort than Lazerowitz's disguised linguistic proposal to redescribe philosophical theories as disguised linguistic proposals. A good deal of wholesome fun can be had by trying to work out precisely what neurosis of its propounder it symptomatically expresses.

Theatre poster by Oskar Kokoschka

The Middle Years

Freud in 1914; drawing by Hermann Struck.

Above Freud at Clark University, Worcester, Massachusetts, in September 1909. With him in the front row are Stanley Hall and Carl Jung. Back row, from left to right, A.A. Brill, E. Jones and S. Ferenczi.
Below The International Psychoanalytical Congress at Weimar, 21 September 1911.

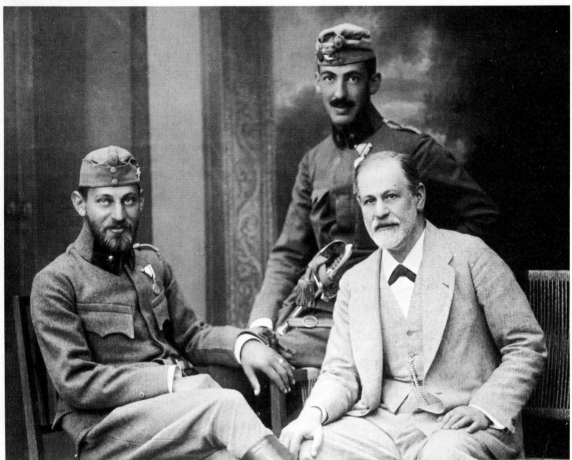

Freud and some of his children: *Opposite* With Anna in the Dolomites, 1912. *Above, top* Fishing with Ernst at Thumsee (Bavaria), 1901. *Bottom* With Ernst and Martin during the First World War.

Title pages of the first editions of *The Interpretation of Dreams* and *Three Essays on the Theory of Sexuality*.

DIE

TRAUMDEUTUNG

VON

Dᴿ SIGM. FREUD.

«FLECTERE SI NEQUEO SUPEROS, ACHERONTA MOVEBO.»

LEIPZIG UND WIEN
FRANZ DEUTICKE.
1900.

DREI ABHANDLUNGEN ZUR
SEXUALTHEORIE

VON

PROF. DR. SIGM. FREUD

IN WIEN

439591-R.

LEIPZIG UND WIEN
FRANZ DEUTICKE
1905

Freud at work in his study.

Top, left Julius Wagner-Jauregg (1857–1940), director of the Psychiatric Division of the Vienna General Hospital, with whom Freud disagreed on the treatment of war neuroses. Wagner-Jauregg was awarded the Nobel Prize for medicine in 1927.

Top, right Stefan Zweig (1881–1942), one of Freud's most assiduous correspondents, who introduced many literary and artistic figures to him.

Bottom Gustav Mahler (1860–1911), the composer, had a brief but extremely successful encounter with Freud in 1910. Freud said of him that he had never met anyone who seemed to understand the workings of psychoanalysis so swiftly.

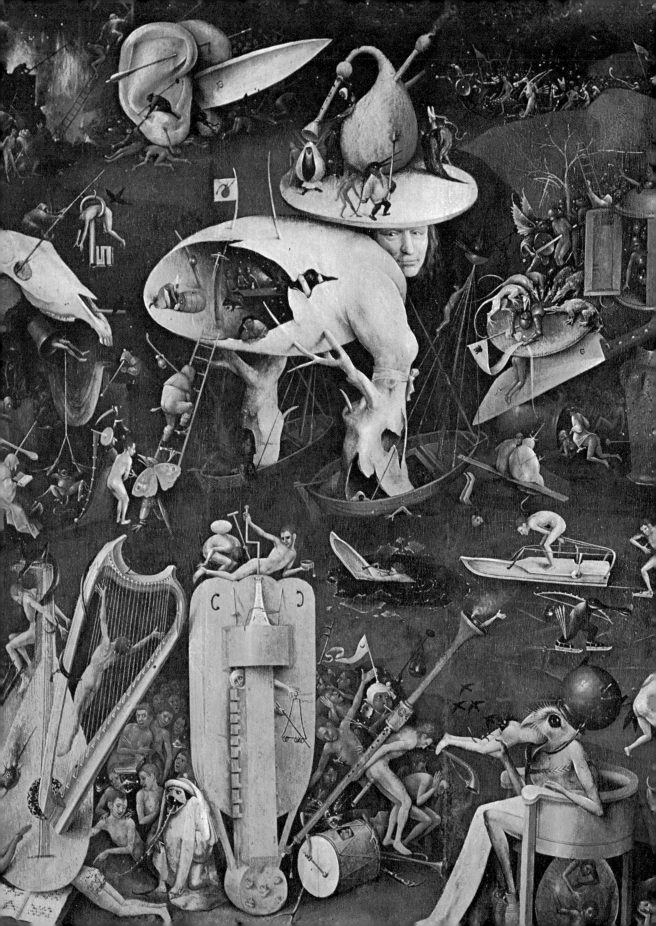

6

Psychoanalysis and the Decolonization of Mankind

Octave Mannoni

(Translated by Nicholas Fry)

Detail of the triptych of the *Garden of Delights* by H. Bosch, a work which both inspired Surrealist artists and post-Freudian analysis.

THE various phenomena which may be described by the term colonization stemmed basically from the political outlook of the civilized countries and were the result of socio-economic forces. If one were sticking to fundamentals, in fact, there would be little point in trying to interpret these phenomena – either in order to explain them or to influence them – by the techniques available to psychology or psychoanalysis. From a political viewpoint such an enterprise would inevitably be dismissed as pure mystification.

But this is not the only possible point of view. And there are many other aspects to the actual situations created by colonization. Moreover, by their very peculiarity, they can show up more general aspects of other, inter-human relationships, although in an exaggerated, sometimes caricatured form.

The Europeans living in the colonial territories did not generally include those who had the power to decide on a policy of colonization – or of de-colonization – nor even those who had the most to gain from such a policy. Many of them thought – or at least believed that they thought – only of the good they could do: converting to the true faith, nursing the sick, feeding the hungry, teaching the ignorant. In a word, bringing the 'benefits of civilization'. It should be remembered that the time is not very far distant when it was still unthinkable that such an expression should contain any ironic overtones. Those who believed in this mission would no doubt have condemned the real policy which they were serving without daring to admit it to themselves. They approved of it above all because of the new territories which it opened up for the exercise of their charitable impulses.

Situations such as this were only possible, in the French colonies at least, as the result of a particular ideology and a particular image of man. The ideology was one of *universalism*. As all men were thought to be universally equal – all created by the same God, possessed of the same immortal soul, capable of the same reason and progress – then savages had to be converted or civilized. The alternative to this ideology was racialism: if certain of the human races were by nature unassimilable, then they could be exploited, reduced to slavery or exterminated. This path was followed also, but it did not lead to 'coloniza-tion' in this same meaning.

Today, we do not see things quite so simply. The relatively rapid changes we have witnessed in our time are due to a large number of factors, the most important of which is that while colonization undoubtedly changed the colonized peoples, it did so in a different manner to that envisaged by the colonizers. Rather in the same way that Caliban explains to Prospero what he has gained from his teaching. But I now want to deal with a different class of factors, namely those which have changed our ideology by giving us a different image of man in general. And more specifically I propose to examine the role played in this change by the discoveries of Freud.

Freud himself, of course, was never directly concerned with the problems of colonization. Those of his disciples who went to observe the so-called primitive peoples at close quarters during his lifetime could be counted on the fingers of one hand, and they were hardly attracted by questions of that sort. They were interested, rather, in a new use of ethnography or anthropology; under the influence of the illusory concept of 'primitivism', they thought they could find the same things in the 'cradle of humanity' as Freud was finding in the childhood of his patients. (Although it was the result of an illusion, they did in fact find them, for reasons which we shall understand later.) They adopted an objective attitude which led them to treat the native as an object of European science, thereby excluding themselves from the situation and systematically neglecting the most essential part of it, namely that it was the meeting point of two different cultures. They did manage to establish, to a greater or lesser degree, the universal value of the more general Freudian theories – but they only obtained confirmation of them in scientific terms. They were not given pause by the fairly obvious objection that *universalism* cannot remain altogether the same once it is founded on the universality of the unconscious instead of the common possession of reason or an immortal soul. They saw well enough that their analytical training gave them a new power of communication with the 'savages'; that they could 'understand' beliefs that had bewildered their predecessors – just as psychoanalysts could interpret utterances in which psychiatry had hitherto only seen nonsense. But they remained satisfied with the capabilities of the tool they were using – like the naturalists with their microscope.

Though he had no experience of this kind, Freud himself said nothing conducive to such a mistake. Analysts chiefly concerned with therapy have easily imagined that Freud merely wished to extend a method originally born of clinical research into other fields of activity. But right from the early years of the twentieth century, Freud knew that his disoveries entailed a radical change in man's conception of his own nature; that they implied, from the beginning, an orientation towards anthropology, and that the therapy of neuroses and ethnography were merely two *applications* of this new anthropology, to which he gave the general name of psychoanalysis. He did not reject the traditional values – reason, science, the civilization of 'underdeveloped' peoples – on the contrary, he justified them by adding something new to them, without which they remained limited in scope. For they could no more reduce or justify the diversity of ritual customs, beliefs and institutions than they had been able to explain delusions and fantasies. In providing the key to neuroses, he showed that on an individual scale, however paltry and exaggerated they might appear, they had basically the same value as the collective solutions through which a people formulates its customs and beliefs. Behind the formation of psychotic delusions he saw the same forces as prophets are possessed by when these forces are manifested in a society which rejects them. Beside the formal belief in the unity of the human species, supported in a somewhat equivocal fashion by biology (despite racial differences) and philosophy (which was unable to face the concept of unreason), he instituted a new foundation to this unity – which he found in the unconscious itself – immediately making it far less formal and more amenable to practical expression. There was a departure from traditional methods of procedure, whether that of fanaticism and activism, which tended to reduce the unwarrantable diversity of cultures in favour of 'European truths', or that of relativism which, since the time of Montaigne, had already been inviting us to view our own forms of truth with scepticism. For a long time, even Marxism had remained embarrassed by these problems; in the mid-nineteenth century (it has revised its attitude since), it accepted the idea of colonization as an accelerating factor in the dialectic movement of history. But the colonized peoples found out for themselves that colonization was withholding from them the real 'benefits of civilization'.

Present-day anthropologists are often critical of Freudian anthropology – even though they almost always owe it far more than they acknowledge. This is the result of a misunderstanding. Freudian anthropology, or the most essential part of it, has nothing to do with what Freud may have said about totemism or the primitive horde. It was not him but the anthropologists of his time who believed in primitivism, totem religion and numerous other illusions. In fact, without knowing it but in a perfectly valid way, they were revealing something of the human unconscious as it was functioning in themselves. Often, the ethnographers' disagreements with Freud appear as disagreements between the ethnographers of yesterday and those of today. If Freud had really built his concepts on the same bases as the ethnography of his time, those concepts would have become outdated at the same time as the bases. This is clearly not the case, and the essence, if not some of the details, of his concepts is by no means condemned to develop hand in hand with the ethnological sciences. The essence, reduced to a minimum, is that the interpretations which he made possible, and even the myths he deliberately invented – such as that of parricide – relate to the unconscious, that is to the possibility of recognizing for ourselves, in ourselves, the meaning of modes of thought or behaviour which at first sight we would declare absurd or unacceptable in ourselves, or shocking when shown to us by others. (The only objection which could be made to this point of view – and I do not exclude it – is that a degree of tolerance and a certain amount of curiosity about cultural differences must have already developed in the world. This is true. A detailed but purely descriptive classification of these differences had already been made, and Freud was able to make use of it. But it was he who drew from it the consequences we know, and who interpreted them.) The theory of repression enables us to understand our attitude when faced with a man who is culturally very different from ourselves, somewhat as it does our attitude towards our own suppressed desires, with all the reactions that this attitude can arouse. The real difficulty cannot be explained in purely cultural terms. How could sorcery, anthropophagy, polygamy and other 'barbarous' customs have disturbed those who observed them if the latter did not carry the temptation or the possibility of these things deeply hidden within themselves? The situation thus created is in some ways similar to paranoia – it is oneself whom one condemns in the other, whom one wishes to convert, to civilize or to educate. The detached and professionally tolerant attitude adopted by ethnographers might be said to resemble that of psychiatrists, who have to put up with their patients' incomprehensible ravings. No doubt both ethnographers and psychiatrists even pride themselves on it to a certain extent – a fact which in itself would be an interesting subject for analysis. It seems in any case that in the colonial situation many of the unconscious aspects of inter-human relationships may be revealed in a more obvious and less sophisticated form than elsewhere, precisely because of the ambivalence inherent in such a situation – because of the particular mixture of tolerance and intolerance, of racialism suffered but not suppressed which the latter necessarily entails.

I happened to find myself in just such a situation at a time when I would have been unable to talk about it exactly as I am now, but when, more interestingly, I was *learning* to do so.

During a very long stay in Madagascar, I had gradually come to take an interest in the country's language and customs. And I had been troubled by the way in which I had reacted to some relatively straightforward ceremonies connected with the cult of the dead. This gave me the idea of undergoing psychoanalysis when I returned to Paris, in the hope of seeing the situation more clearly. I had not got very far with this when I was obliged to return to the country for a short stay; it was at the time of the 1947 rebellion, and during this time of troubles something which had hitherto been concealed in the relationship between the colonizers and the colonized seemed in the process of being revealed. I already knew how to make use of the unconscious as a means of interpretation.

Unfortunately – though I did not even think of it at first and only regretted it later – I was not yet capable of describing my experiences in a personal manner, as a part of my biography, or of my own analysis. Such missed opportunities can never be made up for; I was not well acquainted with Freud's theories – they had changed me, but mostly indirectly, through the medium of personal analysis. I seemed to be ill-prepared, incapable of giving a correct theoretical analysis of the events I was witnessing. In fact, as I finally realized – and several years later I was to regret not having seen it earlier – that was not the real point about the situation. But a small basket at harvest time is better than a larger one at the wrong season, and what I did succeed in gathering related not to the rebellion itself – though this played a revealing role – but to the opinions which the Europeans and Madagascans had of one another. The question was not whether these were right or not, but what they really meant.

The first thing that became clear to me related to the judgements of the Europeans who were accusing the Madagascans of ingratitude. These accusations tied in perfectly with the most serious studies dating from before psychoanalysis. Lévy Bruhl, having no direct experience, could only rely on a consensus of travellers' tales concerning many of the various 'primitive' countries: the attitude of the 'primitive peoples' was 'incomprehensible'; only the hypothesis of a prelogical 'primitive mentality', with no point of contact with our own, could account for it. Our own mentality, of course, went without question; it was logical, and no one thought to examine it. Even when a European traveller thrashed the natives or imprisoned them 'to teach them gratitude', Lévy Bruhl merely saw this as proof of the natives' failings – they must have been ungrateful indeed to drive the Europeans to such extremes. Lévy Bruhl revised his views later under the direct or indirect influence of psychoanalysis – he finally realized that we too had our share of prelogical thinking which was beyond our own comprehension. However, this was not enough in the case of the Madagascans, for in spite of what the colonialists said, the attitude of the natives suddenly appeared quite clear to me. What was taken for a lack of gratitude in fact concealed the opposite – the emergence of feelings of *attachment* which were so strong that the Madagascans did not always manage to accommodate them. Our own feelings of gratitude were no more 'natural' or more logical; we had instituted them in order to avoid the same troublesome unconscious reactions – ranging from attachment to aggression – just as the Madagascans had, like many other peoples, invented a precise and rigid system of rules to regulate the exchange of gifts and counter-gifts. The Europeans violated these rules, either out of heedlessness or sheer ignorance, and then were unable to understand why the Madagascans violated theirs.

Now this simple and easy interpretation threw light on the cult of the dead which had caused me so much embarrassment. Ancestor worship is of course repressed among Europeans. This repression has not been studied in detail, but if one re-reads Freud's case history of the 'Rat Man', looking at ancestor worship in terms of a resurgence of something repressed, with all the symptoms that this implies, then one will get an idea of this repression. I realized, with some astonishment naturally, that the Europeans were without knowing it acting as though they wished to take over the position occupied by the dead in the Madagascan personality as the focus of all hopes and aspirations. The Madagascans were no more aware of this themselves, but it became clear that the rebellion represented an authentic return to the authority of the dead as opposed to the Europeans. I was not seasoned enough to accept such an unbelievable idea lightly, and I might perhaps not have dared to mention it if I had not received confirmation from another source, namely from the ethnographers who were studying the Melanesians. The latter displayed openly what was latent in the minds of the Madagascans, and though scarcely able to believe it, the ethnographers were nevertheless forced to report it. For the Melanesians, the goods brought by the white men's ships are sent from their ancestors. The belief is quite literal, and no doubt stems from the fact that the Europeans have destroyed the ancient barter system which used to be practised between the islands, and have thus caused a resurgence of unconscious beliefs (the phenomenon is known generally by the term Cargo Cult). Various ethnographers have tried to find an acceptable explanation. H. F. Leenhardt, for instance, attempted to solve the problem by pointing out that the natives of New Guinea call the country of the dead *Suné*, while the cargo ships came from *Sydney*. The whole thing, according to him, was based on a confusion of names. The explanation is unlikely enough in itself – whatever the missionaries believe, 'primitive' beliefs are not the result of simple-mindedness. But a more decisive argument is the fact that the cargo cult exists in many other islands where neither Suné nor Sydney are involved.

I have mentioned this brief example, not merely for the sake of quoting from a book of mine – which is now somewhat dated – but to show how analytical interpretation involves the interpreter himself. Our obligation to be grateful prevents us from understanding another attitude – which we are nevertheless acquainted with – and that is the obligation to exchange gifts according to particular rules, which when we find it among 'primitive' peoples we look upon as a curiosity, as a series of arbitrary ceremonies. But behind these obligations there is something common which must be dominated in both cases, and if it cannot be controlled it no doubt makes us regress to the point where the child demands and receives without having anything to give in return, and in particular without gratitude. Gratitude is only learned later.

It was not possible to see things in this way before Freud. All that could have been done – and it was not often done – was to draw up a code of behaviour based on *overt* customs whereby people could learn how to exchange gifts in an intercultural situation so as to avoid possibly disagreeable reactions. When Cook landed in New Caledonia, he offered a native chief a dog as a gift, and was never able to understand why the chief hid from him and was never seen again. He might have gone to look for him, and so been killed without explanation.

Freud's discoveries no longer surprise even those people who have only an imperfect idea of them. Not because they have been popularized – which merely enables them to be disposed of by being assimilated into the mass of superficial information which modern man is submerged in more to the profit of others than of himself. But because they have changed our attitudes without our necessarily being aware of the theories on which these changes are based. Thus it hardly matters whether ethnographers adopt these theories or oppose them, since they still influence their work. It is no longer a question of going to New Guinea to find out if the Oedipus complex is found there, but of realizing that research of this kind is impossible unless one can really communicate with the natives, and that such communication is impossible if one has not first succeeded in communicating sufficiently with one's own unconscious – for without the latter, the Oedipus complex is inaccessible everywhere.

Psychoanalysis and the Decolonization of Mankind

Thus it cannot be said that Freud had no experience of problems of this kind; they were the same ones as he encountered every day in his practice. Jung took the wrong track because he tried to interpret the unconscious as something cultural, as 'collective' and not universal. For this reason he was not entirely free from racialism.

The subject of colonization belongs largely to the past, and will do so entirely one day, in any case. It might be thought that because of this there is no longer any point in studying it. But it is still the pattern for many inter-human situations. In the classic psychiatric situation – with Charcot in 1885, for instance – something similar could be observed, with the doctor playing the role of colonizer and the patients as the colonized people. Freud had arrived at La Salpetrière as a neurologist; he left it a 'hysteric' – having found that he was just hysterical enough to identify with Charcot's patients. This identification is at the origin of the discovery of psychoanalysis, since it made possible Freud's 'self-analysis' with Fliess; Charcot, on the other hand, was not subject to this kind of identification. At the time, nothing resembled a colonized country more than a psychiatric institution; even today, one has only to see two 'stabilized' schizophrenics maintaining the director's tennis court for the similarity to be immediately obvious. Thus the problem of colonization did not only concern overseas countries. The process of de-colonization – which is in any case far from complete in those countries – is also under way at home, in our schools, in female demands for equality, in the education of small children and in many other fields. The development of analytical practice itself should be considered. Insofar as it represents the continuation of psychiatry, it is liable to inherit a 'colonial situation' which is not always easy to get out of. But psychoanalysis goes beyond this technical framework and has some effect on current attitudes. It even modifies the attitudes of churchmen and criminologists. . . . It is difficult to appreciate the importance of an influence which appears very superficial and very deep by turns. There is no cause for optimism in all this, for we now know better than before the extent of the difficulties involved; more often than not one only succeeds in diverting them into other channels. We are merely left with the fact that in interpreting all the various aspects of the world today the ideas of Freud must be allowed a considerable role.

These ideas have naturally evolved, but only in those parts of the doctrine which, as we saw earlier, came too much under the influence of the concepts of the time. Under this influence, Freud made use of 'primitivism' in a way which he believed to be scientific but which does not appear legitimate to us today. We must abandon it. Jung, for his part, had gone much further, making primitivism into a mystique. He believed that a kind of original truth and the natural mental health of mankind had been preserved amongst the 'primitive peoples'. As he wrote: 'Viewed from a relatively safe distance, say from Central Africa or Tibet, it would almost seem as though this fragment of humanity [Europe] has projected upon people still sound in their instincts an unconscious "mental derangement".' The linking of Central Africa and Tibet might seem rather rash to an anthropologist. But leaving aside the Jungian viewpoint, it is a useful reminder that all peoples live equally by their own culture (and not by the normality of their instincts) and that in this respect – i.e. the possession of a culture designed to make life possible under a particular set of circumstances – no people is really more advanced than another.

Moreover, if certain cultures prove capable of destroying others – and colonization is one form of this destruction – we must not fall into the kind of Darwinian judgement which attributes some biological value to this capability or sees in it a guarantee of future progress. For the destructive forces brought forth by these cultures also act internally; they are merely diverted onto others, and the conquering peoples do not move on to more legitimate forms of gratification – on the contrary. These are truths that the civilized peoples are beginning to realize, and the fact that this is happening at the time of decolonization is surely no coincidence.

It is for instance a result of our own culture that we have become more and more intolerant of forms of 'unreason' that past generations accepted far more easily than ourselves, and that primitive societies accept even more. It is taking a superficial view to believe that the stresses and strains of modern societies are pathogenic in themselves; it is our ideals and our elevated concepts, our religion of success and adjustment – that is those things which in history have been our strength – and not the grossness of our materialistic appetites which have caused us to set up those internal colonies which are our psychiatric hospitals and institutions for maladjusted children – hospitals and institutions which the 'primitive' peoples have no need of since their insane have a place in their society and are therefore far less sharply distinguished from those who are 'normal' than are ours. It is us, the sensible people, who have forced this distinction upon them.

Insofar as ethnic differences are concerned, universalism is not sufficient – even though founded since Freud on the unconscious (that is basically on *utterance* and not on the instincts, as is demonstrated throughout *The Interpretation of Dreams*, though this is not the place to expand on this subject). Another aspect of Freudian theory must be invoked, and that is narcissism. For if the first requirement of the human being is to be a man like any other and to be recognized as such, a second follows immediately from it, and that is to be recognized as different from any other and as being himself. We have seen women claiming first of all the right to be equal as human beings. But this demand concealed another one, which was to be recognized in their unique-ness as women, and for each woman to be recognized in her oneness, as her-self – as the woman she feels herself to be and not as men wish to see her. The same thing is happening with the blacks in America. They are violently rejecting the universalism of the liberals, and it is in their uniqueness as blacks that they want to be recognized. The universalist right is accompanied by the right to difference – and the contradiction is only apparent. The differ-ences are *cultural* in every case. The colour of a man's skin, for instance, only counts because of the *meanings* attached to it (and the vaguer they are, the more rigidly they are applied). These meanings are not natural, and therefore not instinctive. In nature, skin colour has no significance.

These problems were not very clearly seen by Freud – though he saw perfectly well the great importance of 'little differences'. His experience in Vienna as a persecuted Jew did not altogether enlighten him, because he felt above all and most profoundly a man like any other, and while remaining faithful to his origins he did not think of cultivating his difference – he did not make any claims specifically as a Jew. Other Jews have occasionally made such claims for him since. It might be said that the whole period was universalist – since it was believed that persecution was due to mere prejudice and that the progress of enlightenment, i.e. the work of reason, should be sufficient to overcome it. Today we know that reason does not really have this power and that the toleration of differences will not come simply from the disappearance of naive prejudices. But if we have to some extent progressed beyond Freud's attitude in this respect, it is to him that we owe the means of doing so.

7

Freud and the
Concept of Parental Guilt

Catherine Storr

Is there any other occupation in the world on which almost everyone is prepared to embark without training, without experience, and without any more specialized knowledge than is provided by having been, so to speak, at the receiving end a good many years before? An occupation, too, which will affect the health and happiness if not the actual survival of one or more people? Which has such a slow gestation that it is necessary for years to pass before it is possible to assess the measure of success or failure attributable to the different measures taken? I am referring, of course, to the job of being a parent, which most of us undertake so light-heartedly, and which, for most of us again, turns out so different from anything we had expected. Our surprise takes innumerable and varied forms, some pleasant, some disagreeable; but what seems to me a comparatively new phenomenon in the history of parenthood is the very prevalent modern feature of parental guilt.

I am not suggesting that the teachings of Freud are solely responsible for this. As it is possible to see from myth, from fable, from history, from fiction and from philosophical writings, guilt has been present in the parent-child relationship since man first began to record the events of his life and his reactions to them. But it is, on the whole, guilt felt for wrongs consciously committed, or, as in the case of Oedipus, for an offence perpetrated under a misapprehension. In general the attitude is one of robust commonsense. Parents who treated their children right were not disappointed in them. The incidence of wicked children born to good parents in the literature of Western Europe is singularly low; the only example which springs instantly to mind is that of Goneril and Regan, and even here it's arguable that Lear was one of those irrational, impetuous characters who so easily alienate their children by demands for extravagant demonstrations of affection. I can't help also suspecting that he was the kind of father who makes a terrific fuss of the new baby, comparing it with the older children to their disadvantage because they are old enough to pit their wills against his and the youngest child is not. Much commoner is the picture of the romanticized child, the innocent, suffering under the ministrations of cruel adults, like so many of the young in Dickens's novels; sometimes these adults are the actual parents, like Mr Dombey, Mr Gradgrind, more often step-parents, like Mr Murdstone, guardians, masters – even, in *Great Expectations*, a sister. How the child preserves his innocence in the face of depravity, his sensitivity and his ideals when surrounded by mentors who have neither, is not fully explained in terms which would satisfy modern psychologists. Something may be attributed to his having had, in early childhood, the experience of security and love; David Copperfield has spent his first years with his loving, if silly, mother and the devoted Peggoty, Pip has had the support of his sister's husband Joe, Florence Dombey had her mother, and little Paul had Florence, to give them values less totally materialistic than those held by their father. But there was, up to the middle or end of the nineteenth century, also a belief in the genetic transmission of what we should now consider acquired characteristics. Little aristocrats, stolen at birth by gipsies, remained apart from their foster brothers and sisters, not only by virtue of their delicate skins and their finely formed limbs, but also by an innate sensibility of feeling and a superior refinement of taste. Little peasants, on the other hand, might be brought up almost on a par with the sons of gentlemen, but they never lost a certain uncouthness which effectually prevented their ever being mistaken for children who had been gently born; Heathcliffe, (although it is true his adoption into the Earnshaw household was in early childhood, not in infancy) is the prime example of the character whose rough, animal nature resists all attempts at civilization, while Jane, in *Jane Eyre*, demonstrates the power of an inborn delicacy of feeling to survive coarsening and brutalizing surroundings.

The belief that you can't make a silk purse out of a sow's ear was, however, not applicable to the more usual situation in which parents or guardians brought up children of their own kind; and here it has always been recognized that the children's development depends on what treatment has been given him in his early years. Apart from the isolated case of Lear, the good characters in Shakespeare's plays have good children, the bad usually, though not always, have children who are also bad. The convention continues unchallenged until the nineteenth century, when some of the great Victorian novelists recognized that it was possible for parents who were not absolutely wicked, but who suffered from the more venial and human failings of pride, stupidity, weakness, to mismanage the rearing of their children with disastrous results. Dickens' Steerforth has been ruined by his mother's pride, George Osborne by his father's ambition, Becky Sharp by the atmosphere of squalor and deceit occasioned by her parents' lack of integrity; and in Mrs Gaskell's *Wives and Daughters*, the beautiful but flawed Cynthia says sadly, 'Oh Molly, you don't know how I was neglected just at a time when I wanted friends most. Mamma does not know: it is not in her to know what I might have been if only I had fallen into good hands', and on another occasion, 'Oh how good you are, Molly! I wonder if I had been brought up like you whether I should have been as good.' The context makes it clear that by 'brought up like you' she means 'loved as you have been'.

But implied in all these and in other fictional relationships is consciousness. The parents of unsatisfactory children have committed their sins of ommission or of commission if not deliberately, at least without consideration of the child's side of the question. The rights of parents were still absolute; they had the power to direct the habits, the thoughts, the feelings, the destinies of their children. A child was a possession as a slave was a possession. A well disposed, kindly owner of slaves, secure in his superior judgement, does not suffer from guilt in his relations with those inferior beings. Nor did our ancestors in relation to their children.

Towards the end of the nineteenth century, however, the structure of family life changed. Medicine, with Pasteur's discovery of the bacterial carriage of infection, with Lister's use of antiseptics, and the subsequent introduction of the aseptic technique in surgery and obstetrics, took a sudden and dramatic step forwards. One of the earliest consequences was the drop in infant mortality. Once it had been established that it was no longer necessary to accept every child that God could send in order to be able to rear three or four to maturity, birth control, though of a fairly primitive kind, had come to stay. The element of choice having been introduced, less responsibility could be laid on Fate, God or the Devil for the outcome, and more taken by the parents; as Adam discovered to his cost, choice involves responsibility and with responsibility goes potential guilt. Parents could now choose not only how many children they had but also the spacing between births, so that jealousy, sibling rivalry, even ill-health became problems which they might themselves, however unwittingly, have created. More than this, the field over which their anxieties, their hopes and their fears were dispersed became very much narrowed, and often one or other sex was represented by only one of their children, so that the only boy or the only girl in a family of three or four had to carry all the parents' ambitions. The pathetically anxious desire to do everything right by each member of a small family inevitably – since the swing of faith from established religion towards science as the saviour of the human race had already begun – led to the creation of a discipline in what had previously been regarded as an almost instinctive activity, that of child-rearing. It was felt that parents could not now afford to make mistakes. It was a complete change from the attitude at the beginning of the century, exemplified by Jane Austen's cool comment on the large family of Musgraves who appear in *Persuasion*. 'The real circumstances of this pathetic piece of family history were, that the Musgraves had had the ill-fortune of a very troublesome hopeless son, and the good fortune to lose him before he reached his twentieth year.'

One more factor now, in our own century, enters into the pattern of family life, and this is the loss, in this country and in America, of the domestic servant class. The dwindling of domestic help in middle-class households began during the First World War, accelerated in the 1920s and 1930s, and ended in 1940 with a total drying up of supply. It is interesting to note that up to 1914 it was assumed to be the right of all but the very poorest families to have some help in the house; the Micawber's 'orflin' is even lodged near the King's Bench prison when Mr Micawber and his family are imprisoned for debt, Trollope's most indigent clergy have some 'little maid of all work' to assist their hard-working wives, and the children in E. Nesbit's stories, though more often than not the family is hardpressed to make ends meet, rely on a girl who cooks them uneatable puddings or, at worst, a full-time visiting daily char. The change affected the middle-class family most; the really affluent could still afford to engage nurses and governesses as they had always done, and the working classes felt no difference since these mothers had always had to care for their own families. It was now the turn of the middle-class mother to keep an eye on her babies while she washed, cooked and ironed; and since these mothers were often from the professional and intellectual classes – were also often themselves professional women – it was second nature to them to look for guidance in this new task by reading. They wanted instruction not only in the physical care of infants, but also in the education of the child's mind. So it was now that the teaching of Freud really came into its own; it had been, as it were, waiting in the wings, enthusiastic-ally adopted by a few, but not yet generally accepted by the lay public. Children in the 1920s were mostly brought up in the old-fashioned way; parents were less repressive than their parents had been, but their word was still conventionally law, however much the children rebelled in private. But with the advent of the domestic revolution, with the increasing popularity of psychology as a 'science', with the gradual surrendering of religious belief, which had before provided reassurance for those who wanted a moral code, with the vogue for psychoanalysis, spread partly by the influx of Continental analysts to Britain and the United States, and partly by the enthusiastic adop-tion of its practice and thinking as a universal panacea in the latter country, the general awareness and acceptance of the teaching of Freud and of his followers was incalculably increased. The enthusiasm was – and virtually still is – confined to the said middle classes, and has only slowly permeated the general public's attitude towards the treatment and education of children; in Britain certainly there is an unwillingness to adopt new attitudes where old ones can still be seen to operate without obvious disaster, and Freud's psychodynamic theory of the human mind is still no more a part of the way of thinking of the man in the street than is the consciousness of Pasteur's discovery of bacteria. Dreams are still interpreted as if they were tea leaves, and the baby's dummy picked up off the railway carriage floor and stuffed back into the infant's mouth. The middle-class mother has, however, been for decades acutely aware of the danger of 'germs', and is now as conscious of invisible threats to her child's psyche; it has always been this class, I suspect, which has had the time, the energy and the interest to consider and to put into practice new approaches to the familiar and the traditional.

It was not until the end of the 1920s, when Freud's writings had been known in his own country for nearly thirty years, and in translation in Britain for more than half that time, that books on child care and child development, written for the general public and not for the specialist, had begun to show traces of Freud's influence. It is interesting to consider the changes which appear in various handbooks of advice for mothers, beginning before the Freudian era, and continuing up to the present day. Mr Pye Chavasse, in *Advice to a Mother*, written some time in the late 1830s, confines his advice almost entirely to the physical aspects of child care; much of what he gives is today unexceptionable. Nor perhaps would one quarrel with his remarks on 'the well-being of the child'. 'A child should be happy; he must, in every way, be made happy; everything ought to be done to conduce to his happiness, to give him joy, gladness and pleasure. . . . Love! let love be his pole star.' And later, when dealing with the problem of peevishness, 'If he be in a cross humour, take no notice of it, but divert his attention to some pleasing object. This may be done without spoiling him. Do not combat bad temper with bad temper – noise with noise. Be firm, be kind, be gentle, be loving, speak quietly, smile tenderly and embrace him fondly, but *insist on implicit obedience,* [author's italics] and you will have, with God's blessing, a happy child.'[1]

Sound sense; advice which, one would think, cannot lead a parent much astray; but it takes for granted the absolute supremacy of the parent and, except for the rather ambiguous clause about God's blessing, the inevitability of a happy result following on judicious action. It also assumes the total self-possession of the parent, a point I'd like to return to later. Eighty years later the attitude has not materially altered. *The Mothercraft Manual* by Mabel

Liddiard, a disciple of the Truby King school, is again mainly concerned with the child's physical well-being, and implies the same belief that as long as the parent follows instructions both she and the child can hardly go wrong. There is, however, a shift of emphasis; now it is not the child's happiness which is of the first importance, but the necessity for strict training from the earliest days. In feeding, for instance, whereas Mr Pye Chavasse recommends gradually reaching the optimum interval between feeds of 'about four hours', Nurse Liddiard insists that 'whatever intervals are decided upon, these must be adhered to strictly. . . . Many mothers and nurses think it cruel to wake a baby for a feed and so live in a constant muddle as to meals, rest, outings, etc. This is a mistaken kindness, the baby and mother should live by the clock.'[2] (More than one of my acquaintances who reared babies in the 1920s and 1930s have told me how they used to sit through their child's frantically hungry yells, waiting till the clock told them that the four hours was exactly up and that they might pacify him.) On toilet training also there is little difference, though Mr Chavasse is again the less peremptory. 'A babe of three months and upwards ought to be held out at least a dozen times during the twenty-four hours. If such a plan were adopted, diapers might be dispensed with at the end of three months – a great advantage. The babe would be inducted into clean habits, a blessing to himself, and a comfort to all around. . . . A DIRTY CHILD IS THE MOTHER'S DISGRACE.'[3] [author's capitals]. This is Mr Chavasse. Miss Liddiard begins the training even' earlier. 'From the third day the nurse should have a small chamber . . . on her knee, and the baby should be held with the back against the nurse's chest. . . . Many nurses train their babies so that they have no soiled napkins after the first week or so, and very few wet ones. . . . Make the child understand that this is a serious business, and do not give him toys to amuse him while sitting on the chamber.' Later, 'As the child grows older a time must be fixed for an attempt at the action of the bowels. The best time is immediately after breakfast. Always insist on their trying to pass urine just before going for a walk; this saves much inconvenience while out.'[4] It is clear that the adults' convenience is the primary consideration. Mother, you could say, is still always right.

But this state of affairs was already doomed. Susan Isaacs published *The Nursery Years* in 1929, only six years after the first appearance of Miss Liddiard's manual, and here already the rights of the child are seen in a very different light. 'So with his training in cleanliness and regular habits of bowel and bladder. We need to be gentle here too, not putting our own standards too rigidly high, nor making our own immediate convenience the first consideration.' She does recommend the mother 'to give the infant an opportunity of regular habits from the earliest days, by putting him on a vessel after each feed' but goes on to say that we shouldn't expect a child to be too docile: '. . . Indeed there are many grounds for feeling distressed about the too-clean and too-docile child even in these earliest days; for he may suffer, in ways that lead to mental illness, under the strain of accepting adult standards too early.'[5] I find this especially interesting, not only because it is the first indication that the child may be regarded as a separate and autonomous being, whose function may be something more than that of fitting in perfectly with his parents' wishes, but also because it seems probable that this threat of possible insanity at some future date is the age-old one of madness and impotence which was used – and probably unfortunately in some circles still is – to discourage masturbation; but here we have the guilt transferred from the child to the parent. Next, after a gap of sixteen years, is the best-seller, *Baby and Child Care*. Sensible Dr Benjamin Spock, writing in the United States, where the knowledge and practice of psychological precepts has always been far ahead of that in Britain, tells us that 'some psychologists think that early training is harmful in certain cases at least . . .'[6] and advises leaving any training until the baby can sit up – 'around seven to nine months'. The whole section on toilet training is anti-disciplinarian. Spock's great contribution to social medicine seems to me, here as elsewhere in his book, to be his ability to combine the comparatively new views on child-psychology with sound common sense. He points out that a 'trained' baby of a few months is not in any normal sense trained; it is only the mother who is trained to have a pot ready at the appropriate moment. He emphasizes the desirability of co-operation between parent and child in this and other matters of adapting to social norms, and, as a final comment on Miss Liddiard's 'serious business' remark, has allowed his illustrator – in my copy at least – to show an unworried infant sitting on 'the vessel' with a teddy bear on the floor within reach.

Finally, by 1957, Dr Winnicott, in *The Child and the Family*, presents an approach which has, presumably, completely integrated the Freudian attitudes. There is no longer any suggestion that the baby should be trained, nor even that it might be 'convenient' for the mother to train herself to avoid dirty nappies. Instead the passing of urine or of a motion have become important emotional experiences which the mother must share with the baby.

Perhaps someone told you to hold your baby out regularly after feeds from the start, with the idea of getting in a bit of training at the earliest possible moment. If you do this you should know that what you are doing is trying to save yourself the bother of dirty napkins. And there is a lot to be said for this. But the baby is not anywhere near being able to be trained yet. If you never allow for his or her own development in these matters, you interfere with the beginnings of a natural process. Also you are missing good things. For instance if you wait you will sooner or later discover that the baby, lying over there in the cot, finds a way of letting you know that a motion has been passed ; and soon you will even get an inkling that there is going to be a motion. You are now at the beginning of a new relationship with the baby ... as if he said, 'I think I am going to want to pass a motion ; are you interested ?' and you (without exactly saying so) answer, 'yes,' and you let him know that if you are interested this is not because you are frightened that he will make a mess, and not because you feel you ought to be teaching him how to be clean. If you are interested it is because you love your baby in the way that mothers do, so that whatever is important to the baby is also important to you. . . . Because what you do is based on the simple fact of your love you soon become able to distinguish between the times when you are helping your baby to be rid of bad things and the times when you are receiving gifts.[7]

Before leaving this comparative study, it might be interesting to look at the changes which took place over this period of more than a hundred years regarding that tender subject, the child and sex. Mr Pye Chevasse ignores the subject completely ; perhaps he felt it not suitable for the mothers who would read his book. Miss Liddiard admits that teaching on the subject of masturbation has changed during her professional life, and that it is now regarded 'only ... as a bad habit and one which usually disappears as intelligence and interest in life appear'. She adds: 'The habit itself should be ignored as much as possible and just spoken of as a thing not done by nice people.'[8] Three years after this comment, which appears in a late edition of *The Mothercraft Manual*, published in 1936, Susan Isaacs writes, 'this is but another expression of the intense inner conflict of the child's feelings towards his parents . . . just because it is bound up with the most hidden issues of the child's emotional life, we must go very slowly in dealing with it; . . . For the child *always* [author's italics] feels ashamed and distressed about it.' Later she writes, 'If the habit persists, and is more than an occasional thing – for this will happen sometimes even with children of excellent parents in the happiest home – then all that remains to us as parents is to ask the advice of a specialist in psychological medicine.'[9] Even the best parents, then, may find that they are responsible for having perpetuated a habit which must be discouraged, though Mrs Isaacs's recommendation – 'Our main task is very definitely to avoid strengthening the fear and guilt . . . for these rivet the child but more firmly in the habit'[10] may seem too indefinite, not to say negative, to help a parent already anxious to cope with the 'ashamed and distressed' child. Winnicott is more explicit about the symptom – if it is still possible to apply this epithet to a universal phenomenon – but not much more precise in his guidance for the mother.

Masturbation is either normal or healthy or else it is a symptom of a disorder of emotional development. . . . Perhaps the most common disorder of masturbation is its suppression, or its disappearance from a child's repertoire or self-managed defences against intolerable anxiety or sense of deprivation or loss. . . . Ordinary masturbation is no more than an employment of natural resources for satisfaction as an insurance against frustration and consequent anger, hate, or fear. Compulsive masturbation simply implies that the underlying anxieties to be dealt with are excessive. Perhaps the infant needs feeding at shorter intervals, or he needs more mothering ; or he needs to be able to know that someone is always at hand, or his mother is so anxious that she ought to allow him more quiet lying in a pram and less contact with her. . . . It must be recognized, however, that in rare cases compulsive masturbation is continuous and is so exhausting that it has to be stopped by repressive measures, simply in order to give the child some relief from his or her own symptom.[11]

I should like to add to this A. S. Neill's remark : 'A child left to touch its genitals has every chance of growing up with a sincere happy attitude to sex.'[12]

These passages illustrate the change which has come about during the last century and a half in the place of the child in adult society. In 1840 the child was to be tenderly cared for, loved and made happy ; his needs are seen as being entirely on an immediate and practical level, he is to adapt himself to the established adult conventions as quickly as possible – 'implicit obedience' ; 'A DIRTY CHILD IS THE MOTHER'S DISGRACE'. The expert, whether it is Mr Pye Chavasse or Dr Truby King, can give detailed and precise instructions to the novice mother which will enable her to do what is right by her baby; there is less difference between these two writers separated by nearly a century, than between the later of the two and her successor, writing only sixteen years afterwards. Now the picture is a different one ; now every aspect of the child's development, physical or emotional, is seen not only at its face value, but also for the symbolic part it plays in the child's psyche. This can be explained to the uninitiated reader, but to tell her how to cope with it is a more difficult matter. Spock solved this problem by preferring the old-fashioned method of giving factual, commonsense advice, which nevertheless incorporates a certain amount of the less controversial psychological theory ;

in consequence he is limited, but as many present-day parents would gratefully agree, practical. Dr Winnicott, however, is more concerned to give
parents a true understanding of the growing child and of the mother-child
relationship; and because he is far too sensitive and perceptive not to recognize the dangers of writing, so that people can read, about what is basically
felt without the need of words, he is constantly at pains to reassure the mother
that 'mothering', the right sort of care of babies and children, is 'natural'. He
specifically states that he is writing not to instruct, but to 'draw attention to
the immense contribution to the individual and to society which the ordinary
good mother . . . makes at the beginning, and which she does *simply through
being devoted to her infant*'.[13] [author's italics].

The trouble is, however, that, as Dr Winnicott would probably agree, no
mother is devoted all the time. Mr Chavasse is not the only writer on child-
care who seems to believe that a mother has only to learn what is the right
course of action in given circumstances for her to follow it. In fact, anyone
who has been personally concerned in the bringing up of children knows that
there are occasions when all the knowledge in the world will not ensure the
mother's doing the 'right' thing, because at that particular moment she isn't
in a frame of mind to care; she, like the child, can be overcome by frustration
and anger – and guilt – and the relief of her feelings comes even before the
consideration of what may be best for the child. Years ago a cartoon showed a
mother furiously addressing her toddler with the words, 'I don't know what
I'm doing to your complexes, but I do know that you're ruining mine!' And
this is where the concept of the unconscious and of psychodynamics which
we owe to Freud have tipped the balance against the probability of present-
day parents feeling confidence in themselves as parents. The suggestion that
every action and every word is making a lasting impression on the infant's
mind, the consequences of which will not appear for years, and may be quite
opposite to what was intended, is enough to alarm all but the very brash. It
is especially inhibiting to the anxious tyro, who had hoped, by consulting
what has been written by experts, to learn how to avoid the worst mistakes;
what he gets instead is a terrifying account of pitfalls he hadn't ever imagined.
The trouble is that when Freud's ideas first began to be adopted in the practice of child care it was optimistically assumed by many that a set of principles
could be drawn up which would ensure the psychic health of the children
whose parents observed them. Parents were encouraged to believe that if they
tried hard enough they could save their children from evil by analytic thought,
rather as earlier generations of babies had been saved by baptism. What was

not allowed for was not only the complexity of the human mind, but also the frailty of the parent. Since no child turns out ideally, and there are bound to be moments when it is clear that a child is unhappy and resentful, or ashamed and angry, or shows other disturbing traits, there are bound also to be moments when parents wonder where to apportion the blame. Before the advent of Freudian teaching, parents may sometimes have blamed themselves for mistakes which, looking back, they recognized, but much more often they blamed the child; either he was ungrateful, or obstinate, or had chosen bad company, or all three. Today's parents, warned in advance of the primary importance of their influence on the child's development, have no such convenient scapegoats. They must blame themselves for everything that goes wrong. The nineteenth-century mother, turning to the pages of Mr Pye Chavasse to discover why her child is not clean and dry at the age of six months can regret that she has not been sufficiently insistent on that 'implicit obedience' and can redouble her efforts without a qualm. The modern mother, whose baby screams at the sight of the pot and is unwilling to part with his motions, finds in Dr Winnicott's text that she has failed in her job; worse than that, the implication that a good mother knows how and when to do the the right thing because 'you love your baby in the way that mothers do', suggests that if she has done the 'wrong' thing it is because she is an unnatural, unloving, 'bad' mother. Later, when the child has night terrors, balks at going to school, is finicky about food, tells lies, is quarrelsome, jealous, rebellious – in short, shows any of the innumerable symptoms of normal childhood, the parents' confidence in their own judgement, even in their own feelings, is gravely undermined. They meant to do so well. They believed everything was going as it should, and now it appears that their good intentions have simply led them along the proverbial downward road, and, which increases their guilt still more, taken the child with them.

Anna Freud, writing later than any author quoted above, has summed up the effects of psychoanalytic thought on the theory of child rearing as follows:

On the other hand, it did not take more than one or two decades of such [psychoanalytic] work before a number of analytic authors ventured beyond the boundaries of fact finding and began to apply the new knowledge to the upbringing of children. The therapeutic analyses of adult neurotics left no doubt about the detrimental influence of many parental and environmental attitudes and actions such as dishonesty in sexual matters, unrealistically high moral standards, overstrictness or overindulgence, frustrations, punishments, or seductive behaviour. . . .

The sequence of these extrapolations is well known by now. Thus, at a time when psychoanalysts laid great emphasis on the seductive influence of sharing the parents' bed and the traumatic consequences of witnessing parental intercourse, parents were warned against bodily intimacy with their children and against performing the sexual act in the presence of even their youngest infants. When it was proved in the analyses of adults that the witholding of sexual knowledge was responsible for many intellectual inhibitions, full sexual enlightenment at an early age was advocated. When hysterical symptoms, frigidity, impotence, etc. were traced back to prohibitions and the subsequent repressions of sex in childhood, psychoanalytic upbringing put on its program a lenient and permissive attitude towards the manifestations of infantile, pregenital sexuality. When the new instinct theory gave aggression the status of a basic drive, tolerance was extended also to the child's early and violent hostilities, his death wishes against parents and siblings etc. When anxiety was recognized as playing a central part in symptom formation, every effort was made to lessen the children's fear of parental authority. When guilt was shown to correspond to the tension between the inner agencies, this was followed by the ban on all educational measures likely to produce a severe super-ego. . . . Finally, in our own time, when analytic investigations have turned to earliest events in the first year of life and highlighted their importance, these specific insights are being translated into new and in some respects revolutionary techniques of infant care. . . .

. . . Some of the pieces of advice given to parents over the years were consistent with each other; others were contradictory and mutually exclusive. . . . Above all to rid the child of anxiety proved an impossible task. Parents did their best to reduce the children's fear of them, merely to find that they were increasing guilt feelings, i.e. fears of the child's own conscience. Where, in its turn, the severity of the super-ego was reduced, children produced the deepest of all anxieties, i.e. the fear of human beings who feel unprotected against the pressure of their drives.

In short, in spite of many partial advances, psychoanalytic education did not succeed in becoming the preventive measure that it had set out to be. It is true that the children who grew up under its influence were in some respects different from earlier generations, but they were not freer from anxiety or from conflicts, and therefore not less exposed to neurotic or other mental illnesses.[14]

Of course all the mistakes and disappointments of the last forty years should not be laid at the door of Sigmund Freud. I hope I have succeeded in drawing attention to the other factors which contributed to make the recent generations of parents particularly susceptible to attacks on self-confidence in their relations with their children. If we, in this century, were not so much addicted to the belief that there must be a 'science' of everything, including of that unpredictable, barely charted area of human behaviour, we should not have fallen so readily into the snare of supposing that we might be able to rear new human beings superior in psychic health to their forefathers. What was not taken into account by Freud's many disciples, who, like St Paul, St Augustine and other organizing secretaries who succeeded another great Jewish prophet, was that the disclosure of a revelation, whether it is that infants have sexual feelings or that all men are brothers, cannot subsequently be translated into a book of rules which will transmute human nature and bring about a millennium. The foundation of the early Christian Church, the drawing up of the Athanasian creed, the threat of punishments, the establishment of dogma, led to the activities of the Inquisition and to massacre on religious grounds, and not to the spread of brotherly love. In the same way, the organization of the rules which were supposed to help parents to rear psychically sound offspring also proved to lead to unexpected and often unwelcome results; and where rules are only partially formulated, and the parent is merely warned of the dangers, but told that his natural instincts will guide him aright, the effect is comparable to that of showing a lone sailor a chart of the currents and winds on the ocean on which he is sailing, but telling him at the same time that his best compass is within his own head. The truth is that most of us learn not so much from theory as by experience; and also that children respond not to what their parents know, but to what they are. The father who has not come to terms with his own aggressive instincts cannot, by carefully adopted attitudes, reconcile his child in turn to his fantasies of destruction; the anxious mother is unlikely to produce an anxiety-free child. I don't mean by this that there is nothing we can do to make ourselves better parents, nor that there are not many invaluable vistas of insight opened up by Freud's work. But I do believe that, partly from a misunderstanding of the application of that work, we have lost confidence in ourselves to an unnecessary degree. Perhaps it is time that we lowered our standards a little. Instead of trying to rear a generation of perfectly un-neurotic, well-integrated, fearless, sexually uninhibited children, we might recognize that such people have never existed. We might remember that, just as we do not expect to give birth to children who are never physically ill, so we might allow our children the common failings of humanity, but hope that we could give them the psychic resilience, the security of being assessed as individuals – which involves hate as well as love – which would enable them to fight for survival; even when this involves a struggle against ourselves.

8

Psychoanalysis:
A Clinical Perspective
Henry Miller

THE pervasive influence of psychoanalysis on twentieth-century thought is evident in the millions of words that continue to be written around the subject, in the plethora of books and journals devoted to it, and especially in the way it has coloured the work of biographers, novelists and playwrights. Why, in contrast, has it had so little impact on medicine and science? There are many reasons but perhaps two are especially germane. They concern its *usefulness* and its *historical background*.

More often than not, contemporary psychoanalytic literature tends to brush aside the simple fact that psychoanalysis had its origin and sought its validation as a method of treating neurotic illness. Since many have tried, but nobody has yet convincingly demonstrated that psychoanalysis (or indeed any form of psychotherapy) is better for psychoneurotic patients than doing nothing at all, this attitude is perhaps not surprising. Certainly attempts to demonstrate the benefits of psychoanalysis by the methods employed to evaluate other forms of medical treatment have invariably proved impracticable, while comparative studies of the various analytic techniques one with another have merely demonstrated a predictable tendency for the patient to produce psychological material that falls conveniently within the conceptual framework of the particular analyst concerned. Furthermore of course the duration and expense of analysis means that even if it were ever shown to be effective, it could not be made available to more than a handful of the thousands of patients with psychiatric symptoms who throng the clinics of every health service. This is one of several reasons for the failure of psychoanalysis to establish itself as a significant clinical discipline in the developed European countries, and for its continued vogue in the great cities of the United States. Payment per item of service is the rule in the medical practice of New York as it was in the Vienna of the 1890s where professional psychotherapy first saw the light of day, and it is difficult to conceive of a therapeutic method more exquisitely suited to such a milieu than psychoanalysis, requiring no equipment, being of virtually indefinite duration, and with the cash transaction between patient and therapist as an integral part of the treatment. Psychoanalysts of course recognize the limitation of numbers and excuse it mainly on two grounds. Some maintain first that analysis should be regarded as a tool of research rather than a generally applicable form of treatment, and secondly that the insight with which they are endowed by personal analysis enables them to treat their patients more effectively even when analytic psychotherapy is not employed. The validity of the first of these contentions relies – if the term research is to mean anything – on the claim of psychoanalysis to be a science. The second rests on both the truth and usefulness of psychoanalytic hypotheses.

The second reason for the failure of psychoanalysis to be widely adopted by physicians is implicit in its historical background. In 1885 Freud left Vienna to work as a postgraduate student of neuropathology in Paris with Jean-Martin Charcot. Charcot had already established a world-wide reputation by defining a number of entirely new diseases amongst the hundreds of neurological patients who filled the chronic wards of the Salpêtrière, and had established, almost single-handed, new clinicopathological entities that were to furnish pabulum for the medical textbooks of the succeeding century. This task completed, he found himself left with a group of hospital patients whose symptoms closely resembled those of the major neurological diseases he had identified, but in whom he could find no evidence of physical disease either in the clinic or in the post-mortem room. At this time such patients were termed malingerers or hysterics in a pejorative sense, and had attracted no serious professional attention. Charcot used the same meticulous and elaborate techniques of neurological examination in the investigation of these cases that he had so successfully employed to define poliomyelitis, multiple sclerosis and neurosyphilis. With such methods and with such patients it is not surprising that he induced the florid symptoms and physical signs that became the hallmark of the hysteria of the Salpêtrière – a histrionic display that significantly disappeared from the hospital after his death in 1893. Charcot threw overboard the general view that most of these patients were cheats and liars, and lent the enormous prestige of 'the Caesar of the Salpêtrière' to the firm pronouncement that they were suffering from a specific disease of the brain – functional instead of structural, and dependent on a localized evanescent and reversible physical abnormality. Extrapolating from his soundly based anatomical findings in cases of stroke and tumour, he postulated an invisible hysterical lesion affecting the cortex of the brain in the patient with hysterical weakness of a hand, the deeper part of the cerebral hemisphere in the patient paralyzed on one side of the body. To Charcot hysteria was neither faked nor psychogenic, but a hereditary degeneration, the emotional and situational factors that were often so conspicuous being no more than provoking factors. Charcot sustained this view even after he had demonstrated that hysterical paralysis could be induced under hypnosis, and indeed he regarded the spontaneously hysterical and iatrogenic hypnotic states as identical. We now know from his contemporaries that some of the chronic patients Charcot regularly demonstrated to audiences of journalists and actresses as well as doctors and medical students in his famous Friday morning clinics were in fact coached and paid for their performances by his assistants. Charcot never suspected this, nor did Sigmund Freud. Distracted from his neuropathological preoccupations, Freud sat at Charcot's feet and was enormously impressed by what is now generally accepted as a meretricious performance that constituted at best a vivid exploitation of the power of professional suggestion. However, Freud was dissatisfied with Charcot's and Janet's mechanistic explanations of these unfamiliar phenomena, and seems to have grasped almost at once the vital fact that hysterical paralysis represented the patient's *idea* of paralysis, and was intrinsically different from and distinguishable from paralysis due to any physical lesion, however transient. Returning to Vienna in 1886 he found academic promotion barred to him by the financial demands of an early marriage, by his Jewish origin, and by a personality that some found captivating, but others unbearably opinionated. Abandoning the clinic and the laboratory he joined Josef Breuer in a private practice that seems to have been quite exceptionally well-endowed with introspective well-to-do psychoneurotics. Denied the advancement his talents richly deserved in orthodox medicine, he proceeded to develop his own highly personal interpretative psychopathology and became its high priest. Had things been even a little different he might easily have become one of those mandarins of internal medicine whose continued rejection of his speculations and affirmations both stimulated and irritated him throughout his long life.

It is no reproach to Freud that his outlook reflected the body-mind dualism that was current at the time, and indeed he deserves particular credit for his early and obstinate prediction that the physical nature of the neuroses would ultimately be established. To begin with at any rate he regarded the interpretation of mental illness in psychological terms as a tactical rather than a strategic move, reflecting little more than the inadequacy of contemporary neurophysiology. In fact he never formally discarded this view. On the other hand he and his successors built up such an enormous superstructure of speculative psychology that many analysts came to accept as axiomatic the palpable pan-psychic nonsense that mental illness was necessarily due to mental causes, that genetic endowment could be ignored, that psychoanalysis was as applicable to psychosis as to neurosis, and that prolonged deep psychotherapy was the only effective as well as the only rational form of psychiatric treatment.

Freudian psychology began in 1895 with a monograph on hysteria, and it is on the precarious foundation of this still controversial disorder that its bizarre superstructure rests. The foundation is insecure for many reasons, not the least being the dubious status of the condition : there are almost as many definitions of hysteria as there are writers on the subject. Charcot himself wrote : 'Keep it well in mind . . . that the word "hysteria" means nothing', and some later writers like Russell Brain have sophisticated this viewpoint to the extent of abandoning the substantive and retaining the adjectival term 'hysterical'. Most definitions comprise the concept of an essentially psychogenic disorder simulating physical illness, unconsciously motivated and often with an element of play-acting. The difficulty of distinguishing the condition from malingering or conscious faking is generally accepted, and in the last resort the differentiation depends on the physician's subjective assessment of the patient's credibility as a witness. Many authorities complicate the issue by stressing the existence of mixed states in which motivation is partly conscious, and many experienced neuropsychiatrists have also had their confidence in the reality of hysteria shaken by occasional otherwise classical cases in which motivation was ultimately exposed as transparently conscious and deliberate.

Rejecting the neurophysiological hypothesis of hysteria, Freud elaborated Breuer's views on the psychogenesis of the condition – that it was an expression of repressed emotion originating in a previous traumatic experience, and that it would be cured by ventilation of the emotional experience (abreaction) under hypnosis. Freud soon discovered first, that free association was as effective as hypnosis in achieving this catharsis, and secondly that abreaction was not invariably effective. Pushing his enquiries further back he decided that the emotional factors concerned with the genesis of hysteria invariably involved traumatic sexual experiences in early life. When it transpired that some such experiences emerging during psychoanalysis were entirely fabricated and had in fact never taken place, Freud did not discard his theory, but postulated with characteristic agility – and after a delay of no less than eight years – that the aetiological factor was the fantasy rather than the reality of early sexual trauma. This piece of casuistry has been greeted as a triumphant revelation by several generations of admirers. There is no need to detail the subsequent elaborations of Freudian psychology. Suffice it to mention the firm and consistent view that all psychoneuroses and not merely hysteria arose from infantile sexual wishes (Freud of course used sex to mean anything he chose it to mean) ; his view of the love-instinct and the death-wish as the two primary instincts (a very unbiological and extremely metaphysical antithesis) ; the metaphorical emphasis on censorship of the unconscious, and the id-ego-superego reification; transference; and the Oedipus and castration complexes. All these of course are everyday matters to the reader of popular psychology. It is worth pointing out that they constitute and depend entirely on retrospective (and introspective) explanation; they have no predictive value that renders them susceptible to objective testing. Several distinguished protagonists have insisted that in its essentials this schema must be accepted in its entirety or not at all – an attitude that is in itself an adequate commentary on the claims of psychoanalysis to be science. In fact of course the whole edifice has the plausible cohesion and internal consistency of a man-made theory. It has more in common with a theology or religious credo than with natural science, which is inevitably characterized by provisional hypotheses, partial understanding, loose ends, and inherent untidiness.

Needless to say neither developmental psychologists nor anthropologists have been deterred by psychoanalytic distaste for critical examination from outside the fold, and both have made valiant but generally unsuccessful attempts to evaluate Freudian theories of personality development. Many such workers have isolated one particular aspect of psychoanalytic belief and have tried to confirm or disprove it by direct observation. The problem is anything but easy, quite apart from such difficulties as those of trying to dissociate the influence of a factor such as breast-feeding from the effects of other social and psychological variables. However the situation is perhaps not quite so intractable as this would suggest. The data of psychoanalysis are subjective, experimental, dependent on nuances of language and expression, and in the last resort liable to tincture by the analyst's suggestions. The techniques of the psychologist and anthropologist on the other hand are largely concerned with observations of behaviour. Direct observation confirms for example Freud's general hypothesis about infantile sexuality. There can be no doubt that pleasurable manipulation of the perineum is extremely common in early childhood. On the other hand there is really no shred of evidence from direct observation that fear of castration or indeed fear of any kind connected with sex is at all common in early childhood, and there is absolutely nothing to suggest that it is a routine feature of normal sexual development.

The universality of the Oedipus situation is of course central to orthodox psychoanalytic doctrine. However, careful direct enquiries have failed to confirm any indication of a universal cross-sex parental preference either in children or adults. No such general pattern has been found by skilled observers of early family life. There can be no doubt that Freud universalized certain family situations that he encountered in the peculiar conditions of his early medicine practice, and that he greatly underestimated the individual variability of the social milieu that surrounds the child. Parental dominance and cultural attitudes to sex are only two of the more obvious variables.

One of the most extended practical applications of psychoanalytic doctrine has been in connection with the upbringing of children, and the infantile disciplines of feeding and sphincter control have been the subject of a good deal of systematic investigation both in Western and in more primitive societies. Freud himself was wisely cautious as to the predictive value of such factors in relation to later life, but subsequent psychoanalytic theorists have been much bolder and have indicated that prolonged breast-feeding on demand, late gradual weaning and a lenient attitude to bowel and bladder training should make a significant contribution to subsequent emotional stability. Hard evidence on these subjects is admittedly scanty but it lends little positive support to these theories. Taken as a whole there is nothing to suggest that in general terms the breast-fed child enjoys inevitable advantages over his artificially fed brother, that prolonged breast-feeding is necessarily better than early weaning, or that feeding on demand induces more (or less) emotional security in the infant than scheduled feeding. Extensive studies on these subjects confirm the robust adaptability of the average human infant to a wide variety of feeding routines, and lend no support to views in which the observer's convictions are clearly read into what he imagines to be the infant's emotional life.

The evil results of bowel-training on personality development have been incriminated by analysts in the genesis of a variety of disturbances ranging from constipation and parsimony through obsessional neurosis to the Japanese national character. These dire sequelae have been linked by some psychoanalytic writers with premature demands on the function of nerve-fibre tracts that have not at this early stage received their fatty myelin sheaths. This sounds attractively rational – except that function appears in advance of myelination and may even facilitate it.

It comes as no surprise to learn that in many primitive tribes where infancy is characterized by unlimited indulgence and complete permissiveness the incidence of anxiety, insecurity and egocentricity in adult life appears to be little different from that with which we are familiar in the developed Western world.

The rational critic of psychoanalysis has a hard task, like trying to grasp a slippery eel. Although psychoanalysis aspires to the status of science, the critic will be told even by its most recent and articulate apologists that the methods applicable in other fields of natural science are not relevant to the study of human psychology, and that understanding of this field depends on special insight that is accessible only to those who have undergone and accepted the discipline of psychoanalysis. Those who have been analyzed and remain unconvinced are left with the rest of us in outer darkness, their failure to acquiesce being complex-determined. Needless to say acceptance of the creed depends on entirely different and more creditable determinants. The critic will also be told that even if a therapeutic test of analysis were feasible it would be irrelevant; that Freud himself, prejudiced by the therapeutic situation, is a rather unreliable guide as to the exact nature of his own work; that his methods and views changed so much during his lifetime that criticism is almost meaningless; and that much the same applies to contemporary psychoanalysis which is continually developing and changing – changes that are rather unconvincingly attributed to the emergence of new data. The remark of one of the greatest physical scientists of the century – that a good theory should be comprehensible to a barmaid – is clearly not applicable in this context. In conclusion the scientific critic is quite likely to evoke the recent reproach of one leading British psychoanalyst – that he should desist, and employ his energies in devising experiments to prove or disprove the psychoanalytic theory. The view that it is the responsibility of the critic to disprove, rather than of the proponent to demonstrate the efficacy of a therapeutic method or the validity of a scientific hypothesis, is the cry of the charlatan in every generation. It is well seen, for example, in the field of cancer, where unorthodox blunderbuss 'cures' comprising a hotch-potch of old and new, sensible and nonsensical methods are floated without any attempt at objective assessment and their critics then challenged to disprove them. In fact psychoanalytic theory does not lend itself to disproof, though its apologists are continually exercised in strenuous and transparent efforts to avoid refutation.

The scientist's first objection to psychoanalysis concerns its claim to universality – that it suffices to explain all the phenomena of psychiatric illness and indeed some of the phenomena of physical illness, which Freud more than once equated with guilt. This claim depends on a highly-wrought theory based on fragmentary clinical evidence drawn from the peculiarly matriarchal Austrian Jewish society of the turn of the century. And the history of medicine is littered with the debris of universal theories. The Greeks attributed disease to disturbance in the balance of the humours. In the early nineteenth century, Broussais and Cruveilhier in France considered gastroenteritis and phlebitis respectively the causal agents of every human disease, while the more philosophical Scot, Cullen, characteristically attributed them all to neurosis. Within living memory the hypotheses of focal sepsis and auto-intoxication have enjoyed similar vogue. Medicine is almost as subject to fashion as education, and today auto-immune disease is incriminated in every otherwise inexplicable physical illness. There is no need to dwell on the ludicrous results of attempts to force every kind of psychiatric disorder into a psychoanalytic mould, but a personal favourite of mine is drawn from a contribution of the revered Fenichel; dealing with the florid psychoneurotic syndrome that is sometimes encountered after a claim for financial compensation following accidental industrial or traffic injury, he dismisses the financial implications of the situation as having little importance, the primary cause of this as of other neuroses being 'avoidance of the Oedipus situation ... activating one's infantile sado-masochism or one's castration anxiety, or both'. The options are charming and very characteristic of psychoanalytic sophistry. Until the claimant was involved in his road accident he was presumably coping with these knotty problems, at any rate to his own satisfaction.

The second medical objection concerns the perpetuation even in current psychoanalytic thinking of psychological determinism based on a body-mind dualism that now seems singularly old-fashioned. There are a few diseases, like Huntington's chorea, to which the patient is irrevocably doomed by his genetic endowment. At the other end of the spectrum there are some like typhoid fever in which constitutional factors play a small part, provided the infective dose is large and the organism virulent. However most illnesses represent the result of an inter-play of constitutional, physical and emotional factors, without the high wall that the analyst erects between organic and psychogenic disorders. Severe anxiety may cause bleeding from a chronic peptic ulcer. Anger may provoke a fatal heart attack in an anginal patient. On the other hand thyroid deficiency afflicts the patient with mental and physical torpor, while a small structural lesion in the left temporal lobe of the brain may lead to attacks of causeless fury. The importance of the constitutional factor cannot reasonably be gainsaid even by those who embrace psychoanalytical theory. If all undergo the ordeals of infantile sexual development in the way the analyst suggests, why do only some become psychoneurotic? More than once, and especially to explain away apparent clinical inconsistencies, Freud himself mentions the obvious – that there are varying degrees of constitutional susceptibility, which takes us back to the factor that represented the whole truth to Charcot, but which the committed analyst so often professes to ignore.

The third objection concerns the imbalance in psychoanalysis between the scanty data, which is in itself almost entirely subjective, and the weight of interpretation it is asked to bear. Freud himself soon ceased to anchor his increasingly fanciful speculations even to anecdotal evidence from clinical observation. Most of his interpretations are no more than affirmations attached to snippets of highly selected data. The explanations are too complete, too specific, too neatly dovetailed, too literary, and sustained with too much fervour. Unlike the hypotheses of science they cannot be refuted. Nor of course can they be shown to be true. Everything is satisfactorily explained, and with what Medawar has epitomized as Olympian glibness. Perhaps hysterical vomiting does mean a pregnancy wish. Perhaps squeezing blackheads is a substitute for masturbation. Perhaps the falling cart-horse does symbolize parturition. Perhaps the snake in the dream of the patient with ulcerative colitis really does represent the penis and vagina (as well as the patient and the diseased bowel). But the nagging question recurs – how does he *know*? and the answer is of course that he *doesn't*, and that these are no more than speculative interpretations, plausible only to the prepared mind.

Not only has interpretation outweighed observational data, but analysis is obsessively concerned not to test its hypotheses against evidence drawn from outside itself. Freud himself issued dire warnings against any attempt to seek outside confirmation of statements made during psychoanalysis, and when he states that infantile sexuality is supported by evidence drawn from infancy, he refers not to findings based on the direct observation of infantile behaviour, but to nothing more than selective recollections of infancy dredged up during the loaded sessions of psychoanalysis. And the later studies of such child analysts as Melanie Klein and Anna Freud have been directed more to proving and illustrating psychoanalytic theories than to testing them. In particular, and despite its profound influence, Melanie Klein's exegesis of children's play owes practically nothing to the children and everything to highly slanted interpretation.

It would of course be unfair to castigate Freud for failing to control his therapeutic observations. Even by the end of his long life medicine had hardly learned the technique of the controlled therapeutic trial from agriculture. However it is revealing that after nearly eighty years of psychoanalysis, no such controlled evaluation has been completed. Untreated psychoneurosis shows a striking tendency to improve with the passage of time. Without well-designed therapeutic trials, how can we be sure that the results claimed from several years of psychoanalytic treatment have anything to do with the treatment, and might not have occurred either spontaneously or in response to some quite different form of treatment? After all, psychoanalysis is more lengthy than any other form of psychotherapy and furnishes proportionately increased opportunities for spontaneous cure. This is not to minimize the difficulties inherent in a controlled trial of psychotherapy and especially of psychoanalysis, though it is disappointing that analysts have not made more serious attempts to overcome these difficulties. It is particularly remarkable that Freud nowhere thought it worthwhile even to compare the infantile recollections of the 'normal' men and women whose training analyses he undertook with those of his psychoneurotic patients. To the best of my knowledge these baselines have never been established by analysis of a random sample of the population – yet those presenting themselves for this form of treatment and furnishing the data on which its theoretical formulations rest represent beyond question a highly self-selected group. It may be an exaggeration to suggest that only an odd-ball would submit to psychoanalysis, but its clients can hardly be regarded as representative. Furthermore psychoanalysis is dispensed for money, and the 'control' patient could hardly be expected to pay for nothing.

This clinical evaluation of psychoanalysis is highly critical and unfavourable. To the physician analysis represents in the first instance a therapeutic method the value of which remains doubtful after three-quarters of a century of use. Severe depressive illness can for example be viewed either as 'a reaction to loss of the love-object' or as due to a deficiency of brain catecholamines. The occurrence of depression after bereavement, especially in middle life, supports the psychoanalytic interpretation; its high incidence after influenza or the administration of reserpine is less easy to explain in psychopathological terms. Evidence for the catecholamine hypothesis is drawn from man and experimental animals and is elegant though in the last resort admittedly incomplete. Nor does one hypothesis utterly negate the other: perhaps the desolating grief of bereavement in the susceptible subject disturbs the sufferer's physiology to the point of producing a reversible and treatable change in cerebral metabolism. But if we consider the operational usefulness of the two hypotheses the story is very different. There is no convincing evidence for the value of psychotherapy in depressive psychosis, but three-quarters of all patients can be offered rapid and effective relief of symptoms with modern drugs and without any change in the environment, or any adjustment of or even attention to psychopathology. Secondly, the theoretical formulations that have been based on psychoanalytic findings represent a paradigm of pseudoscience: they are affirmative, subjective, unprovable and irrefutable. Furthermore they have diverted the energies of many gifted people from the tangible problems of serious mental illness to the speculative interpretation and dubious therapy of minor disorders.

The analysts are perfectly correct in their insistence that the therapeutic test alone is far from conclusive. There are highly effective forms of treatment based on entirely erroneous theory and some on no theory at all, while there have been therapeutic regimes founded on scientific bases which proved in the event to be wholly ineffective. The therapeutic test is useful but not definitive.

What does remain of value to medicine from the massive literature of Freud and his disciples? Shorn of jargon, it demonstrates that ideas and behaviour are often determined by influences quite different from those to which they are attributed in the patient's spoken rationalizations. Neither the patient's statements nor the surprise with which he greets the psychotherapist's explanations can be regarded as a reliable guide to the consciousness or unconsciousness of his motivation, and in one sense Freud did little more than make explicit what had been implicit in the work of poets and novelists from Shakespeare to Balzac. However this emphasis helped psychiatry to escape from a hopeless attempt to account for the phenomena of mental illness in superficial and purely rational terms. Freud's contributions to normal psychology are more convincing and more impressive than those to psychopathology, though again it must be stressed that this is at a literary and interpretative rather than a scientific level. Some 'Freudian slips' in which what is at the back of the speaker's mind pushes its way to the front seem to be very revealing – though no one has ever succeeded in showing how often this is the case, how much the interpretation owes to the listener, and how often such slips are meaningless and truly accidental. As with the brilliant diagnostician, the felicitous triumph is remembered and recorded, the larger number of boss shots ignored. Freud's studies on dream interpretation too, though unduly dominated by the wish-fulfilment theory, comprise some first-class clinical observations – such as that whatever their narrative content, dreams are built of the bricks of the previous day's experiences. But if I were briefed to plead in defence of the Freudian contribution to clinical psychiatry I would concentrate on the role of psychoanalysis in helping us to understand the symptomatology of mental illness by extrapolation from the symbolism so vividly displayed in the world of dreams. Admittedly some of the symbolization claimed in psychoanalytic literature is so speculative and so far-fetched as to be unconvincing, and its interpretation owes much to the theorist's preconceptions. However, the serious attention paid to the nature of dreams may help us for example to recognize the diagnostic significance of the guilt-ridden depressive delusion that the body is rotting away or that it is being eaten by worms. To produce a plausible explanation of symptomatology is admittedly a limited contribution. Indeed it is one of the strongest criticisms of analytic psychiatry made by clinical colleagues in the United States that the analyst's report interprets the patient's symptomatology in fascinating detail, but does absolutely nothing to explain why he was well last week and is mad today – still less what can be done about it. The concept of the disease-entity is admittedly old-fashioned, but like physical illness most mental disorders sort themselves into groups each of which has a core of fairly well-defined clinical features, and a pattern of natural history that soon declares itself to the trained mind. Except in the presence of psychosis or serious organic disease, for example, hysterical symptoms (begging the question of their nature) are a feature of adolescence and immaturity and arise *ab initio* in the stable adult only under overwhelming provocation. Except in a handful of cases depressive illnesses show ultimate spontaneous recovery, a tendency to recur, and a striking symptomatic response to drugs or electroconvulsive therapy. Certain forms of schizophrenia respond similarly if less impressively to phenothiazines. We know of course that in the last resort there are no illnesses in the abstract, but merely sick people. Nevertheless classification, always provisional, permits shorthand description and facilitates conceptual manipulation. More important still at the operational level, it often points the way to effective empirical treatment.

To the clinician then the contribution of Freud and psychoanalysis to psychiatry is a limited one, with something on each side of the balance sheet. I first encountered the works of Freud as a medical student forty years ago and I reacted with a mixture of fascination and suspicion. These feelings were revived during a much longer period of more intensive study as a war-time neuropsychiatrist. Subsequent readings in the literature of psychology and anthropology, together with the continued failure of the analysts to validate their hypotheses, have deepened these suspicions. And the recent triumphs of psychopharmacology bid fair to make analytic theories irrelevant to clinical medicine long before anybody can discover how far they are true and how far false.

9

Art and Freud's
Displacement of Aesthetics
Michael Podro

THE *Interpretation of Dreams* is incomparably rich in the use it makes of theories of art and insights into works of art, yet neither here nor elsewhere does Freud offer what could be described as a theory of art or aesthetics, that is, a theory which marks out the role of art within mental life.

In the philosophy of mind and the studies of psychology out of which Freud developed his own thought, aesthetics had a central place, for instance in the theories of the mind of Kant and Schiller at the end of the eighteenth century and the major revisions and adaptations of them by J. F. Herbart and Schopenhauer in the nineteenth. These theories echo continuously through Freud's thought. His own explicit reference to them or – more often – to those who relayed them is extensive. Herbart, for instance, had depicted the mind of any individual as developing through the conflict and fusion of mental impressions and chains of remembered impressions formed by association. One impression or complex of impressions would inhibit the entry of another into consciousness, or facilitate its entry by fusing with it, depending on how they were related to each other and to past experience.[1] Notions like 'repression', and patterns of the 'dream-work' which Freud will call 'condensation' and 'overdetermination,' were developed out of ideas from Herbart, and it was from basic ideas of Schopenhauer that Freud developed his notions of the mind eluding its own rational procedures, and of thought in language, as closely tied to action.

But it is not a matter of 'spare parts' from discarded theories which Freud takes up and re-uses in his own construction of the mind; rather – to change the analogy – it is as though what had originally been learned as a game had become something more important – ideas developed with particular clarity with respect to art were no longer related primarily to art but are seen to characterize the procedures of mental life as a whole. I want to examine Freud's use of aesthetics, particularly in *The Interpretation of Dreams*, and then the problems of carrying his enrichments back into the discussion of art.

Freud frequently compares the construction of a dream to a poem – not the motive for dreaming, but the meaning of a dream when the analyst has finally managed to get past its apparent sense or nonsense but the organization of its components. It is not the latent content or the wishes concealed behind the images of the dream which he compares with the poem, it is the way the sleeping mind constructs its artefact, or the way the analyst reconstructs it. There is one account of a dream which leads quickly to the analogy with poetry and is a convenient starting point. Freud first reports his dream: 'I had written a monograph on an (unspecified) genus of plants. The book lay before me and I was at the moment turning over the folded colour plate. Bound up in the copy was a dry specimen of the plant.'[2] He then notes that the element in his dream which stood out most was the *botanical monograph*. Freud then goes through a series of chains of association which connect the botanical monograph with a Dr Königstein whom he had met the previous day.

> A fresh topic touched upon in my conversation with Dr Königstein – my *favourite hobbies* – was joined through the intermediate link of what I jokingly called my *favourite flower*, the artichoke. . . . Behind 'artichokes' lay, on the one hand my thoughts about Italy, and on the other hand a scene from my childhood [being allowed by his father to tear pages out of a book] which was the opening of what have since become my intimate relations with books. Thus 'botanical' was a regular nodal point in the dream. Numerous trains of thought converged upon it which, I can guarantee, had appropriately entered into the conversation with Dr Königstein. Here we find ourselves in a factory of thoughts where, as in the 'weaver's masterpiece', –

> > . . . a thousand threads one treadle throws
> > Where fly the shuttles hither thither,
> > Unseen the threads are knit together
> > And an infinite combination grows.
> >   (Goethe, *Faust*, Part I, Sc.4.)[3]

Each element in the dream thoughts is interconnected in numerous ways and in this way represented many times over. For the moment I am not concerned with what Freud sees as the *function* of this richness of interconnection: I want to amplify the way he characterizes the complexity by reference to poetry. On the reciprocal adaptation of dream thoughts he writes:

> Any one thought, whose form of expression may happen to be fixed for other reasons, will operate in a determinant and selective manner on the possible forms of expression allotted to the other thoughts, and it may do so, perhaps, from the very start – as is the case in writing a poem. If a poem is to be written in rhymes, the second line of the couplet is limited by two conditions: it must express an appropriate meaning, and the expression of that meaning must rhyme with the first line. No doubt the best poem will be one in which two thoughts have, by mutual influence, chosen from the very start a verbal expression which will allow a rhyme to emerge with only slight subsequent adjustment.
> In a few instances a change of expression of this kind assists dream condensation even more directly, by finding a form of words which owing to its ambiguity is able to give expression to more than one of the dream thoughts. There is no need to be

astonished at the part played by words in dream formation. Words, since they are the nodal point of numerous ideas, may be regarded as predestined to ambiguity. . . .[4]

And later

It is, indeed, not easy to form any conception of the abundance of the unconscious trains of thought, all striving to find expression, which are active in our minds. Nor is it easy to credit the skill shown by the dream-work in always hitting upon forms of expression which can bear several meanings – like the little tailor in the fairy story who hit seven flies at a blow.[5]

Now this multiplicity of meaning, the interpenetrating senses which we find in the components of a dream, are too obviously similar to the confluences and interpenetrations of sense in literature for the point to need labouring. The similarity is not only in the sense of compression, of the multiplicity of sense, but also in another sense of *unity* which Freud assumes in dreams.

This other sense of unity is central for us. Freud assumes that the dream thoughts, the meanings which are striving for expression in a dream, are mutually enforced by association; this reciprocal enforcement appears to be one factor in giving them strength to avoid repression : several connected or associated trains of thought will get through into consciousness where an isolated one would lack the power to do so. Although even when supporting each other they cannot enter consciousness undisguised. Compression both strengthens and disguises. But Freud's view of this has another dimension :

There is often a passage in even the most thoroughly interpreted dream which has to be left obscure ; this is because we become aware during the work of interpretation that at that point there is a tangle of dream thoughts which cannot be unravelled and which moreover adds nothing to our knowledge of the content of the dream. This is the dream's navel, the spot which reaches down into the unknown. The dream-thoughts to which we are led by interpretation cannot, from the nature of things, have any definite endings ; they are bound to branch out in every direction into the intricate network of our world of thought. It is at some point where this meshwork is particularly close that the dream wish grows up, like a mushroom out of its mycelium.[6]

It is the place where the mesh of threads is particularly close which enables ideas otherwise stranded or repressed to gather force and emerge into consciousness, and where that mesh is particularly close is determined by urgencies which are earlier than those which, if only in their disguised form, are allowed to appear in our consciousness. From this earlier unconscious urgency our dream is given an underlying unity, and this urgency in turn makes use of, and precipitates, the unity of the associative chains in consciousness.[7]

At this point I think it is worth recalling a passage of Kant which is not so very far from that of Freud and is, in a way, its mirror image. Kant introduced a notion he termed 'aesthetic ideas': this had two characteristics and clearly, in Kant's mind, these characteristics came together in serious art. On the one hand 'aesthetic ideas' are suggestive representations of things like heaven or supernatural powers or the most complete and unlimited realization of some idea, none of which could ever be met with in actual experience. On the other hand an 'aesthetic idea' involved a multiplicity of interrelated facets or images with which the mind could never get on level terms. Kant connected these two characteristics of the 'aesthetic idea' by regarding the use of our minds when trying to cope with this richness – a richness which resisted our unifying grasp – as an appropriate analogy for the confrontation of the human mind with the divine or transcendent.[8]

If we turn back to the passage from Freud we find the same two components, but now much more interestingly connected. For Kant it was a matter of the profusion of interconnected imagery being a suitable exercise of our minds for hinting at the realm of the supersensible. For Freud that profusion was a means by which ideas readily available to us could be organized in such a way as to allow associated thoughts, otherwise too disturbing for us to consider, into consciousness; and these thoughts, in turn, were indicative of something with which we could have no immediate acquaintance yet which was within us not outside us: not a reality to which our knowledge aspired, but a reality from which our urgencies derived.

But the parallel with Kant has not bridged the gap between what we might perhaps call the interpretation of the dream and that of the work of art, because in the dream the fabric of words or images is not present for the interpreting mind is an equivalent way: we are both internal to our dreams and external to them in a different way than we are to works of art.

One way of distinguishing between the dream, the dream-and-its-interpretation, and the work of art, suggests an analogy for considering how they are related. We can construct a series of senses which can give to the notion of the consonance of notes: we can start with consonance in the sense of the coincidence of the upper partials of two notes, a fact about sounds independent of any hearer; next to this we can place the sense of the consonance or harmonic relations which we hear, which involves our expectations but without effort; next to this comes the harmonic relations we have to learn to attend to, to habituate ourselves to, and finally those harmonies which we can understand conceptually but do not perceive sensuously. On a series of this kind the dream before it is interpreted is like the second and its interpretation is like the last of these, while art seems to occupy a place in between. In art simultaneous accessibility to perception and reflection. is necessary. Perhaps Freud had the idea of some such series in one of his underlying conceptions of the mind, when he sees the conceptual and action planning activity as one end of the picture of the mind and sense perception toward the other end, and sees the flow of activity coming from the instincts and perceptions toward concepts and action. Our confrontation with art shows us progressing less far toward conceptual analysis and action than interpreting dreams (which is diagnostic and purposive). In two connected senses art is more regressive, not than dreams, but than the interpretation of dreams. It is not under the constraint of logical thought and it is not purposive, in the sense of seeking results.

If we have linked the nature of the organization of dreams as interpreted and poems, how far can we regard the forms of satisfaction of dreaming and of art as similar? One special example of the transition to art of the emergence into consciousness of repressed material (although not a dream) was suggested by Freud in *Psychopathic Characters on the Stage*.[9] Here Freud discusses the kind of involvement the audience has with the action of the play and holds that in certain cases the nature of the audience's involvement depends upon the *displacement* of our attention from the real springs of action: thus in Hamlet we do not attend to the real source of Hamlet's difficulties which is his Oedipal relation to his mother:

... psychological chance turns into psychopathological drama when the source of suffering in which we take part and from which we are meant to derive pleasure is no longer a conflict between two almost equal conscious impulses, but between a conscious impulse and a repressed one.

In the case of Hamlet the repressed impulse is one which Freud assumed is shared by all of us:

It appears as a necessary pre-condition of this form of art that the impulse that is struggling into consciousness, however clearly it is recognizable, is never given a definite name; so that in the spectator too this process is carried through with his attention averted, and he is in the grip of his emotions instead of taking stock of what is happening.

I am extracting one point from this short but compressed paper – that of the need not to name the neurosis or repressed element, if the drama is to afford us pleasure, that is if we are to be emotionally carried along by it. On Freud's account naming is a way of raising the sentries of the mind so that we resist the material and can no longer participate in the struggle of the character, no longer identity with him. Freud makes this point with a certain diffidence: 'A certain amount of resistance is no doubt saved in this way.' But need naming this source of the disturbance significantly raise our resistance to participation? *If* the Oedipal component is regarded as the source of the drama, the single generating force, then to name it may be to reduce the interest of the plot to that of diagnosis, to press us toward the practical attitude which discharges itself in action. (Freud himself notes in this paper that if disturbed behaviour is exhibited on the stage, without our involvement or identification, we feel like calling for the doctor.) But if this component is only one of many – which merge and separate so that we are unable to sustain all in mind at the same time, then we might be able to name it without thereby curtailing our involvement: for then to explain Hamlet's relation to his mother would not mean we would have succeeded in 'taking stock', for we would not have taken stock, we would not have reduced the character and conflicts of Hamlet to a single conflict or to a case history: for Freud himself to name the source of conflict was to reduce *his* sense of the play to a diagnostic discovery.

This raises a further point: is our involvement with the play adequately described in terms of 'identification' with the central character? That this is an essential part of how we respond to drama, and to people with whom we are in serious contact in ordinary life, seems clear, but it seems equally clear that the otherness of other people, our seeing them as confronting us, making a relationship with us or potentially doing so, is no less essential a part of our experience: Hamlet and Claudius and Polonius are all people we could know as well as be. They are presented to us not only psychologically in the sense Freud discusses of Hamlet, but socially and politically. There is then another matter: they are linked in a fabric which we do not attend to simply literally, but are connected by figuring in metaphors and the devices of self-reference which are irreducible to the literal plot.

There are two connected issues here: the propensity to see the play merely literally is clearly going to make it easier to see it purely diagnostically – to treat the central character as a potential patient. And to treat the play literally and even to name the source of psychological disturbance will tend to short-circuit our involvement the more the psychoanalytic interest constitutes our whole interest in the protagonists.

A notion related to that of displacement of attention was given a critically brilliant visual application nearly twenty years ago by Ernst Gombrich in his paper, 'Psycho-Analysis and the History of Art'.[10] The paper brings together a large number of connected problems which concern the distinction between private urgencies and public meaning in works of art, and our response to erotic subject matter. In part of the paper Gombrich suggests that historically the rise in erotic content or erotic aggressiveness toward the spectator, the eroticism which we find threatening, is something which only became acceptable in art when it was accompanied by the demand for visual sophistication on the part of the spectator. Increase in erotic content, say between Raphael and Titian, demands a corresponding rise in perceptual difficulty if we are not to find the image repellent. And Gombrich adduces, among his evidence, our sense of repugnance when confronted by erotic or emotionally charged subject matter where the artist is not sharing with the spectator the productive procedure with which he builds up his charged image. The result is that we reject the painting as sentimental or vulgar or insincere. Gombrich finds something suspicious about this rejection: what, after all, has sincerity got to do with it? The point I want to take up is that of the emotional appeal needing to be counteracted by difficulty. The assumption here is that in principle there are two sources of mental urgency – one libidinous or emotional, and one concerned with self-control, and that we cannot accept something which appeals only to the former. Gombrich takes his examples to show that increasingly the gratifications of the first urgency or agency – the emotional appeal – require compensating the second, by granting it a commensurate role in our involvement with the picture.

It is possible, I believe, to keep Gombrich's critical insight here substantially in play while calling into question one aspect of his balancing or compensation theory. *Does* Titian demand more visual sophistication from us than Raphael: and *did* Raphael demand less from his contemporaries (for whom his art was new) than Titian from his contemporaries? Gombrich as historian alerts us to the difficulty of seeing the objects of the past as their contemporaries saw them.

I should like to suggest first that the kind of participation which Gombrich points to in the case of Raphael's *Galatea* and Titian's *Rape of Europa* are kinds of participation also demanded, for instance, by Titian's *Urbino Venus*, which, surely, is both very lucid and very seductive. In each case we have to attend not only to the subject but also to engage in the movement between the subject and the means of representation: the brush strokes and the flesh in the *Europa*, the symmetries of the form and the energy of the turning *Galatea*, the

Chardin, *Boy with Playing Cards* (see p. 133–4).

Paul Cézanne, *Card-Players* (see p. 134).

Freud and Surrealist Painting

Above, top André Masson: *Automatic Drawing*, ink, 1925 (see p. 144).
Bottom Oscar Domínguez: *Decalcomania*, gouache, 1937 (see p. 144).

Opposite Yves Tanguy: *Il faisait ce qu'il voulait*, oils, 1927 (see p. 145).

Overleaf René Magritte: *Personal Values*, oils (see p. 145).

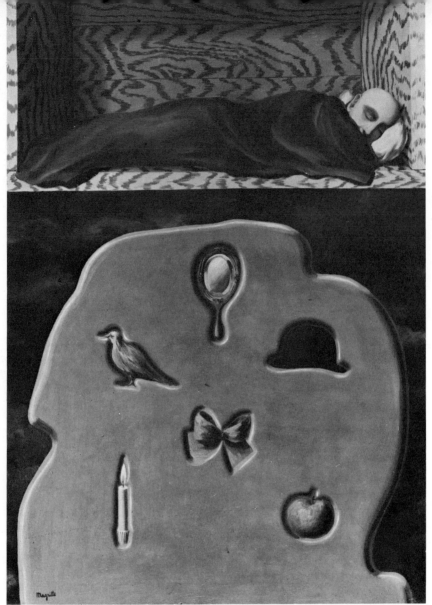

René Magritte: *Le dormeur téméraire*. In Magritte's work, the recurrent figure of the man with the bowler hat may represent his own self, oils (see p. 145).

René Magritte: *Les amants*, oils (see p. 145).

Max Ernst, from
Une semaine de bonté (see p. 147).

Max Ernst, from
La femme 100 tête (see p. 147).

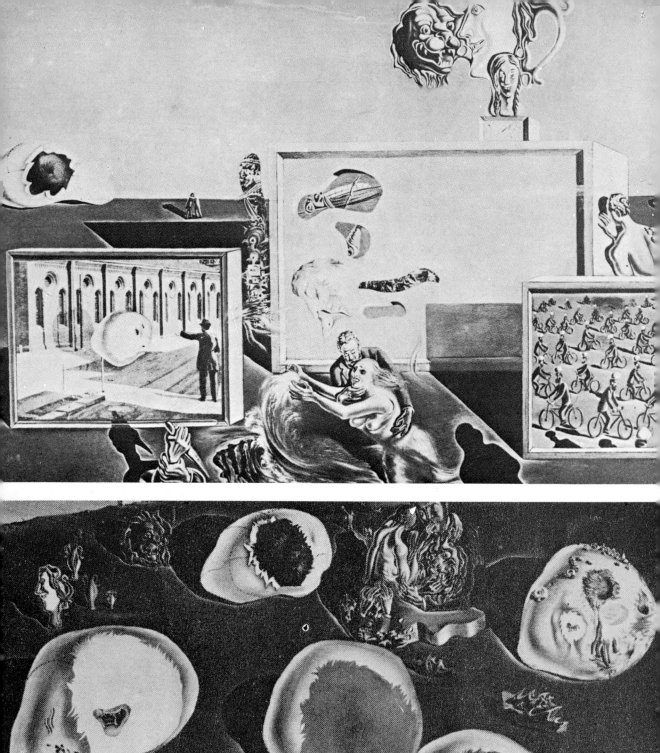

Art and Freud's Displacement of Aesthetics

absurd simplicity of outline which nevertheless takes in the incredibly exact three-dimensional and gestural connotation of the *Urbino Venus*. What we have in each case is the impossibility of taking the work simply as its most obvious subject-matter suggests: we cannot just look through the painting at the subject. On this point we have not yet parted company with Gombrich. But could we not press the point further? Is the sheer demand on our perception in these cases merely something which prevents our looking at the subject matter uninterruptedly: is its demand not itself constitutive of our excitement in the subject? Let us spell out the problem again still keeping Gombrich's examples. The question here is, how emotional urgencies provoked by very obvious erotic images, differ from the urgencies elicited in attending to a painting by Titian. Perhaps the comparative discomfort in front of the sentimental or erotically obvious painting can be seen as frustration in two ways: first, that the picture does not provide enough visual suggestions to work on. The power from what Freud called the navel of the dream fabric does not press itself into our consciousness that easily. My point here is just that the metaphor of the opposition, seductiveness versus complexity, may lead us away from seeing their interdependence. Second our response to the too obviously erotic may be the result of what Freud calls fore-pleasure being of the wrong kind, or that the image is too literal in its appeal for us to gain any satisfaction other than the satisfaction we want from reality.

So far I have talked about ideas of, or derived from, Freud in connection with works of art which make very obvious claims to emotional importance. And yet it is one of the most obvious facts about art that a great deal of the art we treat as of greatest importance has quite unimportant subject matter. Do the lines of thought from Freud help us to understand the importance we attach to a still-life by Chardin or Cézanne? There are two traditional theories dominant on the interest of such works: one is that the very absence of important subject matter means that we can be rid of our ordinary action planning attitudes, or moral concerns, our tangential intellectual activity which interferes with the pure perceptual attention. This is the view most forcefully expressed by Schopenhauer and later by Roger Fry. The other view is that the interest lies in our mental activity, for instance our pleasure in making analogies. The two views are not necessarily exclusive. I believe both are given a new force taken in conjunction with some points made by Freud.

One way into this problem is perhaps through paintings like Chardin's *Boy with Playing Cards* at the National Gallery. Our satisfaction surely contains

Top Salvador Dali: *Illumined Pleasures*, oils, 1929 (see p. 148).
Bottom Salvador Dali: *Accommodation of Desire* (see p. 148).

the pleasure in the way the very simple passages of paint are placed side by side, and in the way these patches of paint take on, at the same time, such exact spatial and textural connotations; furthermore those textures, of leather, or baize, or wood, have about them a sense of luxury and neatness like the fitting together of the painted planes. The boy sits there accomodated within a composition which has the exactness of marquetry, and with a corresponding lightness and exactness of touch, builds a house of cards, even the plane surfaces of which coincide with defined areas of paint.

Our sense here of poise or control may require no less activity of the shuttles of the mind than is involved with highly charged subject matter. And, indeed, it is not clear that our sense of poise could have the satisfaction it does have if it were not something which allowed us to entertain material which was potentially disturbing. But what sources of disturbance relate to this picture? As a start one can suggest that the sense of regression, absorption in what is sensuous and in childlikeness is surely built up here simultaneously with the composure. This interpretation is merely a tentative sketch of how such criticism might proceed. It still needs to be placed in an historical context, within painting and within eighteenth-century France.

I turn to Cézanne's card-players next partly because it has been felt to demand psychoanalytic consideration and because for many of us Cézanne is the artist who is most readily associated with the notion of inward repression.[11] But I have another reason. There is a contrast between the Chardin *Boy with Playing Cards* and the painting by Cézanne that I want to exploit in the cause of critical tactics. That consonance between paint and the objects depicted which was so characteristic of the Chardin is missing in the Cézanne. Not that we simply disregard the paint and look at the players. Perhaps we might even try to do the reverse – ignore the represented objects and attend to the firm pressure of the overlapping brush strokes. We can try, but do neither for very long – we have to move with the emphasis of our attention now slightly more on the brush strokes, now slightly more on the dour-faced players or the uncertainly placed bottle in the centre. What the comparison with Chardin's painting of the boy brings out is the lower level of consonance between paint areas and objects – the minor key, the element of dissonance, where this must be carefully distinguished from disconnection. Paint and the object represented are in extremely close relation, but not one of easy cadence. A second feature of Cézanne's card-players which is unlike that of the painting by Chardin is the nature of the composition: the men play the game dead-pan, and we the spectators can just glimpse the 'hand' only of the man on our left. The subject and the perceptual alertness of the observer have at least this superficial connection. But can we characterize the kind of satisfaction here? Where do our threads converge? In that confident way in which (as he developed these paintings) the figures became more inscrutable? In the way incongruities of proportion within each figure and the increasing elusiveness of literal detail in the setting enforce our sense that the player's concentration on his game, and the painter's concentration on his, cannot be disturbed?

To ask for unity in this way may be thought to be a mere return to old-fashioned notions of 'appropriateness' and 'decorum', or even an 'essence' of the painting. Not only. For the force of the question asked in the context of the discussion of Freud is this: what kind of pleasure are we getting? In what way is the work satisfying? And neither historians nor philosophers can ignore this question about works of art for long, nor dissociate it from the question, in what does the work's unity reside?

10

Freud and
Surrealist Painting

Dawn Ades

THE title of this essay will suggest one of two things to the reader – either an attempt to apply Freudian techniques of analysis to Surrealist paintings, or an account of the influence Freud had on the Surrealist painters via his influence on the formation of Surrealist theory. The former would it seems to me be impracticable on its own for several reasons, reasons which I hope will become clear in the first part of this essay, in which I shall try to assess the extent and exact nature of Freud's influence on Surrealism.

It has always been assumed that Freud bore some sort of parental responsibility for Surrealism. The Surrealist writers, in particular André Breton who wrote the first *Surrealist Manifesto* in 1924, have frequently supported this idea. Freud held a high place in the Surrealist pantheon beside, among others, Marx, Rimbaud, Lautréamont and the Marquis de Sade. When for example, the Surrealists redesigned the pack of playing cards they replaced the court cards with more relevant symbols : in the Revolution suit the Genius was de Sade, the Syren Lamiel and the Magus Pancho Villa; in the Dream suit the Genius was Lautréamont, the Syren Alice, and the Magus Freud. In 1938 Breton wrote that Freud had led 'a whole life of shining comprehension, of exclusive devotion to the cause of human emancipation conceived in the most generous form. . . '.[1] But this kind of homage tells us little about the precise nature of Freud's influence, other than that it was not exclusive.

'Transform the world' (Marx), 'Change life' (Rimbaud) – if Marx had provided a framework for Revolution, Freud seemed to the Surrealists to provide a framework for man's psychic liberation, and for freeing him from certain kinds of sexual guilt and inhibition (see for example *Totem and Taboo*). In trying generously to embrace both Marx and Freud, Surrealism built into itself tensions which led to bitter quarrels. Dada, which had been a formative experience for several future Surrealists, was hostile to Freud, seeing him as contributing to the preservation of bourgeois society by helping man to adjust to his social situation. Tzara, the impresario of Zurich Dada, censured him as 'someone who constructed his mystery on a kind of bourgeois ideal, a prototype of the normal man',[2] the opposite of Tzara's Nietszchean ideal. This objection to Freud was felt by certain Surrealists, in particular by Aragon, one of the few Surrealists who remained for a long time a member of the Communist Party, who attacked him viciously in 'Traité du Style'.

'Thus Freud, outrageously rouged, in a suggestive outfit surveying the asphalt of surprise, walks the streets like any writer past his prime. . . . *Paul et Virginie* would pass for an astonishing new work today, provided Virginie made a few reflections on bananas and Paul now and then absentmindedly yanked out a molar. . . . All the Austrian psychiatrist needs now is Papal consecration, with Thomist reconciliation of psychoanalysis and religion. . . .'[3]

Surrealist painting has been accused of consisting in a wholesale application of a sexual symbolism based on Freud and of the rather facile kind pilloried above by Aragon.[4] (A painting of Magritte's, *The Explanation*, delights in mocking his idea through its deliberately obvious symbolism: a carrot and a bottle lie on a table beside an imaginary fusion of the two, with the carrot inserted in the neck of the bottle.) This idea of it is obviously inadequate; it neither explains the real nature of Freud's influence on the formation of Surrealist theories, nor that this influence was manifested in many diverse ways in Surrealist works.

The discovery of whole new areas of man's existence that were hitherto unknown or shrouded in mystery, and which were shown by Freud to be in some way uncontaminated by the constraints of logic and reason, enormously excited the Surrealists. Under the influence of these discoveries, they set out to explore the unconscious, and the two most important methods they chose of doing this were automatism and the dream. These would seem to be close counterparts to Freud's psychoanalytic techniques of free association and dream analysis, but the exact nature of the connection between Freud's techniques and the Surrealists' ideas is rather more complex.

In the first *Surrealist Manifesto* Breton, who had trained as a medical student, claims that automatic writing was suggested to him by Freudian methods he had used on his patients during the war. 'Wholly occupied as I still was with Freud at the time, and familiar with his methods of examination which I had had some opportunity of practising on patients during the war, I decided to obtain from myself what one tries to obtain from them, a monologue delivered as rapidly as possible over which the subject's critical mind may not impose any judgment, unhampered by any reticence, and which should be as exactly as possible *spoken thought*.'[5] Breton and Philippe Soupault both experimented with this 'automatic writing' and published the results in collaboration in 1919. *Les Champs magnétiques* (Magnetic Fields) thus appeared under the auspices of Dada rather than Surrealism which was not launched as a movement for another five years. However, Breton goes on in the *Manifesto* to show how the experiment was so successful – producing 'a considerable choice of images of a quality such that we could not have prepared a single one by long hand'[6] – that he bases his definition of Surrealism on automatism:

Freud

SURREALISM, n.m. Pure psychic automatism by which it is intended to express, either verbally or in writing, or in any other way, the true functioning of thought. Thought dictated in the absence of all control exerted by reason, and outside all aesthetic or moral pre-occupations.

ENCYCL. PHILOS. Surrealism is based on the belief in the superior reality of certain forms of association heretofore neglected, in the omnipotence of the dream, and in the disinterested play of thought. It leads to the permanent destruction of all other psychic mechanisms and to its substitution for them in the solution to the principal problems of life. [7]

There are several reasons, however for pausing before assuming that Freud is in fact the primary source, as Breton suggests, of Surrealism. Significantly, what they had all found so exciting about *Les Champs magnétiques* were the images, the emphasis being thus upon a poetic rather than a psychic revelation. One could in fact say that it is one of the last works of Symbolism; the imagery, at least of those parts attributed to Breton, is, like Breton's contemporary poems, Mallarmean. Breton was not, anyway, the first to experiment with automatic writing, for both Arp and Tzara had done so during the days of Dada independently of any application of Freud's ideas about free association. Finally, during the long gap between the publication of *Les Champs magnétiques* in 1919 and the first *Manifesto*, Breton had not decided that automatism was a solution. In an article written in 1922, 'Entrée des médiums', he at least temporarily rejects both 'psychic automatism' and reciting dreams as fruitful 'Surrealist' activities in favour of the hypnotic trance used by mediums, [8] When in the *Manifesto* he says, 'But we . . . who made ourselves in our works into the hollow receptacles of so many echoes, modest recording devices'[9] . . . it is clear that there is still a strong spiritualist influence. It was not until the *Message automatique* of 1933 that Breton explained in detail the distinction between the automatic drawing and writing practised by the mediums and drawing and writing that was automatic in the Surrealist sense – a distinction muffled in the *Manifesto* by the use of the phrase 'recording devices'. Mediums are completely unaware of what they write; either their hand is 'as though anaesthetized' and guided by another, or they copy an inscription which 'appears' to them. Surrealist automatic writing, contrary to what spiritualism proposes (the dissociation of the psychological personality of the medium), proposes the unification of the personality. Breton had, needless to say, no time at all for the claims by spiritualists to receive messages from beyond, communications from the dead. It is necessary to mention this because the Surrealists were in the habit of talking about 'the beyond' in various contexts, but almost always in reference to something beyond our mind's *conscious* range, and thus to beyond external reality in that sense, not because of any supernatural quality. Automatic writing was in theory open to anyone to practise, not just to those, as in spiritualism, who have a 'gift' for it. The Surrealists in fact much preferred the drawings of mediums, such as Victorien Sardou and Helen Smith, which they reproduced in Surrealist periodicals, to their writings. The two years from the dissolution of Dada to the birth of Surrealism (1922 to 1924) are known as the '*période des sommeils*'. The future Surrealists practised hypnotism, and men like Robert Desnos discovered that they could fall into a trance at will during which they produced sentences and drawings of startling originality. Desnos even claimed that some of the phrases, frequently elaborate puns, that he produced in this way were transmitted to him by Rrose Sélavy, Duchamp's female alter ego. Breton himself, though, was not successful at getting into hypnotic trances. This period of experiment ended after a series of disturbing incidents, but spiritualism had exerted a determining influence on Surrealism, Breton later described automatism as 'inherited from the mediums. . .'.[10]

A more fundamental question is how far the Surrealist concept of the unconscious is modelled on Freud. Freud believed that our sanity relies on the dynamic *balance* between the forces of the conscious mind, the preconscious and the unconscious. Breton does not discuss the preconscious at all, preferring to restrict his theory to a more generalized idea of the unconscious, returning in a sense to a philosophical rather than a psychological definition of it. The concept of a creative unconscious was not new, either among Freud's predecessors or among artists and poets. As Freud himself said, 'We are probably inclined greatly to overestimate the conscious character of intellectual and artistic production. . . . Accounts given us by some of the most highly productive men, such as Goethe and Helmholtz, show rather that what is essential and new in their creation came to them without premeditation and as an almost ready whole.'[11] But it was not until Freud published *The Interpretation of Dreams* in 1900 that a direct connection was established between dreams and the unconscious. During a dream the contents of the unconscious have an opportunity of forcing their way through into the ego and into consciousness. So it is through the dream that we have the best chance of tapping the unconscious, once we have succeeded in interpreting the true but latent content of the dream via its 'façade' or manifest content. It was this discovery that fascinated the Surrealists.

Freud

It is apparently by the greatest chance that light has recently been thrown on a part of the intellectual world, and to my mind by far the most important part, which people were in the habit of no longer caring about. For this, we must thank Freud's discoveries. Founded on these discoveries, a current of opinion is finally emerging thanks to which the human explorer will be able to extend his investigations, authorized as he will be no longer to have to take account only of summary realities. Imagination is on the point of regaining its rights.[12]

Freud described the world of the dream as the Realm of the Illogical : 'The governing rules of logic carry no weight in the unconscious.'[13] For the Surrealists, it was a matter of overwhelming importance to release experience from its cage of immediate utility and common sense, where it was governed by logic and rationalism, for logic and rationalism had shown themselves incapable of solving the major problems of contemporary life (witness the First World War) and even to be responsible for them. This embracing of the illogical for its own sake was inimical to Freud. Freud had also interpreted the dream as the *fulfilment of a wish,* and this confirmed its importance for the Surrealist, although not in a sense Freud would have understood : 'It is up to man to maintain the increasingly formidable band of his desires in a state of anarchy.'[14] The dream could be valued as a part of man's psyche, in itself, but not as an instrument of psychoanalytic treatment. 'I believe in the future resolution of those two states, apparently so contradictory, of dream and of reality, into a sort of absolute reality, of *surreality.* . . .'[15]

So the two main paths by which the Surrealists chose to bypass conscious control were automatism, hybrid offspring of Freud and the mediums, and the dream. In an attitude of expectancy, not of scientific investigation, they lay in wait for the 'marvellous', trying to surprise in themselves new and startling images to rival Lautréamont's 'as beautiful as the chance meeting on a dissecting table of a sewing machine and an umbrella'. Such images, they claimed, which disrupted normal relationships between familiar objects and thus contributed to a sense of *dépaysement*, could not be produced consciously. It was a matter of dispute among them whether the graphic and plastic productions of artists connected with the group could be called Surrealist painting. Breton answered that such painting already existed.

For young painters like André Masson, Joan Miró and Yves Tanguy, the promise of new and revolutionary discoveries held out by the group of poets and painters centred around Breton seemed much more exciting than the unprofitable relationship with Cubism in which other current artistic circles seemed to be locked.

'Rather than setting out to paint something, I begin painting and as I paint, the picture begins to assert itself, or suggest itself under my brush. The form becomes a sign for a woman or a bird as I work . . . the first stage is free, unconscious.'[16] Thus Miró describes the origin of such canvases as *Birth of the World* (1925), but he goes on, significantly, 'the second stage is carefully calculated'. Breton, although he recognized that by Miró's abandonment to 'pure automatism . . . he could pass as the most Surrealist of us all'[17] had reservations about him, fearing that he had 'only summarily verified the value, the profound reasons for automatism. Miró is more or less accused of being too much a painter, of using automatism for aesthetic ends, of taking pleasure in what Aragon called his '*harmonies personelles . . . imbéciles harmonies*'.[18] This reserve *vis-à-vis* Miró betrays Surrealism at its most doctrinaire. Miró may have remained indifferent to the philosophical and psychological tenets of Surrealism, but the release of his imagination, bodied forth in the increasingly flowing, organic morphology of his paintings after 1923, was very close to what Breton describes in the following passage :

A work cannot be considered Surrealist unless the artist strains to reach the total psychological scope of which consciousness is only a small part. Freud has shown that there prevails at this 'unfathomable' depth a total absence of contradiction, a new mobility of the emotional blocks caused by repression, a timelessness and a substitution of psychic reality for external reality, all subject to the principle of pleasure alone. Automatism leads straight to this region.[19]

It was not just automatism that led to Miró's sudden pictorial and mental freedom, however, but a whole atmosphere of uninhibited activity. He felt free to draw upon his childhood for inspiration, upon Catalan folk art, children's art, Spanish proverbs and superstitions, and could release his erotic imagination. He made use of the fantasy world of Bosch, so that echoes of the strange plants and animals in Bosch's *Garden of Delights* appear in Miró's *The Tilled Field*. Miró wrote the following poem about *Harlequin's Carnival* with imagery as turbulent as in a piece of automatic writing :

The ball of yarn unravelled by the cats dressed up as Harlequins of smoke twisting about my entrails and stabbing them during the period of famine which gave birth to the hallucinations registered in this picture beautiful flowering of fish in a poppy field noted on the snow of a paper throbbing like the throat of a bird at the contact of a woman's sex in the form of a spider with aluminium legs. . . .[20]

For Masson, however, Surrealism intervened in a much more complete and disruptive way. Masson, whose intelligence and wide reading brought him very close to Breton, adopted the principle of automatism wholeheartedly. His automatic drawings of 1924–6 are a fine web of lines out of which rise a breast, a fish, a hand. He let his hand wander over the paper until it suggested an image to him which he then allowed to grow. However this process, with its non-pictorial origins, proved barren for him. 'The danger of automatism is without any doubt that of often associating only inessential connections whose content, as Hegel said,' 'does not go beyond that which is contained in the images".'[21] It did not seem to lead anywhere for him, and he found it 'a fallacy to believe that the resistance of the material can be overcome by denying that resistance'.[22] He abandoned automatism after a few years.

More mechanical automatic processes were in some ways more successful. *Frottage*, invented by Max Ernst, consisted in rubbing a pencil across a paper laid on a textured surface such as floor boards, and the resulting marks suggested images to the artist. This method had the advantage, he said, of 'resting on nothing more than the intensification of the mind's faculties by appropriate technical means, excluding all conscious mental guidance (or reason, taste, morals), reducing to the extreme the active part of that one whom we have called, up to now, the "author" of the work' and 'this procedure is revealed . . . to be the real equivalent of that which is already known by the term "automatic writing" '.[23] Ernst's method, unlike Masson's, manages to eliminate the personal aesthetic baggage of the artist, and the learned skills which must to some extent be involved in a drawing by hand, which was one of the aims of the Surrealists. However, the *frottages* were subsequently carefully composed into images, rather as the poets used images from automatic writing in their poems, often relying on subtle visual puns.[24] *Decalcomania* was a process devised by Oscar Domínguez, in which a sheet of paper was spread with black gouache, and a second sheet was laid on top, and stripped off when the paint was nearly dry. The resulting configuration was the interpreted, and the result would be 'to express yourslf in the most personal and valuable way'.[25] Ernst said: 'Thanks to studying enthusiastically the mechanism of inspiration, the Surrealists have succeeded in discovering certain essentially poetic processes, whereby the plastic work's elaboration may be freed from the sway of so-called conscious faculties . . . amounting to a bewitching of either reason, taste or the will.'[26] It is clear that these 'graphic appearances of thoughts and desires'[27] have a primarily poetic, not psychoanalytic, interest.

The other route offered to Surrealism, the 'so-called trompe-l'oeil fixing of dream images', brings us closer again to Freud, but, except in certain particular cases that I shall discuss below, in an oblique sense. In calling paintings 'dream paintings', is one implying that, as dreams, psychoanalytic techniques can be applied to them ? Freud certainly did not think so. When asked by Breton to contribute to an anthology of dreams, he replied, 'A mere collection of dreams without the dreamer's associations, without knowledge of the circumstances in which they occurred, tells me nothing and I can hardly imagine what it could tell anyone.'[28] For the Surrealists dream paintings stand alone, as windows onto another world. Their illusionistic technique is vital, because it provides a semantic bridge for the spectator. (Tanguy's paintings, however, could not strictly be called dream images, because they do not, particularly the later paintings, deal with objects in the real world, while dreams always do. Only if one had seen a Tanguy painting would one dream of such objects.)

The source for many Surrealist 'dreams' is in fact not so much Freud, as the hypnotic, enigmatic paintings of de Chirico. His silent canvases, filled with arcades, towers (which to some critics have yielded their secret, being respectively vaginal and phallic symbols), trains, unrelated objects like a ball and an antique statue placed together, have a theatrical spatial organization, like a stage, which Ernst, Magritte and Dali all use.[29] Sometimes he uses conflicting perspectives, as in *The Anxious Journey* which becomes a nightmare of arcades with a train rushing towards us, and has the terrifying and inescapable spatial ambiguity of a dream. But in de Chirico the sexual symbolism remains innocent, while in Dali's case, for instance, it has a heavy, knowing quality.

Magritte hated symbols – or at least hated talking about them. In his paintings objects stand for themselves. There is no 'fantasy' in them, and although there is mystery it does not provide an escape. It springs from the argumentativeness of his paintings. '*Ceci n'est pas une pipe*', he wrote under a painting of a pipe. In *Personal Values* with its wild scale, the walls are sky – but objects cast shadows on them. Such things are possible in dreams, but Magritte suggests we contemplate them in a waking state.

Seldom is there a personal reference in his paintings (apart from the enigmatic bowler-hatted man which may be himself), but in the case of *Les Amants*, where the lovers' heads are muffled in white shrouds, one can suggest a memory of the death of Magritte's mother when he was a child. She drowned herself, and when her body was rescued her nightdress covered her head. The painting seems to refer to it in the muffled way of complex dream disguise.

Freud

Max Ernst and Dali both offer us childhood memories and dreams which are directly relevant to their paintings and to the way in which we are invited to interpret them.

Max Ernst relates a vision of half-sleep provoked by an imitation mahogany panel opposite his bed. A man wearing the turned-up moustaches of his father is in front of the panel, and

... after having executed leaps in slow motion, legs spread, knees drawn up, torso bent forward, he smiles and draws from the pocket of his trousers a fat crayon in a soft material I find I cannot describe more precisely. He sets to work: panting violently he hurriedly traces the black lines on the panel of false mahogany. He quickly imparts to it new forms, forms which are at once surprising and abject. He accentuates the resemblance to ferocious or viscous animals to such a point that he extracts from it living creatures that fill me with horror and anguish. Content with his art, the fellow tosses his creations in the air, then gathers them in a kind of vase by stirring it, faster and faster, with his fat crayon. The vase itself, in whirling, becomes a top. The crayon becomes a whip. Now I realize that this strange painter is my father. ...[30]

This vision helps us towards an understanding of several of Ernst's paintings of 1923–4, the period of his finest Surrealist paintings, *Woman, Old Man and Flower 1* and *Ubu Imperator* in particular. On the left side of the former a man with a moustache is seated with a tiny naked woman reclining on his arm, and in the background is a curious object that balances on a pointed end like a top. In *Ubu Imperator* this object, which is clearly in some way a spinning top, dominates the painting. The father and the top have become one, and also are identified with Jarry's monstrous anti-hero Ubu, who dominates and terrorizes everyone with his enormous sexual and territorial greed. That Ernst's vision was provoked by sexual fear and jealousy of his father (the pencil being a phallic symbol?) would seem to be confirmed, particularly when he tells us that he remembered this dream, which he originally had between the ages of five and seven, at the age of puberty, 'in examining the question of how my father had conducted himself in the night of my conception. ... For a long time afterwards I was unable to disengage myself from a quite unfavourable impression of [his] conduct on [that] occasion.'[31] Ernst's relationship with his father would seem to be the basis of at least two other paintings from this period, *Pietà or Revolution by night* and *Oedipus Rex* of 1922. The moustached man in *Pietà* is clearly Ernst's father, but also bears a striking resemblance to the father figure in de Chirico's painting *The Child's Brain*. In the background is a line drawing of another bearded man, and this drawing is the prototype of all Dali's father figures in his paintings of 1929–30.

Freud and Surrealist Painting

There are many other dreamlike works of Ernst which are more enigmatic, but will perhaps one day be interpreted more fully. It is significant that some of his paintings derive their imagery from his collages (*Oedipus Rex* is based on a collage illustration to Eluard's *Répétitions*) for the collage is the ideal medium for the 'culture of systematic displacement and its effects'. The coupling of unrelated objects, of two distant realities, as in Lautréamont's image quoted above, or in Rimbaud's 'I accustomed myself to simple hallucination: I saw quite deliberately . . . a salon at the bottom of a lake'[32] is similar to processes in the dream in which contraries can exist side by side. Ernst's collage books, *La femme 100 Tête, Rêve d'une petite fille qui voulait êntrer au Carmel, Une semaine de bonté*, are like the unfolding of a dream, but of a dream which has its own poetic value, not a dream which is useful as a further aid to analysis of the dreamer.

The problem of the 'dream' painting becomes more complex with Dali. He was the only Surrealist painter who escaped Freud's scorn. Freud wrote to Stefan Zweig, 'I really owe you thanks for bringing yesterday's visitor. For until now, I have been inclined to regard the surrealists, who have apparently adopted me as their patron saint, as complete fools (let us say 95%, as with alcohol). That young Spaniard, with his candid, fanatical eyes and his undeniable technical mastery has changed my estimate. It would indeed be interesting to investigate analytically how he came to create that picture. . . .'[33] In approving of Dali's technical mastery Freud did not understand that his 'ultra-retrograde technique', a deliberate return to nineteenth-century academicism, was also a deliberately anti-painterly, anti-aesthetic gesture ('instantaneous and hand-done colour photography').[34] He did however understand the paradox of Dali's paintings, which is that while presenting all the symptoms of a deranged, obsessive personality, Dali himself is (comparatively) sane. 'The only difference between myself and a madman,' he said, 'is that I am not mad.' 'It is not the unconscious I seek in your pictures, but the conscious', Freud told Dali. 'While in the pictures of the masters – Leonardo or Ingres – that which interests me, that which seems mysterious and troubling to me, is precisely the search for unconscious ideas, of an enigmatic order, hidden in the picture. Your mystery is manifested outright. The picture is but a mechanism to reveal it.'[35] Unlike de Chirico's, Dali's pictures are conscious records of his own self-analysis. The analysis *becomes* the subject of the painting. Dali read Freud's *The Interpretation of Dreams* while a student at the Academy of Fine Arts in Madrid: 'This book presented itself as one of the capital discoveries in my life, and I was seized with a real vice of self-interpretation not only of my dreams but of everything that happened to me, however accidental it might seem at first glance'.[36] His paintings are therefore never records of a single dream, or a single image from a dream, as Magritte's sometimes are, but a complex compilation of memories, 'visions' ('Thus I spent the whole day seated before my easel, my eyes staring fixedly, trying to "see", like a medium . . . the images that would spring upon my imagination'.)[37], interpretations of himself and other myths, references to the works of de Chirico or other Surrealist painters. Also, just as James Thrall Soby observed that his pictures 'swarm with fetishes direct from Krafft-Ebing's case histories, slippers, keys, hair and so on'[38] so they also begin more and more to look like illustrations to Freud or Lacan, so that it is almost impossible to tell where his own experience ends (or begins) and he begins to draw material from psychotic case histories.

In his book *Tragic Myth of Millet's Angelus*, which itself is almost a parody of a Freudian dream analysis, Dali tracks down the cause of the irrational fascination Millet's painting exercised on him, through a series of associations, in a 'delirium of interpretation', to the threat it poses to him of being devoured during the sexual act. Apart from the sexual symbolism Dali finds in the pitchfork and wheelbarrow, Dali is reminded by the pose of the two figures of seeing the male praying mantis being eaten by the female immediately after the sexual act. In *Atavism of Twilight* Dali represents the young man as a skeleton. As a child, Dali tells us, he was terrified of being eaten ; he also had an irrational fear of locusts. The locust that appears on the mouth of the young man (Dali) in *The Great Masturbator* and the *Lugubrious Game* is synonymous with a praying mantis. The fear of sex, (cf. The *Spectre of Sex Appeal*) leads to onanism (the young man hiding his head in shame in *Illumined Pleasures* and *The Lugubrious Game*, but this brings with it the threat of castration. Dali painted several versions of William Tell which he interprets as a castration myth, and in *William Tell* the bearded father figure (which we traced back to Ernst and de Chirico) brandishes a pair of scissors at his shrinking son, whose sex is replaced by a leaf. The same bearded father appears in the foreground of *Illumined Pleasures*, embracing a woman who is trying to wash blood off her hands. The lions' heads that recur in Dali's paintings are also identified with the father (*Accommodation of Desire*). In *Illumined Pleasures* the lion's head is linked to the head of a woman, which is the double image of a woman and a jug – a reference to the Freudian commonplace of a woman symbolized as a receptacle. Dali's canvases have a total lack of unity in the aesthetic sense, the figures and images isolated in separate areas of the canvas, as though taken individually from dreams.

Dali's debt to Freud is clear, but there is one major part of his activity that he owes not to Freud but to Jacques Lacan – his paranoiac-critical activity. Lacan published *De la psychose paranoiaque dans ses rapports avec la personnalité* in 1932, but Dali had met and discussed his ideas with him when he first went to Paris in 1929. The paranoiac suffers from hallucinations and delusions of grandeur, persecution and castration, and can be cured by autopunition. Dali's paranoiac-critical activity, acclaimed by Breton as an instrument of the first importance for Surrealist activity, consisted of the hallucinatory ability to look at one object and 'see' another. It has little in fact to do with real paranoia, being rather an induced state of mind. The double images it produced proliferate in Dali's paintings. In *Impressions of Africa,* for instance, Gala's eyes are also the arcades of the building behind her, a donkey's head becomes a priest with arms raised, and so on.

This has been a bare account of the kind of influence Freud exerted on Surrealism, and Surrealism itself has only been discussed in its relationship with Freud, which makes it an unbalanced description of a widely ranging movement which contained forces often contradictory with one another. However, I hope that I have indicated how Freud's influence was both more restricted and more diffuse than might at first be supposed. Knowledge of his work usually filtered second-hand to the painters; while close acquaintance with his work could prove a double-edged weapon. Finally, Freud's interests are in many ways opposed to those of the Surrealists, as Aragon indicated, and it is Jung who seems in greater sympathy with them:

Far therefore from being a material world, this is a psychic world, which allows us to make only indirect and hypothetical inferences about the real nature of matter. The psychic alone has immediate reality, and this includes all forms of psychic, even 'unreal' ideas and thoughts which refer to nothing 'external'. We may call them imagination or delusion, but that does not detract in any way from their effectiveness. Our much vaunted reason and our boundlessly overestimated will are sometimes powerless in the face of 'unreal' thought.[39]

11
Freud,
Morality and Responsibility
Jonathan Glover

AT times it seems as if Freud made no impact on moral attitudes. For in the moral pronouncements of bishops and headmasters, or in letters to the newspapers about 'permissiveness', the appropriate post-Freudian note of self-doubt is not often heard. The sense that human acts are often more complicated than they seem, the awareness of the ambiguities of our own motives when moralizing or denouncing, are arguably as rare as ever. Yet it may be mistaken to suppose that Freud has had no influence here. Causal links in such matters are notoriously hard to establish, but there is often to be found in our culture a variety of moral scepticism which is perhaps partly traceable to psychoanalytic thinking. It is often said or implied that argument about right and wrong is pointless, since our conduct is determined always by factors other than our professed moral beliefs. It is also sometimes suggested that morality is a kind of fraud by which people are duped into behaving in socially convenient ways. Another form of moral scepticism suggests that holding people responsible for what they do is a practice that will fade away as old superstitions are replaced by a 'scientific' view of man.

Even if it is hard to be sure how widespread such scepticism is, or how much it is influenced by Freud, it is worth asking to what extent, if any, Freud's theories provide a justification for changes of moral attitude. Three aspects of Freud's thought are relevant here : his own account of the origin of conscience and morality, his determinism, and his claims about unconscious motivation.

Freud holds a Hobbesian view of man, who is seen, not as a social animal, but as one whose dangerous instincts must be restrained. One crucial restraining factor is morality. In *The Future of an Illusion,* Freud discusses the prohibition of murder.

> It is manifestly in the interest of man's communal existence, which would not otherwise be practicable, that civilization has laid down the commandment that one shall not kill the neighbour whom one hates, who is in one's way, or whose property one covets. . . . Insecurity of life, an equal danger for all, now unites men in one society, which forbids the individual to kill. . . . We do not, however, tell others of this rational basis for the murder prohibition ; we declare, on the contrary, that God is its author.

If the social function of morality is a Hobbesian one, how does it work ? Why do people take notice of what morality commands or forbids ? Here

Freud's account is entirely original. There is a psychological process which consists in 'many developments, repressions, sublimations and reaction – formations by means of which a child with a quite other innate endowment grows into what we call a normal man, the bearer, and in part the victim, of the civilization that has been so painfully acquired'. The key to this process is the Oedipus phase, when the young boy sees his father as a rival for his mother, and has to repress his own unsatisfiable desires.

Freud describes this in *The Ego and the Id*:

Clearly the repression of the Oedipus complex was no easy task. The child's parents, and especially his father, were perceived as the obstacle to a realization of his Oedipus wishes, so his infantile ego fortified itself for the carrying out of the repression by erecting this same obstacle within itself. It borrowed strength to do this, so to speak, from the father, and this loan was an extraordinarily momentous act. The superego retains the character of the father, while the more powerful the Oedipus complex was and the more rapidly it succumbed to repression . . . the stricter will be the domination of the superego over the ego later on – in the form of conscience or perhaps of an unconscious sense of guilt.

He goes on to refer to the superego's 'compulsive character which manifests itself in the form of a categorical imperative'.

Some of the difficulties of this account of conscience are well known. The existence of the Oedipus phase itself is a matter of dispute. Even if the Oedipus phase does exist it is unclear what would count as testing the claim that conscience is the outcome of repressing the Oedipus desires. Apart from these doubts about the postulated psychological mechanism, there are also familiar problems of defending both the functionalist account of morality and the large Hobbesian generalizations about innate human nature with which its Freudian form is interwoven. How do we know what men who somehow escaped all current forms of socialization would be like? Are all moral beliefs socially useful in the way the prohibition on murder is? But these are doubts rather than refutations. The point is not that Freud is wrong, but that there are not clearly established answers. We cannot yet go beyond agnosticism on these matters.

In response to these commonplace objections, it may be said that in the study of man little is clearly established, and that the Freudian account of morality has, at least in part, a certain intuitive plausibility. Our parents give us commands when we are young and the 'commands' of conscience may be shadows of these. We imitate our parents in many ways, and giving commands to ourselves may be one such way. And from where do the commands of conscience get their authority? May it not be that we obey them because, if we do not, we will feel guilty? And is it not likely that this guilt is the result of childhood conditioning?

All this does have some plausibility, even if being plausible is not the same as being true. But even if the account is true as far as it goes, it is important to see that it will not do as an explanation of the whole of morality. It can only be taken for that if a narrow and crude view of morality is presupposed. If morality is thought of as a series of arbitrary commands, backed up by the sanction of guilt feelings, then perhaps a Freudian account will be all that is required. But this view of morality will at best only fit people whose moral thinking is itself simple and crude, and in particular who altogether exclude reasoning from their morality.

There certainly are people whose morality consists in an arbitrary list of commands, which are thought of as having an authority that is obscure but unchallengeable. (Freud's own use of the Kantian term 'categorical imperative' suggests that he thought of morality in terms of authoritative internal commands.) But more reflective people often start to reason about ethics. Should I be a pacifist? What would be a just distribution of income? Can I justify abortion without also justifying infanticide? Moral questions are often hard to answer: we do not have a set of inner commands which always tell us what to do. And thinking about such questions does not consist in a kind of intent listening, in the hope that the inner voice will speak loudly enough for us to hear its commands. Nor does it consist in inspecting what makes us feel guilty. In a sophisticated morality, it may be considered wrong to be swayed by feelings of guilt in cases where we know these feelings to be the result of conditioning in values we reject. Guilt feelings are often harder to give up than the beliefs that go with them: the atheist who had a heavy childhood conditioning in religion may be unable to escape irrational guilt feelings when he spends Sunday morning in bed instead of in church.

A fuller account of morality than that presupposed by Freud would allow for people standing back from the childhood set of commands and guilt feelings, and modifying their beliefs in the light of experience, reasoning and imagination. We may see the consequences of our beliefs (as when the supporter of a war visits a hospital for wounded children), find those consequences unacceptable, and set about modifying our beliefs. Or we may find our beliefs about right and wrong to be inconsistent or arbitrary (as most people's are about the ethics of killing) or that they presuppose factual beliefs that we no longer hold. Developed moral thought is not a static state of imprisonment within social norms imposed by childhood, but a process of interaction between general beliefs and particular responses. In the light of our responses to new experiences, we modify our stock of general moral beliefs. But equally, in the light of our general beliefs we may sometimes reject some of our particular responses as crude or perhaps sentimental. There is no reason why this process should leave us accepting the assumptions either of our upbringing or of our society.

But, despite the possibility of a moral autonomy and sophistication unrecognized by Freud, it may well be that the primitive system of commands and guilt feelings is the necessary basis out of which a developed morality must grow. It may be that, without the social pressures and internalization of parental commands Freud describes, no moral attitudes would develop, and we would all be like psychopaths. It is not clear that this is so. Again, we know virtually nothing with certainty here, but the speculation once more has some plausibility. It may also be that an explanation such as Freud's of the social function of this embryonic morality is correct. Yet, even if all this were true, no grounds would be given for the moral scepticism sometimes thought to be based on Freud's account of the superego. The claim that this account shows morality to be a fraud practised by society, and a way of imposing conformity to norms not of one's own choice, tacitly presupposes that all moral thinking can be reduced to the embryonic morality discussed by Freud. So crude a reductionism is tempting only to the degree it is not made explicit.

It may be said that Freudian theory has, or should have, modified our attitudes because of the support it gives to a determinist view of man. We do not have to think Freud's view of morality adequate, but we may be more impressed by the powerful case he made for psychological causal mechanisms underlying behaviour previously thought mysterious or the product of a somehow uncaused will. If explanations of at least some persuasiveness can be provided in terms of psychological mechanisms for slips of the tongue, dreams, jokes and various neurotic disorders, it is then more convincing to suggest that the human mind is one vast and complex mechanism. This is a presupposition of the psychoanalytic view of people, and is also a presupposition of many of those who are either sceptical about morality in general, or in particular about our moral responsibility for what we do.

The mere fact that Freud's approach to people was a determinist one need not detain us long. For Freud was by no means the first person in history to take such a view, and the status of determinism in his work is unclear. It is not certain whether Freud thought his work had provided evidence for the truth of determinism, or whether he merely adopted a kind of methodological determinism, resolving never to give up the search for causes of behaviour.

But if, for the sake of argument, we assume that Freud's explanations add to the plausibility of determinism, we are not forced by this increased plausibility to regard people as less likely to be acting freely or less responsible for their actions. This is because the truth of determinism is not by itself sufficient to show that no one ever acts freely. I often have both the ability and the opportunity to do things I do not in fact do. I could have gone to the zoo today, although I did not. The reason I did not was because I did not want to go, not because I was unable to do so. And this remains true even if my lack of enthusiasm for the zoo turns out to be causally explicable. In thinking of human acts, we contrast motivation on the one hand with abilities on the other. If I had sufficient motive for doing something but did not do it, I must have lacked the ability or opportunity. If I had the ability and opportunity but did not do it, I must have lacked the desire. Lack of freedom, and hence non-responsibility, comes from limited opportunities or abilities. Where I knowingly do something normally considered bad, the question of whether I am to blame for it is largely a question of whether I did it because I wanted to do it, or whether I did it, despite not wanting to do it, as a result of inability to do otherwise.

There are special cases, where I do what I want but am still unfree. These are cases of desires I cannot help having or cannot resist. Drug addicts, alcoholics, compulsive hand-washers and others have such desires. But the reason that such people are not acting freely has nothing to do with any general thesis of determinism. It is not *any* causal explanation that shows that a desire is unavoidable or irresistible. There must be reason to think that the person could not give up or resist the desire if he wanted to do so. The compulsive hand-washer cannot give up his desire to wash even if he wants to do so. Other desires are more easily mastered. Freedom is a matter of degree, so any drawing of boundaries here is a rather blurred affair. But there remains a substantial difference between acts which I would have altered if given some incentive to do so, and acts I would not have altered however much I wanted to do so. This difference, between freedom and unfreedom, is not obliterated by the fact that both acts may be causally determined.

The basis for saying that freedom and responsibility are not undermined by determinism is the distinction between two sorts of causal explanation of why

The Later Freud

Freud in 1926; from a drawing by Ferdinand Schmutzer.

Above Anna, Freud's youngest
daughter, in 1930.
Above, right Martha Freud and her
daughter Sophie, *c.* 1912.
Right 19 Berggasse, where Freud lived
and worked from September 1891 to
June 1938. Victor Adler, 'the grand
old man of Austrian democracy' had
lived there before him.

Opposite Freud and his grandson
Stephen Gabriel, eldest son of Ernst.

Freud psychoanalyzing
Freud. Drawing by Charles B.
Slackman.

The 'Seven Rings' Committee
– back row, from left to right,
Otto Rank, Karl Abraham,
Max Eitingon, Ernest Jones.
Front row, Freud, Sandor
Ferenczi and Hans Sachs.
Freud had given his
colleagues rings like his own,
set with similar stones, hence
the name of the Committee.

Freud at work in his study, 1937.

Freud with two of his chows. His interest in dogs was a late discovery, made in 1928 when Dorothy Buckingham presented him with his first chow.

Freud in London : June 1938–9

Freud's arrival in his first London home, at 39 Elsworthy Road. With him are his daughter, Mathilde Hollitscher, Ernest Jones and Lucie Freud, wife of Freud's son Ernst.

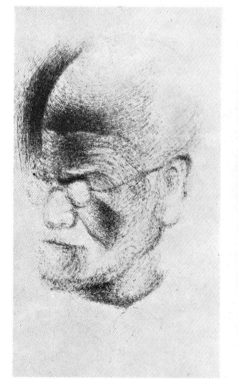

Top Freud's consulting-room at Elsworthy Road, rearranged by his son Ernst, with the furniture brought from Vienna.

Bottom, left The ornaments on Freud's desk were placed by his maid Paula in exactly the same order as they had been in Vienna.

Bottom, right Sketch of Freud by Salvador Dali whom Stefan Zweig took to visit Freud in July 1938. Freud rather liked his 'candid fanatical eyes and his undeniable technical mastery' and Dali made a sketch of him.

Freud in his study at 20 Maresfield Gardens, reading his MS of *Moses and Monotheism*.

a person does one thing rather than another. It may be that he wants to do the other act but cannot, or it may be that he performs this act because he wants to, although he is able to do the other thing. In the first case he cannot help the outcome, while in the second case he can. We identify people with their desires, rather than with their abilities or opportunities. Moral praise and blame can appropriately be applied to a person's desires and motives, but not to his abilities and opportunities. (This is subject to two qualifications: some desires or motives are ones a person wants to give up but cannot, while some limitations on our abilities and opportunities are the result of our own previous decisions, for which we can be blamed or praised.)

But if holding people responsible is based on making moral judgements in terms of their motives and desires, it is clear that motives or desires which are unconscious pose a special problem. It seems a serious moral criticism of someone to say that his actions are always motivated by self-interest and that all his desires are selfish. But are we equally, or at all, justified in disapproving of someone whose desires and motives, while just as selfish, are unconscious? For, surely, if he does not identify with these desires, and does not even know of their existence, it is odd for us to identify him with them? Should our attitudes to him be based on our attitude to desires and motives he might repudiate if he became aware of them?

Freud himself never directly confronts the problem of responsibility for actions that are unconsciously motivated. But he does discuss the links between his account of the unconscious and responsibility in the content of a note about the curious problem of *Moral Responsibility for the Context of Dreams*. His remarks there about the unconscious impulses that determine our dreams seem to rest on considerations that could apply equally to any unconscious desires.

Freud confidently says: 'Obviously one must hold oneself responsible for the evil impulses of one's dreams. What else is one to do with them?' The fatuity of the rhetorical question does not increase the obviousness of the view it is intended to support. But Freud partly recovers after this unpromising start, and puts forward some arguments that are worth quoting in full.

His first argument is that I am not entitled to identify myself with only the conscious part of my mind. He says:

Unless the content of the dream (rightly understood) is inspired by alien spirits, it is a part of my own being. If I seek to classify the impulses that are present in me according to social standards into good and bad, I must assume responsibility for both sorts; and if, in defence, I say that what is unknown, unconscious and repressed in me is not my ego then I shall not be basing my position upon psychoanalysis, I shall not have accepted its conclusions – and I shall perhaps be taught better by the criticisms of my fellow-men, by the disturbances in my actions and the confusion of my feelings. I shall perhaps learn that what I am disavowing not only 'is' in me but sometimes 'acts' from out of me as well.

What exactly is Freud rejecting here? We are normally willing to regard some desires as alien to the person who has them. We do not hold the alcoholic responsible for drinking because we believe that he is neither capable of resisting his desire to drink nor of giving up the desire. He may well wish he did not have any desire to drink. We are prepared to regard the possession of an unwanted desire that a person cannot eliminate or resist as a form of incapacity, and not to hold him responsible for what he does as a result. (We may hold him responsible for becoming an alcoholic, but that is another matter.) The view which Freud is arguing against is that we should regard unconscious desires as alien to a person in a similar way.

Freud's argument is not clear. He says that if I adopt the view he rejects 'I shall not be basing my position upon psychoanalysis'. But what does this mean? If we decide that actions coming from some kinds of motive are not blameworthy, this is a moral decision of ours. The only way in which it could be undermined by any psychoanalytic findings would be if it depended on some factual assumption that turned out to be false. What is this assumption, and what is the evidence that it is false? The only clue Freud gives is his remark that 'what I am disavowing not only "is" in me but sometimes "acts" from out of me as well'. This seems to mean no more than that I do have the unconscious motive, and that it does influence my behaviour. But the alcoholic also does have his desire to drink, and it does influence his behaviour. Freud does not show that the decision to treat unconscious motives as similar to the unwanted but inescapable desires of the alcoholic is based on any false beliefs.

Freud has a second argument for saying that we are responsible for unconsciously motivated acts. This is his claim that acceptance of such responsibility is psychologically inescapable. He says: 'Moreover, if I were to give way to my moral pride and tried to decree that for purposes of moral valuation I might disregard the evil in the id and need not make my ego responsible for it, what use would that be to me? Experience shows me that I nevertheless *do* take that responsibility, that I am somehow compelled to do so.'

This argument depends on the belief that feeling guilty about something is the same as believing oneself to be blameworthy. But we have seen that it is possible to think one's own guilt feelings irrational, as in the case of the atheist with reflex guilt feelings about not going to church. If it is true that we feel guilty about acts even when we see that they were unconsciously motivated, it still seems an open question whether or not we ought to regard such feelings as rational. And, if we came to think them irrational, might we not perhaps find that these feelings of guilt started to fade away? Freud says about my accepting responsibility that experience shows me that I am somehow compelled to do so. But without trying to give up such guilt feelings, we cannot be sure that the feeling of compulsion is not an illusion.

The argument is also unsatisfactory in treating questions of responsibility as though they only concerned whether or not we ought to blame ourselves for what we do. No consideration is given to the question of what attitudes we ought to adopt towards other people who act out of possibly disreputable unconscious motives. Even if it were true that someone could not help feeling guilty about something, this would not establish that others were entitled to blame him. It is the avoidability of a bad act that makes blame reasonable, not the unavoidability of guilt feelings afterwards.

If we cannot accept that Freud's own remarks settle the question of responsibility for what is unconsciously motivated, is there any other way of approaching the problem? In outlining an alternative approach, one may start by asking what difference it should make to a person's decision how to act if he knows of the possibility of unconscious motivation. For it is arguable that knowledge of one's own motives is less relevant to such decisions than it is often taken to be.

Consider someone wondering whether he ought to give some money to Oxfam. He may well suspect that if he gives the money his motives may be less purely unselfish than they seem at the conscious level. Is it not possible that his most powerful motives are below the level of consciousness? Perhaps he wants to feel a glow of virtue, and to act in a way that flatters his picture of himself. Or it may be that he wants to avoid the feelings of guilt induced by reading the Oxfam advertisement and then doing nothing about it. Suppose, on the other hand, he decides not to send any money. At the conscious level his reasons may be those of a radical political kind. He may think that Oxfam does more harm than good by easing the conscience of the rich, and thus being a substitute for more effective action at government level. But, even here, he may suspect that powerful unconscious motives are at work. May the political case against Oxfam perhaps be functioning as a rationalization for an unconscious determination to preserve his own standard of living ?

In a case like this, the motives involved in either course of action may be suspect. But there seems no reason why this should lead to any kind of paralysis. There is something unattractively self-absorbed about treating the purity of one's own motives as a prime consideration when deciding what to do. This is part of the case for saying that decisions about right and wrong ought to be based on the consequences of the acts being considered, with questions of motivation left largely on one side. If giving money to Oxfam leaves the world a slightly better place than not doing so, one should give the money. This holds even if one suspects that one's motives for giving are, whether at a conscious or unconscious level, a bit dubious.

But this needs some qualification. If our motives are unconscious, they may well distort our view of the likely consequences of what we do. Perhaps self-deception about our motives is in itself not of great moral importance, but where it is linked with self-deception about the facts of our situation it becomes more relevant. Consider a question related to the one about giving to Oxfam. Should a country like Britain give more aid to economically poorer countries ? Some people argue either that such aid is always a concealed form of exploitation, or else that the most effective way of improving the lot of people in backward countries is for advanced ones to forget aid and concentrate on increasing their own prosperity. I have not the knowledge to assess with any certainty the truth of such views. But it is reasonable to say that beliefs so obviously convenient to so many of us ought to have their credentials very thoroughly examined before being accepted.

This point can be generalized. Knowledge of the possibility of unconscious factors distorting our view of our situation places on us a special duty of sceptical scrutiny. This duty is not primarily to examine our own motives, but is rather a duty to look with special care at our grounds for holding factual beliefs that are suspiciously convenient to us.

We can now return to the problem of whether or not we are justified in holding other people responsible for acts that are unconsciously motivated. The various excuses that absolve people from responsibility for what they do can broadly be classified, as they were by Aristotle, under the headings of ignorance or compulsion. I am not blameworthy when I do not know certain crucial facts about what I am doing, nor am I blameworthy when I am compelled to act, either by external pressures or by irresistible desires. Both of these factors, ignorance and compulsion, function as excuses only where they are not themselves the result of my own relevantly blameworthy act or omission. If I fire a gun in a busy street without bothering to look and see if anyone is in the line of fire, my ignorance does not excuse me from blame for killing someone. And irresistible impulses are not an excuse if they result from my deliberately taking a drug knowing it would have that effect.

To what extent do unconscious motives involve either compulsion or ignorance? It does not seem likely that all unconscious motives are irresistible. Addicts, whose impulses sometimes really are irresistible, are not open to any normal degree of persuasion to act differently. But there seems no reason why unconscious motivation should always be as powerful as this. Perhaps a man's unconscious motive for buying his cigarettes at a certain shop is that he finds a girl who works there attractive. Although the whole thing is unconscious, it may still be that he finds her only so mildly attractive that he could be persuaded to go to another shop by being told that it gave double green shield stamps.

Perhaps unconscious motives are more often irresistible than conscious ones, though even this would not be easy to prove. But if they do not always involve compulsion, do they always involve excusable ignorance? We have seen that unconscious motivation can involve ignorance, not only of one's motives, but also of relevant facts of one's situation. We may 'overlook' what unconsciously we do not wish to know. I have argued here that knowledge of one's own motives is normally not centrally relevant to the right and wrongs of a decision how to act. It follows from this that ignorance of one's motives will normally not be sufficient to clear one of the charge of knowingly doing wrong. So any claim that people never ought to be held responsible for unconsciously motivated actions will have to depend on the view that unconscious desires always cause a relevant and excusable ignorance of some other kind.

The assertion that whenever I do not know my own motives there is always something else I also do not know seems a sweeping one. And even in cases where unconscious motivation clearly does distort someone's way of seeing things, it is not clear that this distortion is always excusable. It has been argued here that we have a special duty to resist such distortions in cases where there is a possibility that suspiciously convenient beliefs are self-interested rationalizations. Some kinds of self-deception are not excusable ignorance, but a kind of semi-deliberate negligence.

It may be said that this sort of criticism can only be made in cases where motives are not really unconscious. There is a duty to resist our view of things being distorted by selfish motives which we suspect may be present But many people suppose that motives whose presence may be suspected by the person who has them are not genuinely unconscious.

This seems to be based on an over-dramatic view of unconscious motivation. Some of the most convincing cases of unconscious motives occur with post-hypnotic suggestion. The person under hypnosis may be told to take his shoes off an hour after recovering normal consciousness, and also be told to forget the whole episode of being hypnotized. When the time comes he will remove his shoes, perhaps explaining to anyone present that his feet hurt. This kind of case is dramatic partly because, without knowledge of the post-hypnotic suggestion, no one would suspect any unconscious forces to be at work.

But there is no reason to think that most unconscious motives are as deeply inaccessible as this. Where external observers have good evidence for ascribing such motives to someone this evidence is usually available to himself. His behaviour falls into a pattern that does not fit his officially declared goals but does fit the postulated unconscious aims. Such cases are far more common than those where the external observer has access to a dramatic episode such as the post-hypnotic suggestion. And, in these more common cases, the pattern into which his behaviour falls should be visible to the agent himself, if he cares to look for it.

It is sometimes thought that during the process of psychoanalysis, many motives as deeply inaccessible as those supplied by post-hypnotic suggestion are discovered. But the difficulty here is to see what sort of inaccessible evidence such 'discoveries' could be based on. If the unconscious motives cannot be suspected from the patterns of conduct of the person who has them, what counts as testing the claim that they exist? The fact that the patient comes to accept his analyst's interpretation is not enough, for this may be the result of a kind of indoctrination. The fact that the patient feels helped by his psychoanalysis is not enough, for being given a coherent view of oneself, even if a false one, could still be beneficial. The truth of the analyst's claims about motivation can only be judged by how plausibly they fit the patient's habitual patterns of behaviour. And this evidence is available to the patient himself, independently of his psychoanalysis.

If we are sceptical about the evidence for inaccessible unconscious motives, outside such special contexts as post-hypnotic suggestion, we will be less inclined to take the view that people cannot help it when their view of their situation is distorted in ways described by Freud. For, if most of our unconscious motives can at least be suspected when we take the trouble to think about the matter, we ought to be fairly successful in noticing self-deception if we keep a look out for it. And it has been argued here that at least where its influence may have an important effect on our actions, self-deception is something which we ought to try to detect.

References

Any student of Freud must necessarily be indebted to three authors : to Erna Lesky, the historian of Viennese medicine for her authoritative *Die Wiener Medizinische Schule im 19. Jahrhundert* (1965), Ernest Jones for his comprehensive biography, *Sigmund Freud : Life and Work* (3 vols., 1953–7) ; and to Henri F. Ellenberger's monumental history of dynamic psychiatry, *The Discovery of the Unconscious* (1970).

Freud and Medicine in Vienna

1 W. Trotter, *Instincts of the Herd in Peace and War,* 2nd edition, London, 1919, pp. 77–8.

2 J. Breuer and S. Freud, *Studien Über Hysterie,* Leipzig and Vienna, 1909, p. 140.

3 L. R. Grote (ed.), *Die Medizin der Gegenwart in Selbstdarstellungen,* Leipzig, 1925, p. 2.

4 Sigmund Freud, *Briefe 1873–1939,* Frankfurt a.M., 1960, p. 9. 'To flay animals or to torture people' echoes the phrase 'To tease people, to torture animals' (*Menschen necken, Tiere quälen . . .*) from the preface to *Max und Moritz* by the German humorist Wilhelm Busch (1832–1908).

5 Hermann Nothnagel (1841–1905) was professor of medicine at Hamburg, Jena and Vienna, and the leading clinician of his time. Neuropathology, chronic diseases, gastro-intestinal disorders and cardiac conditions were of major interest to him. He was an authority on angina pectoris, and it was from this disease that he died. Nothnagel was a clinical scientist to the very last, as shown by the notes found on his night table, undoubtedly written shortly before his death, recording the signs and symptoms of his heart attack.

6 Freud, *Briefe,* p. 33.

7 Hermann Bahr (1863–1934), Austrian dramatist, critic and theatre manager, influential as the leader of a Viennese literary group ; Hugo von Hofmannsthal (1874–1929), poet and dramatist, whose *Elektra* (1903) was set to music by Richard Strauss ; Richard von Schaukal (1874–1942), lyrical poet ; Arthur Schnitzler (1862–1931), Austrian physician, dramatist and novelist.

8 Ernest Jones, *The Life and Works of Sigmund Freud,* vol. 1, New York, 1953, p. 332.

9 Egon Friedell, *Kulturgeschichte der Neuzeit,* London and Oxford, 1947, vol. 3, p. 573.

10 Fritz Wittels, *Sigmund Freud : his Personality, his Teaching and his School,* New York, 1924, p. 20.

11 Jones, *op. cit.,* p. 29.

12 Grote, *op. cit.,* p. 3 ; Jones, *op. cit.,* pp. 28–9.

13 Grote, *op. cit.,* p. 3.

14 Ernst von Fleischl-Marxow (1846–91), physicist and physiologist, worked on nerve and muscle physiology and discovered the electrical activity of the brain, thus initiating research that eventually led to electro-encephalography. Sigmund Exner von Ewarten (1846–1926) succeeded Brücke as professor of physiology and head of the Institute. He investigated the physiology of perception, particularly vision.

15 Johannes Müller (1801–58) was professor in Bonn and Berlin. He was not only a physiologist but also a comparative anatomist, embryologist, and pathologist. See Rudolf Virchow, *Johannes Müller,* Berlin, 1858 ; Martin Müller, *Ueber die philosophischen Anschauungen des Naturforschers Johannes Müller,* Leipzig, 1927.

16 Rudolf Virchow, 'Ueber das Beduerfnis und die Richtigkeit einer Medicin vom mechainschen Standpunkt', *Virchows Archiv,* 1907 pp. 188 ff, 1907 ; Erwin H. Ackerknecht, *Rudolf Virchow. Doctor, Statesman, Anthropologist,* Madison, 1953, p. 49.

17 Virchow, *Die Einheitsbestrebungen in der wissenschaftlichen Medizin,* Berlin, 1849, pp. 14, 21.

18 Karl Sudhoff (ed.), *Rudolf Virchow und die*

deutschen Naturforscherversammlungen, Leipzig, 1922, p. 261.

19 Ludwig and his friends were all born within a period of five years, and they died within the space of four years: Carl Ludwig (1816–95), Emil du Bois-Reymond (1818–96), Ernst Brücke (1819–92), Hermann Helmholtz (1821–94).

20 E. Th. Brücke, *Ernst Brücke*, Vienna, 1928, p. 19.

21 Contributions to a Theory of the Mechanism of Urinary Secretion.

22 The substance of the dissertation was published the following year as 'Beiträge zur Lehre von der Diffusion tropfbar flüssiger Körper durch poröse Scheidewände', *Poggendorffs Annalen* 58 :77–94, 1843.

23 The Theory of Sound Perception.

24 Ludwig Traube (1818–76), graduated M.D. in 1840, was a student of Johannes Müller, and became professor at Berlin in 1857. Devoted attention to experimental pathology and clinical medicine as in the relationship between heart and kidney disease, the effects of digitalis, and the changes produced by section of the vagus nerve.

25 *Beiträge zur experimentellen Pathologie und Physiologie* (Contributions to Experimental Pathology and Physiology), herausgegeben von Dr L. Traube, Berlin, 1846, pp. iv-v.

26 Gas, water and electricity were not supplied to the Institute until 1885, when it was expanded further.

27 E. Lesky, *Die Wiener medizinische Schule im 19. Jahrhundert*, Graz-Köln, 1965, p. 259.

28 Siegfried Bernfeld, 'Sigmund Freud, M.D., 1882–1885', *International Journal of Psychoanalysis* 32 : pp. 204–215, 1951 (see particularly pp. 206–8).

29 Jones, *op. cit.*, p. 62.

30 Certain wards or sections in the hospital were run by the professors in the University medical school, and were used for teaching. Each professor who headed such a *Klinik* chose his assistants. Other wards not used for teaching were headed by a *Primarius*, or senior resident, who was assisted by *Sekundarärzte*, junior residents. Any physician could apply for such a position if one was vacant.

31 Sigmund Freud, *The Interpretation of Dreams*, in *The Basic Writings of Sigmund Freud*, translated and edited by Dr A. A. Brill, New York, 1938, p. 417 ; Jones, *op. cit.*, pp. 365 ff ; Peter Amacher, *Freud's Neurological Education and its Influence of Psychoanalytic Theory*, New York, 1965, pp. 9–20.

32 Freud, *Briefe*, p. 130.

33 Jones, *op cit.*, p. 144.

34 Freud, *Briefe*, p. 35.

35 *Ibid.*, p. 94.

36 *Ibid.*, p. 139. Nothnagel was a widower, his wife having died in 1880 of puerperal fever, and was left with four children. He had a very large and lucrative practice which took most of his time from noon to 4 pm and again from 5 to 8 or 9 pm. See Max Neuburger, *Hermann Nothnagel. Leben und Wirken eines deutschen Klinikers*, Vienna-Berlin, 1922, pp. 149–52.

37 Freud, *Briefe*, p. 196.

38 Freud, *Briefe*, p. 35.

39 Bernhard Naunyn, *Erinnerungen, Gedanken und Meinungen*, Munich, 1925, pp. 234–7, 249.

40 William H. Welch, 'The Evolution of Modern Scientific Laboratories', *Bull. Johns Hopkins Hosp.* 7, 1896, pp. 19–24.

41 Knud Faber, *Nosography. The Evolution of Clinical Medicine in Modern Times*, 2nd. ed., revised, New York, 1930 ; pp. 59–94, 116–71.

42 Adolf Kussmaul (1822–1902), son and grandson of medical men, received his medical education at Heidelberg, where he later taught from 1855 to 1859. Thereafter he was professor of internal medicine at Erlangen (1859–63), Freiburg (1863–76), and Strassburg (1876–88). Kussmaul was an outstanding clinical observer, describing the peculiar respiration associated with diabetic acidosis (Kussmaul's air hunger), as well as the conditions designated as progressive bulbar paralysis and periarteritis nodosa.

43 Neuburger, *op. cit.*, p. 141.

44 *Ibid.*, pp. 107, 146.

45 Freud, *Briefe*, p. 130.

46 Nothnagel's position in research on the nervous system may be indicated by the fact that his work was cited by such investigators as Hughlings Jackson (1876, 1887), *Selected*

References

Writings of John Hughlings Jackson, ed. James Taylor, New York, 1958, vol. 1, pp. 150–1, vol. 2, p. 105; William James, *Principles of Psychology,* London, 1901, vol. 1, pp. 40, 51, 56, 60; C. S. Sherrington, *The Integrative Action of the Nervous System,* New Haven, 1906, pp. 65, 254, 396.

47 Freud: *Zur Auffassung der Aphasien,* Leipzig and Vienna, 1891; English translation by E. Stengel – S. Freud, *On Aphasia,* New York, 1953, p. 28.

48 Neuburger, *op, cit.,* pp. 168–70. Contrary to Bernfeld's assertion (see note 28 above, p. 213), Nothnagel did present numerous neuropathological cases to his students. Clearly Bernfeld did not read Neuburger's biography of Nothnagel which has a number of references to just this point. Apparently he simply accepted Freud's statement in his 'Autobiography', which is not fully reliable.

49 Electrodiagnosis and therapy were not peculiar to Nothnagel; they were part of the medical scene of the period, having been introduced in Paris and Berlin in the 1850s, and in Vienna a decade later. See Lesky, *op. cit.,* pp. 389–93.

50 According to Bernfeld (note 28 above, p. 211) it was December 1883; Jones gives the date as 1 January 1884 (*op. cit.,* p. 68).

51 Grote, *op. cit.,* pp. 3–4.

52 Lesky, *op. cit.,* pp. 373–405.

53 Freud, *Aus den Anfängen der Psychoanalyse,* London, 1950, p. 66.

54 Neuburger, *op. cit.,* pp. 338–9.

55 J. M. Charcot, *Poliklinische Vorträge.* I. Band, *Schuljahr 1887/88,* übersetzt von Dr Sigm. Freud, Leipzig and Vienna, 1892, pp. IV–V.

56 Heinrich Obersteiner (1847–1922), psychiatrist and neurologist, professor at Vienna, had undertaken research on the nervous system in Brücke's laboratory while still a student. He established the first neurological institute in 1882, with research centering chiefly on neuroanatomy and pathology. A lecture on cerebral anatomy which Freud delivered on 12 May 1885 was intended, as he wrote to his fiancée, 'actually only for one person, Professor Obersteiner' (Freud, *Briefe,* p. 139). The latter helped Freud that

year to obtain a position as *locum tenens* for three weeks in the *Heilanstalt* in Oberdöbling, a private mental hospital run by Obersteiner's father together with Max Leidesdorf, professor of psychiatry at Vienna.

57 Jackson, *op. cit.,* vol. 1, p. 52.

58 The phrase 'a dependent concomitant' was borrowed by Freud from Hughlings Jackson's study 'On Affections of Speech from Diseases of the Brain', *Brain* 1, 1878–9 pp. 304–30; 2, 1879–80, pp. 203–22, 323–56.

59 Jones, *op. cit.,* pp. 367–9.

60 For detailed analysis of the influence of Meynert and Exner see Amacher, *op. cit.,* pp. 21–54.

61 Theodor Meynert, *Klinische Vorlesungen über Psychiatrie,* Vienna, 1890, pp. 38–43.

62 Freud: *Gesammelte Werke,* vol. 13, London, 1940, p. 3.

63 Sketch of a physiological explanation of psychological phenomena.

64 Henri F. Ellenberger, *The Discovery of the Unconscious. The History and Evolution of Dynamic Psychiatry,* New York, 1970, p. 478.

65 Freud, *Anfänge, op. cit.,* pp. 94–5.

66 Freud, *Gesammelte Werke,* vol. 10, p. 273; a similar passage occurs in vol. 6, p. 165.

67 Breuer and Freud, *op. cit.,* p. 161.

68 Jones, *op. cit.,* p. 235.

69 George Rosen, 'History of Medical Hypnosis', in *Hypnosis in Modern Medicine,* ed. Jerome M. Schneck, 2nd edition, Springfield, Ill., 1959, pp. 3–27.

70 Freud, *On Aphasia,* pp. XI-XII.

71 Imre Herman, *Gustav Theodor Fechner. Eine psychoanalytische Studie über individuelle Bedingtheiten wissenschaftlicher Ideen,* Leipzig-Vienna, 1926.

72 Ellenberger, *op. cit.,* p. 542.

73 Iago Galdston, 'Freud and Romantic Medicine', *Bull. Hist. Med.,* 30, 1956, pp. 489–507.

Freud and Marx

1 Z. A. Jordan, 'Karl Marx as a Philosopher and a Sociologist', in Jordan (ed.), *Karl Marx: Economy, Class and Social Revolution,* London, 1971.

2 Alfred Schmidt, *The Concept of Nature in Marx,* London, 1971.

3 Jordan, *op. cit.*, p. 11.

4 Marx to Engels, 18 June 1862 and 7 July 1866; see Karl Marx – Friedrich Engels, *Gesamtausgabe* (MEGA), section III, vol. 3, pp. 77 and 345.

5 For a translation of the Preface see Marx–Engels, *Selected Works*, London, 1968, pp. 181 ff.

6 Schmidt, *op. cit.*, p. 134.

7 Albert Einstein and Sigmund Freud, *Why War?*; cited by Sylvia Anthony, in *The Discovery of Death in Childhood and After*, 2nd revised edition, London, 1971, p. 220. For Freud's original text see *Gesammelte Werke*, vol. 16, pp. 13 ff.

8 Ernest Jones, *Sigmund Freud*, London, 1955, vol. 2, p. 149.

9 Ernest Glover, *Freud or Jung?*, London, 1950, p. 31.

10 Herbert Marcuse, *Eros and Civilisation*, Boston, 1955; see also the debate between Fromm and Marcuse in the essay collection *Voices of Dissent*, New York, n.d., pp. 293 ff.

11 *Voices of Dissent*, p. 294.

12 *Ibid.*, pp. 313–5.

13 *Times Literary Supplement*, 8 January 1971. For Marcuse's standpoint see, in particular his *Psychoanalyse und Politik*, Frankfurt, 1968. For a critique of Marcuse's *One-Dimensional Man* see Peter Sedgwick, 'Natural Science and Human Theory', *Socialist Register*, London, 1966, pp. 163 ff.

14 Karl Korsch, *Karl Marx*, New York, 1963, pp. 129 ff.

15 Eugene Kamenka, *The Philosophy of Ludwig Feuerbach*, London, 1970, p. 79.

16 Marx, *Capital*, London, 1946, vol. I, p. 51.

17 *Die Zukunft einer Illusion*, in *Gesammelte Werke*, vol. 14, pp. 325 ff.

18 Leo Strauss, *Spinoza's Critique of Religion*, New York, 1965, p. 45.

19 Kamenka, *op. cit.*, p. 78.

20 T. B. Bottomore (ed.), *Karl Marx – Early Writings*, New York, 1964, pp. 43 ff.

21 Kamenka, *op. cit.*, p. 120.

22 Kamenka, *op. cit.*, p. 59.

23 *Ibid.*, p. 128.

24 *Ibid.*, p. 111; for Engels's treatment of the subject see his essay on Feuerbach in Marx- Engels, *Selected Works*, London, 1968, p. 596 ff.

25 Marx, *The Holy Family*, London, 1957, p. 170.

26 *Ibid.*, p. 175.

27 Schmidt, *op. cit.*, p. 21.

28 Marx, *Holy Family*, p. 177.

29 Jordan, *op. cit.*, p. 26.

30 Marcuse, *Hegels Ontologie und die Grundlegung einer Theorie der Geschichtlichkeit*, Frankfurt, 1932.

31 Marcuse, *Reason and Revolution: Hegel, and the rise of Social Theory* (London, 1941, 1955).

32 See in particular *One-Dimensional Man*, Boston, 1964; also 'Repressive Tolerance' in *A Critique of Pure Tolerance*, London, 1969. For a critique of Marcuse's standpoint see Alasdair MacIntyre, *Herbert Marcuse*, New York, 1970; London, 1970.

33 *Op. cit.*, p. 57.

34 See Habermas, *Erkenntnis und Interesse*, Frankfurt a.M., 1968; Mitscherlich, *Krankheit als Konflikt*, Frankfurt a.M., 1966.

35 *Capital*, vol. III, pp. 799–800.

36 Marcuse, 'The Obsolescence of Marxism', in Nicholas Lobkowicz (ed.), *Marx and the Western World*, Notre Dame, Indiana, 1967, pp. 409 ff.

37 *Ibid.*, p. 413.

38 *Op. cit.*, p. 31.

39 *Ibid.*, p. 32.

40 *Marx and the Western World*, p. 416.

41 *Ibid.*

42 See Sedgwick, 'Natural Science and Human Theory', *passim.*

43 Stuart Hampshire, *Spinoza*, London, 1956, p. 108.

44 *One-Dimensional Man*, pp. 172–3.

45 *Hegels Ontologie*, p. 8.

Freud and the Concept of Parental Guilt

1 Pye Henry Chavasse, *Advice to a Mother*, 14th ed., London, 1896.

2 Mabel Liddiard, *The Mothercraft Manual*, 10th ed., London, 1936.

3 Chavasse, *op. cit.*

4 Liddiard, *op. cit.*

References

5 Susan Isaacs, *The Nursery Years*, 5th ed., London, 1936.

6 Benjamin Spock, *Baby and Child Care*, New York, 1946.

7 D. W. Winnicott, *The Child, the Family and the Outside World,* London, 1957.

8 Liddiard, *op. cit.*

9 Isaacs, *op. cit.*

10 *Ibid.*

11 Winnicott, *op. cit.*

12 A. S. Neill, *Problem Family,* London, 1940.

13 Anna Freud, *Normality and Pathology in Children,* London, 1966.

Art and Freud's Displacement of Aesthetics

1 I have given an account of Herbart's view of the mind and related theories in the tradition from Kant, which are mentioned in this paper, in *The Manifold in Perception*, Oxford, 1972.

2 Freud, *The Interpretation of Dreams*. Standard Edition of *The Complete Psychological Works of Freud,* London, from 1953, vol. IV, p. 282.

3 *Ibid.,* p. 283.

4 *Ibid.,* vol. V, p. 340.

5 *Ibid.,* p. 523.

6 *Ibid.,* p. 525.

7 *Ibid.,* vol. IV, p. 280 f.

8 I. Kant, *Critique of Judgement*, § 49.

9 Freud, *op. cit.,* vol. VII, pp. 305–10.

10 E. H. Gombrich, 'Psycho-Analysis and the History of Art', *Meditations on a Hobby Horse and Other Essays on the Theory of Art,* London, 1963. See particularly pp. 35–7.

11 Kurt Badt, *The Art of Cézanne*, London, 1965, Chapter II. See also the review in the *Times Literary Supplement,* 27 May 1965, p. 416.

Freud and Surrealist Painting

1 André Breton, Preface to *Cahier consacré au rêve*, Cahiers G.L.M., 7th Cahier, Paris, March 1938.

2 Tristan Tzara, quoted by Aragon in Garaudy, *L'Itinéraire d'Aragon*, p. 88.

3 Louis Aragon, 'Traite du Style, *Nouvelle Revue Française*, 1928.

4 The Surrealists themselves had of course helped to familiarise the public with his kind of symbolism. There could no longer be the naiveté manifested at the Dada exhibition in Cologne, where, after complaints of obscenity, the only offending item the authorities could see was a Dürer print of *Adam and Eve*, in spite of the fact that the room was filled with suggestive and grotesque objects.

5 Breton, 'Manifeste du Surréalisme', *Sagittaire*, Paris, October 1924.

6 *Ibid.*

7 *Ibid.*

8 Hypnotism was practised by Freud and Breuer as an aid to uninhibited speech before the latter developed his techniques of free association. The Surrealists also held sessions of collective analysis, possibly under the influence of American writers like Matthew Josephson. New York had enjoyed a fashion for Freud for six or seven years, while France lagged behind.

9 Breton 'Manifeste', *op. cit.*

10 Breton, 'Artistic Genesis and Perspective of Surrealism', 1941 (in *Le Surréalisme et la Peinture*, new ed. Paris, 1965, p. 68).

11 Sigmund Freud, *The Interpretation of Dreams*, London, 1900 (trans. James Strachey, p. 613).

12 Breton, 'Manifeste', *op. cit.*

13 Freud, *An Outline of Psycho-analysis*, (trans. Strachey, p. 25), 1940.

14 Breton, 'Manifeste', *op. cit.*

15 *Ibid.*

16 Quoted in James Johnson Sweeney, 'Joan Miró; Comment and Interview', *Partisan Review*, New York, February 1948, p. 209.

17 Breton, 'Le Surréalisme et la Peinture Nouvelle', *Nouvelle Revue Française,* Paris, 1928.

18 Aragon, 'La Peinture au défi', 1930, in *Les Collages*, Paris 1965, p. 70.

19 Breton, *Artistic Genesis and Perspective of Surrealism*, p. 70.

20 Joan Miró, untitled article on *Harlequin's Carnival, Verve*, Paris, January-March, 1939, p. 85.

21 André Masson, 'Le Plaisir de Peindre' *La Diane Francaise,* Paris, 1950, p. 16.

22 *Ibid.,* p. 40.

Freud

23 Ernst, *Beyond Painting,* New York, 1948, p. 8

24 Ernst, *L'Histoire Naturelle,* Paris, 1926.

25 Breton 'D'une décalcomanie sans object préconçu, (Décalcomanie du désir)', *Le Surréalisme et la Peinture* new ed. 1936, p. 129.

26 Ernst *op. cit.,* p. 20.

27 *Ibid.,* p. 21.

28 Transition, 1951, 1.

29 The period of de Chirico's paintings they were interested in was 1910–7.

30 Ernst, *op. cit.,* p. 3.

31 *Ibid.,* p. 4.

32 Rimbaud, *Une Saison en Enfer,* quoted by Ernst, *op. cit.,* p. 12.

33 Jones, *Life and Work of Sigmund Freud,* vol 3., p. 251. The drawing Freud refers to was done on the spot by Dali, who made an analogy between Freud's cranium and a snail.

34 Salvador Dali, *Conquest of the Irrational,* New York, 1935.

35 Reported by Dali to William Rubin; see Rubin, *Dada and Surrealist Art,* London, 1969, p. 216.

36 Dali, *The Secret Life of Salvador Dali,* London, 1942, p. 167 (note).

37 Dali, *op. cit.,* p. 220.

38 James Thrall Soby, *Salvador Dali,* New York, 1941.

39 C. G. Jung, 'The real and the surreal', *Structure and Dynamics of the Psyche,* London, 1933, p. 382.

Chronology

This chronology is based on Ernest Jones's biography of Freud (3 vols., London, 1953-7).

1856   Birth of Sigmund Freud on 6 May at 117 Schlossergasse, Freiberg, Moravia.

1859   The Freud family moved to Leipzig.

1860   The Freud family settled in Vienna, at first in the Pfeffergasse, in the largely Jewish quarter of Leopoldstadt, then (in 1875) in the Kaiser Josefstrasse.

1865   Sigmund passed an examination which gained him entrance to the Sperl Gymnasium, the local high school in the Leopoldstadt.

1873-4   He graduated from the Sperl Gymnasium with the distinction *summa cum laude*
In the autumn of 1873 he entered the University of Vienna as a medical student. His first-year course included anatomy, chemistry, botany, microscopy and mineralogy.

1874-5   Freud's second-year course had, in addition, dissection, physics, physiology and zoology. He also attended weekly seminars on philosophy and logic where his teacher was Professor Brentano. Freud's Professor of Physiology was Ernst Brücke who was later to become one of his mentors and friends.
In 1875 Freud visited England where his half-brothers, Emmanuel and Philipp had settled in 1859.

1876   In March Freud embarked on the first of his original researches on the advice of Professor Carl Claus, head of the Institute of Comparative Anatomy. He was given a travel-cum-research grant which enabled him to work on the gonadic structure of eels in Claus's Zoological Experimental Station at Trieste. That summer also Freud first came into contact with Ernst von Fleischl-Marxow, who was to become one of his closest friends
In the autumn of 1876 Freud entered Brücke's famous Institute of Physiology as a research scholar and started working on the histology of nerve cells.

1877-8   Freud's research led to a major discovery connected with the spinal ganglion of the *Amoecetes* (Petromyzon), a genus of fish belonging to the Cyclostomatae. Brücke presented his pupil's findings to the Academy in July 1878 and they were published in its *Bulletin* the following month. It was Freud's first professional success. Among the friends he made at that period was Joseph Breuer.

1879-80   Freud continued his research at Brücke's Institute. In the latter part of the year he was called up for his year's military service during which he lived at home and carried on with his medical studies.

1881-2   On 30 March Freud passed his final examinations with the grade 'excellent'. He was promoted to the post of Demonstrator in Brücke's Institute, a post which involved some teaching, and he stayed there until July 1882. In that period he became intensely interested in Breuer's famous case of Anna O. and the birth of the 'cathartic method.'
In April 1882 Freud first met Martha Bernays whom he was later to marry. By June of that year they were secretly engaged. At the end of July Freud entered the Vienna General Hospital where he first started working in surgery. In October he moved to the department of Internal Medicine, run by Professor Nothnagel.

1883   On 1 May Freud was transferred to the Psychiatric Clinic of the General Hospital where he was promoted to the rank of *Sekundarazt* and where his chief was Professor Theodor Meynert.

Chronology

1884   On 1 January Freud entered the department of Nervous Diseases. Among his researches he investigated the possible clinical uses of cocaine but his discoveries were taken up by two colleagues, Carl Koller and Leopold Königstein, who took the lion's share of the glory.

1885–6   Freud worked for a while in the Ophthalmological and Dermatological departments but in August he left the General Hospital for good.

In September he was appointed *Privatdozent* in neuropathology, a long sought-after goal. Having obtained a travel grant to study under Charcot in Paris, he spent the winter of 1885-6 there; he attended Charcot's demonstrations of the use of hypnosis on hysterical patients at the Hôpital de la Salpêtrière and worked in the laboratory. After Paris he spent a few weeks in Berlin where he studied children's diseases.

1886   In April Freud rented a suite at 7 Rathaustrasse, in the best professional quarter of Vienna and started his private practice in neuropathology. He also researched in anatomy in Meynert's laboratory, lectured on the use of hypnosis and worked in Dr Max Kassowitz's clinic for children.

On 13 September Freud married Martha Bernays in the town hall at Wandsbeck. Back in Vienna they settled in a flat at 5 Maria Theresienstrasse.

1887   Birth of Freud's eldest daughter, Mathilde, on 16 October.

In December Freud started to use hypnotic suggestion on some of his patients with some success. This year marks the beginning of his friendship with Wilhelm Fliess which was to end in 1902.

1889   Birth of Freud's son Martin on 6 December.

1891   Birth of Freud's son Oliver on 19 February.

In August the family moved to a larger house at 19 Berggasse where Freud was to live until his final departure from Vienna.

Publication of Freud's first book, *Aphasia*, dedicated to Breuer. Also a massive monograph on unilateral paralyses in children.

1892   Birth of Freud's son Ernst on 6 April.

Very slowly and gradually from that year onwards Freud began to formulate the theory of 'free association'.

1893   A further two monographs on children's paralyses were published as well as a paper, written with Breuer and entitled 'The Psychical Mechanism of Hysterical Phenomena'. Birth of Freud's daughter Sophie on 12 April.

1895   Freud, by now the leading authority on children's paralyses, was asked by Nothnagel to write the section on infantile cerebral paralyses for his new *Encyclopaedia*.

Publication of *Studies in Hysteria*, written by Freud and Breuer together and which marks the beginning of psychoanalysis.

In July another momentous event took place: the analysis by Freud of one of his dreams, which led eventually to his *Interpretation of Dreams*. Birth of Freud's youngest daughter, Anna, on 3 December.

1896   The term 'psychoanalysis' was first used by Freud in two papers. Freud spent the summer holidays with his family at Aussee in Styria, then travelled to Italy with his brother Alexander.

Death of Freud's father, Jakob Freud, on 23 October.

1897   Freud began the long and laborious psychoanalysis of his own subconscious which was to engross him for several years.

In the summer he made an extensive tour of Europe.

1898   Freud published a paper on 'Sexuality in the Aetiology of the Neuroses' which contained the first pronouncement of the theme of infantile sexuality.

Chronology

Once again Freud took an extensive tour of Europe in the summer.

1899   Freud rented a large farmhouse near Berchtesgaden in Bavaria where the family was to spend many summers. That particular summer he wrote most of *The Interpretation of Dreams*. The book was published on 4 November (although the publisher put the date 1900 on the title page). It was, however, a long time before it received the recognition it deserved.

1900   Freud began to give a course of lectures on dreams at the University.

1901   In the late summer Freud and his brother Alexander visited Rome, which he had longed to do for years, for it played an extensive part in his dream life. He called the visit 'the high-point of my life'.

1902   Beginning of the Psychological Wednesday Society, a weekly meeting in Freud's waiting-room between Freud, Max Kahane, Rudolf Reitler, Wilhelm Stekel and Alfred Adler. Later others joined the circle, including Sandor Ferenczi and Otto Rank, and many guests were invited: C. G. Jung, Ernest Jones, Max Eitingon and A. A. Brill among them.
At the end of the summer Freud went to Italy with Alexander. That year marked the end of Freud's relationship with Fliess; they had not met since 1900 but had continued to correspond.

1904   Publication of Freud's *Psychopathology of Everyday Life*. In the summer Freud went to Greece with his brother; it was a memorable visit.

1905   Publication of *Jokes and their Relation to the Unconscious* and *Three Essays on the Theory of Sexuality*; the latter caused a sensation and made Freud very unpopular, mainly because of his theories on infantile sexuality.

1906   By 1906 Freud was so well established that his private practice was flooded with patients, especially from Eastern Europe. His theories also made an impact in medical circles abroad, notably in the Anglo-Saxon countries. Among his champions were Havelock Ellis and Wilfred Trotter.
In April a regular correspondence was started between Freud and Jung.

1907   Freud was visited by some of his professional admirers: Max Eitingon, Jung and Earl Abraham from Zurich and Sandor Ferenczi from Budapest; the latter was to become one of his closest friends and collaborators, but, as with so many of Freud's colleagues, the relationship became strained towards the end.
Publication of Freud's study on Wilhelm Jensen's *Gradiva*.
A Freud Society was founded in Zurich.

1908   On 15 April the old Psychological Wednesday Society (*see* 1902) was rechristened the Vienna Psychoanalytical Society. Its first international Congress took place in Salzburg on 26 April and marked the first public recognition of Freud's work.
In the summer Freud went to Holland and England and visited Jung in Zurich on his way back.
That year he published five papers, one of which, on anal sensations in infancy, was to have wide-reaching results in the development of modern psychology.
A Psychoanalytical Society was founded in Berlin.

1909   On 7 February Freud's eldest daughter Mathilde was married to Robert Hollitscher. In the later summer Freud, Ferenczi and Jung were guests of Stanley Hall, the President of Clark University, Worcester, Massachusetts, where they gave lectures on the occasion of the tenth anniversary of the University. The first official recognition of Freud's achievements came when he was given an honorary doctorate.
Among the works published that year was the case history of 'Little Hans' and 'The Family Romance of Neurotics'.

Chronology

1910 The second International Psychoanalytical Congress took place at Nuremberg at the end of March.

In May the American Psychopathological Association was founded, with Freud and Jung as honorary members.

Publication of Freud's Worcester lectures, *Five Lectures on Psychoanalysis*, as well as a book on *Leonardo*.

In the late summer Freud and Ferenczi toured southern Italy and Sicily.

1911 Break with Alfred Adler. This was the first of several breaks with colleagues with whom Freud disagreed.

The third International Psychoanalytical Congress was held at Weimar in September. Freud founded a periodical, *Imago*, and wrote a little that year.

1912 Freud founded another periodical, *Zeitschrift*.

In the summer he visited Rome again. He published some short papers but was mostly occupied in writing *Totem and Taboo*.

Break with Wilhelm Stekel.

1913 On 14 January Freud's daughter Sophie married Max Halberstadt of Hamburg.

Publication of *Totem and Taboo*.

The Budapest and London branches of the Psychoanalytical Society were founded in May and October respectively, with Ferenczi and Ernest Jones as respective Presidents. Once again that year Freud visited Rome and at Christmas went to see his daughter Sophie in Hamburg.

First meeting of the so-called Seven Rings' Committee, whose main aim was to fortify Freud against the numerous attacks which were being made against him.

Break with Jung.

1914 Birth of Freud's first grandchild, Sophie's eldest son.

Freud's sons Martin and Ernst enrolled at the outbreak of war whilst Oliver was engaged in engineering work.

1915 Freud worked on a series of essays, several of which were never published. Among those which were was a pair on Thoughts for the Times on War and Death'.

The first part of Freud's *Introductory Lectures* was published.

1916 Marriage of Freud's son Oliver.

Freud spent part of the summer at Salzburg.

1917 Another dismal war year for Freud. He spent the summer at Csorbato where he had rented a villa.

Publication of the second half of the *Introductory Lectures*.

1918 The fifth International Psychoanalytical Congress was held in Budapest in September; it was attended by official representatives of the German, Austrian and Hungarian governments who were interested in the possibility of treating war neuroses through psychoanalysis.

1919 In January the publishing house Internationaler Psychoanalytischer Verlag was founded, with Freud, Ferenczi, von Freund and Rank as its directors.

In October Freud was given the title of Professor of the University though it did not bring him a seat on the Faculty Board.

Birth of Sophie's second son, Heinz Rudolf.

1920 Death, in January, of Freud's daughter Sophie.

In February the Berlin Policlinic was opened, thus making Berlin the main psycho-analytical centre in the world.

Freud was asked by a Commission of the Austrian military authorities to submit a report

Chronology

on the electrical treatment of war neurotics which they were investigating. In October he gave evidence before the Commission but his opinions prejudiced them against him. In September the sixth International Psychoanalytical Congress was held at The Hague. That year Freud worked mainly on *Beyond the Pleasure Principle* and *Group Psychology and Analysis of the Ego*.

Birth of two more grandsons: Anton Walter, son of Martin Freud and Stephen Gabriel, son of Ernst.

In December Freud was made an Honorary member of the Dutch Society of Psychiatrists and Neurologists.

1922 Anna Freud, Freud's youngest daughter, was made a member of the Vienna Society on 31 May.

The seventh International Psychoanalytical Congress was held in Berlin in September. Birth of Ernst's second son, Lucian Michael.

1923 The first signs of the illness (cancer of the jaw) which was slowly to kill Freud appeared in February. He underwent a small operation in April, the first of thirty-three.

Death of Sophie's second child, Heinz Rudolf, of milary tubercolosis on 19 June.

In the summer Freud spent his holidays at Lavarone with his family, then went to Rome with Anna. In October he underwent another two operations, then another two in November.

Publication of *The Ego and the Id*, and, among other papers, of Remarks on the Theory and Practice of Dream Interpretation', A Seventeenth-Century Demonological Neurosis' and The Infantile Genital Organization of the Libido'.

1924 Birth of Freud's sixth grandson, Clemens Raphael, son of Ernst; and of two grand-daughters, Eva Mathilde, daughter of Oliver, and Miriam Sophie, daughter of Martin. Publication, among other papers, of 'Neurosis and Psychosis' and 'The Economic Problem of Masochism'.

The eighth International Psychoanalytical Congress was held in Salzburg in April, but Freud was too ill to attend.

1925 In the summer Freud underwent some minor operations on his jaw. Death, on 20 June, of Joseph Breuer.

The ninth International Psychoanalytical Congress took place in Hamburg in September, but once again, Freud was unable to attend.

Death, on 25 December, of Karl Abraham, a life-long friend and colleague of Freud's. Publication of Freud's *Autobiography*.

1926 On Freud's seventieth birthday the amount of letters, telegrams and tributes which showered 19 Berggasse attested to the fact that his name had become an international household word. The day after his birthday Freud held his last meeting with the Committee. Freud spent the summer at Semmering with his family and continued to treat two patients a day although he was in much pain and discomfort.

In December Freud and his wife travelled to Berlin to see their grandchildren (Sophie's sons) and there Freud met Albert Einstein.

Publication of *Inhibitions, Symptoms and Anxiety*. In June Freud began to write *The Question of Lay Analysis*.

1927 Publication of the controversial *The Future of an Illusion*.

1928 A particularly painful year for Freud.

Publication of the essay 'Dostoyevsky and Parricide'.

1929 Publication of *Civilization and its Discontents*.

1930 In July Freud was awarded the Goethe prize which gave him great pleasure.

Death on 12 September at the age of 95, of Freud's mother.

Chronology

On 10 October, Freud underwent another operation and a week later had broncho-pneumonia. But by November he was back at work, treating several patients a day.

1931   Freud underwent yet another operation in April but was back at home for his seventy-fifth birthday celebrations.

Publication, among other papers, of 'Libidinal Types' and 'On Female Sexuality'.

1932   Final break with Ferenczi who, for some years, had been showing signs of antagonism towards Freud.

Freud underwent five operations that year, one of which, in October, was extensive.

1933   At the onset of Nazi persecutions, Freud was begged by his friends and colleagues to flee from Austria, but he did not consider it seriously, partly because of his lack of mobility.

Death, on 24 May, of Ferenczi.

At the end of May Freud's books were burnt in the Nazi bonfire in Berlin, and the German Society for Psychotherapy came under Nazi control. The new editor of its official organ, the *Zentralblatt fur Psychotherapie*, was C. G. Jung who was joined in 1936 by Hermann Göring.

1936   In March Freud had another operation performed on his jaw. He spent his eightieth birthday celebrations relatively quietly. Among the highlights were a letter from Einstein, a visit from Thomas Mann (which particularly pleased him) and an Address signed by Mann, Jules Romain, Virginia Woolf, Romain Rolland, H. G. Wells and many other writers and artists who admired his work.

Freud was made an honorary member of several international psychoanalytical and psychological associations, including the Royal Society.

In July Freud underwent two very painful operations.

On 13 September Freud and Martha celebrated their golden wedding anniversary.

Another operation was performed in December.

1938   Austria was invaded by the Nazis on 11 March. Freud's flat at 19 Berggasse was visited by the S.A. and a week later by the Gestapo. Thanks to the diligence and help of some friends and admirers — among whom were Ernest Jones, Marie Bonaparte, W. C. Bullitt (the American Ambassador to France) and President Roosevelt — the Nazi authorities eventually granted the Freud family an exit permit.

On 4 June Freud, with his wife, Anna and two maidservants (Martin, Mathilde and their families had left a little earlier) left Vienna for good. The next day they crossed into France and thence into England.

Freud's reception in England was enthusiastic. On 23 June the official Charter Book of the Royal Society was brought for him to sign, and he received letters and presents from many admirers.

His first London home was at 39 Elsworthy Road, but later in the autumn he moved permanently to 20 Maresfield Gardens.

Publication, in August, of the German edition of *Moses and Monotheism* on which Freud had been working since 1934.

In September he had to undergo another operation, but by the end of the year he was seeing up to four patients a day and working on *An Outline of Psychoanalysis* which was never completed. At Christmas, however, he underwent yet another operation.

1939   Publication, in March, of the English edition of *Moses and Monotheism*.

Freud's health grew steadily worse during the year and no further operation was feasible. He was visited by many of his friends, including Marie Bonaparte and Hans Sachs. He was alive when the Second World War was declared but died shortly before midnight on 23 September. His body was cremated at Golders Green on 26 September.

Index

Index

Index

Index